实用主义研究

PRAGMATISM STUDIES

| 第一辑 |

刘放桐　陈亚军◎主　编

陈　佳　孙　宁◎副主编

人民出版社

本书由复旦大学哲学院资助

发　刊　词

　　《实用主义研究》计划每年出版一期。作为一个供国内外学者开展学术交流的平台,集刊将及时反映国内外学术界关于实用主义和美国思想文化的研究成果,并有意识地引导学界对相关的一些重要问题展开深度的探讨和建设性的合作。

　　在实用主义研究方面,集刊的主要内容有以下四个方面:

　　1. 及时反映国际学术界的最新实用主义研究成果。集刊将以每期 1/3 的篇幅刊登国际著名实用主义研究学者的文章,并将这些文章整合在一个特定的主题下。

　　2. 及时反映国内学术界的最新实用主义研究成果。集刊将刊登国内资深学者和青年学者的最新研究成果,并和国际学者的文章形成良性的互动和对话。

　　3. 介绍国内外学术界的最新实用主义研究动态,其中包括实用主义最新著作的书评、著名实用主义学者的访谈,以及国内外相关会议的综述等。

　　4. 译介实用主义研究的经典文章。集刊将组织一批优秀的译者组织编译一批具有重要学术价值、国内学界尚不熟悉的经典文章,并将文章整合进当期的主题中。

　　除此之外,集刊还将在每期中插入一个美国思想文化的研究的专题。此专题的范围不再限于实用主义研究,而是试图将美国哲学、思想、政治、文化研究广泛地整合起来。

　　所有文章的质量将由实用主义专业委员会成员严格把关，争取让集刊真正具有让国内外学界认可的学术价值，在国内外学界产生一定的影响，并成为我国实用主义和美国思想文化研究的前沿阵地。

目 录
CONTENTS

Pragmatism Studies

实用主义研究

再论重新评价实用主义

——兼论杜威哲学与马克思主义哲学的同一和差异①

刘 放 桐

复旦大学哲学学院

我在 1987 年写过一篇以《重新评价实用主义》为题的文章,对长期流行的全盘否定实用主义的评价模式提出了全面的质疑,引起了一些同行专家的共鸣,中国现代外国哲学学会因此于 1988 年在四川成都举行了全国实用主义讨论会,就如何对之作求实评价达成了与我的观点非常接近的共识,它们成了我国几十年来对实用主义研究的一个重要转折点。从 1996 年发表《西方哲学近现代转型与马克思主义哲学和当代中国哲学的发展道路(论纲)》起,我的研究重点转向现代西方哲学与马克思主义哲学的比较研究,发表了系列论著,主要是提出和论证了如下两个观点:第一,西方哲学从近代到现代的转化是西方哲学发展史上一次具有划时代意义的哲学思维方式的转型,标志着西方哲学发展到了一个新的、更高的阶段。第二,这一转型与马克思在哲学上的革命变更在阶级基础和理论形态上都有原则区别,但又存在着重要的共同之处。这两个观点与国内外马克思主义学界长期流行的关于马克思主义和现代西方哲学关系的观点同样大相径庭,也引起了哲学界的广泛关注。它们实际上是我重新评价实用主义观点的进一步发挥,但反过来又深化了我对实用主义的重新评价,特别是对马克思在哲学上

---

① 本文是作者主持国家社科基金重大招标项目"杜威研究与《杜威全集》翻译"(12&ZD123)的阶段性成果。

的革命变更的背景下来重新评价。本文就是这种深化了的重新评价之一。

一、实践的观点是杜威实用主义哲学的基本观点

实用主义是一个广大的家族。其中各个成员的某些观点互不相同,同一位实用主义哲学家在各个时期的观点也不尽一致。但所有的实用主义者在不同程度上都强调人的实践在哲学上的首要的、核心的地位和作用。这一点在杜威哲学中表现得更为突出。

杜威从不同角度明确地把实践的观点当作其整个哲学的基本观点。他在《确定性的寻求》第一章中就指出了传统哲学的各种片面见解的根源"都是由于人们(为了寻求绝对的确定性)把理论与实践、知识与行动分隔开来了"①,而他这本书的主题正是"考虑到用通过实践的手段追求安全的方法去代替通过理性的手段去寻求绝对的确定性的方法",②也就是从实践的观点出发来研究哲学,论证理论(认识)与实践的统一、知识与信仰(价值)的统一。在杜威看来,人作为整个自然界的一种生物处于永远活动之中。人的认识(感觉、思维)、情感(喜怒哀乐)和欲望(理想、目的)以至人的整个生活世界,都是从人的活动中产生的,也都是通过人的活动本身而得到实现。当人生活着的时候,"在他的行动中有些行动产生了理解而有些事物发生了意义,因为这些东西成为互相间的记号了;成为期望和回想的手段、对于未来的准备和对于已经过去的东西的赞美了。活动具有了理想的性质。引力和斥力变成了对于优美东西的爱好和对于丑恶东西的憎恶。这种活动寻求着和创造着一个人们可以在里面安全生活的世界。希望与恐惧、欲望与厌恶和认知与思维一样,都是对事物的真正反应"③。由于杜威把人的所有这些活动都看作是实践的表现形态,因此他实际上是把实践当作人

---

① LW 4:19.本文所引杜威著作均出自 John Dewey, *The Collected Works of John Dewey*, 1882–1953, ed. Jo Ann Boydston (Carbondale: Southern Illinois University Press, 1969–1991).EW 为早期著作, MW 为中期著作, LW 为晚期著作,冒号前为卷数,冒号后为页码。下同。

② LW 4:20.

③ LW 4:237.

的全部生活的杠杆。也正是在这种意义上,他明确提出"我们应该把实践当作是我们用以在具体可经验到的存在中保持住我们判断为光荣、美妙和可赞赏的一切事物的唯一手段"。①

杜威的哲学有经验自然主义、工具主义、实验主义等不同的名称,也有存在论、真理论、方法论、政治理论、教育理论、美学、伦理学、社会学等各个不同方面的理论。贯彻于所有这些名称和理论中的则是行动、活动、行为、生活、生命、探究(探索)的决定性作用,而这些在他那里都是实践的别称。

例如,杜威的经验自然主义从名称上说具有存在论意义,但是他的这种存在论与传统哲学的存在论有根本性的区别。它的经验所涉及的不是作为具有实体性存在意义的物质或精神,它的自然也不是与人无牵涉的自在的自然界(尽管他并不否定人以外的自然界本身自在地存在),而是与人的活动、行为、生活直接相关(牵涉)的对象,后者也只有在与人相关时才具有现实意义。在杜威看来,真正的经验即现实的和活生生的经验只能是作为有机体的人与作为环境(自然环境和作为自然一部分的社会环境,甚至也包括思想环境)的对象之间的一种交互活动。任何人都不可能孤立地、抽象地存在,他总是生活在一定的环境(情境)之中,受到环境(情境)的制约;而环境也总是人所处的环境,离开了人,作为环境的自然就不能作为现实的环境而存在,而只能是抽象的、自在的存在。人所处的环境总要对人产生刺激,而人对环境的刺激也必然要产生反应。这种刺激和反应是不能分开的,总是形成为一个相互作用的过程,而这正是生命、生活、活动、行动、行为,即实践的过程。这种过程是不断延续的。人的生命正是在人与其环境的相互作用中存在并得到延续的。因此,杜威的经验自然主义中的经验与传统哲学的认识论中谈论的经验也具有完全不同的意义。它不是指认识论中的某一个环节或者阶段,而是人的整个生命、生存所牵涉的一切。这种牵涉正是与环境(自然)的交互作用,即生活、行动、过程,也就是实践。

又如,杜威的真理论与传统哲学的真理论虽然大致用同样的词句来指称,却有完全不同的意义。杜威所谓真理既不是以往唯物主义者所谓对不

---

① LW 4:26.

以人为转移的客观事实或规律的正确反映,也不是以往唯心主义者所谓绝对精神的体现或人的主观感觉,而是人在探究(实践)中得出并使人的生活、行动、行为、实践得以进行的某种观念、理论、方法、手段,或者说适应环境的工具。杜威由此称他的真理论是一种工具主义理论。换言之,按照杜威工具主义真理论,观念、理论等不是个人主观自生的,而是处于环境(境遇、情境)中的人为着适应环境(发现和解决环境给人所提出的问题以及对人的行动所造成的困难,找到解决这些问题和克服这些困难的方法,使人的行动、实践得以继续进行下去)而探究出来的。他认为,人总是处于一定的环境之中,人为了生存和发展,必须探究应付环境的手段、方法和理论。如果这些手段、方法和理论能够帮助我们应付环境,克服环境所加的障碍(困难、问题),使我们得以生存和发展,或者说使人得以有效地行动、生活、实践,那就是经得起实践的检验,那它们就是真理。杜威的这种真理论也就是他的探究理论,而这是一种特殊形式的实践论。因为它是指真理以实践的需要为背景,通过实践(探究本身也属于实践)而获得,经由实践来检验,以达到为实践服务的目标。

在杜威看来,人们建立科学和哲学的目的归根到底都是为了探究出使人们得以生存和发展的适当的方法、手段和理论。人的生存和发展都是一个延续的过程,会不断地碰到新的环境、新的问题和困难,需要人们不断地探究出应付新环境、解决新问题和克服新困难的新的工具。杜威由此倡导不断地发展科学、改造哲学,使它们不断地符合人的生存和发展的目的。也正因为如此,杜威在真理问题上坚决反对一切封闭的、静止的、绝对化的观点,肯定对真理的探究是一个开放、多样化、发展的过程。

应当指出,对杜威关于真理是行为(行动、生活、实践)的工具、真理就是具有效用的观点,常常被人作了极端利己主义的解释,似乎只要能满足个人的私利,就可把任何荒诞的观念和理论都宣布为真理。过去人们指责实用主义是垄断资产阶级和帝国主义的哲学也正是基于这一点。这种指责用在粗俗的实用主义上是有根据的,用在杜威身上就不妥当了。因为把真理看作是满足个人私利的工具根本不符合杜威本人的旨意。杜威在许多著作中都一再指出他所谓有效、有用都是相对于行动、行为、生活、实践本身,而行动、行为、生活、实践并不仅仅是属于个人的,更重要的是属于社会或者说共同体的。他一再明确指出私利必须服从公益。关于这方面的情况,杜威本人在《哲学的改造》、《确定性的寻求》、《新旧个人主义》等论著中作了许多声辩,此处就不列举了。

杜威等实用主义哲学家其他方面的理论同样以生活和实践为中心。例如,杜威的探究方法既不同于传统的经验派和理性派哲学家的方法(例如传统逻辑的经验归纳法和理性演绎法),也不同于现代分析哲学家的逻辑或语言分析方法和现象学家的现象学方法,其根本之点就在于把探究过程当作是知和行、认识和实践统一的过程,而这正是行动、生活和实践的过程。如果说皮尔士和詹姆士等其他一些实用主义哲学家对现实生活和实践的强调大体上只是当作哲学的一般原则的话,杜威哲学的突出特色就是把这一原则贯彻于人类现实生活和实践的各个重要领域。与胡塞尔、海德格尔等人通过曲折的道路才返回生活世界不同,与只关注逻辑和语言的意义分析的分析哲学家更不同,杜威的哲学直接面向现实生活。杜威一生在哲学上所关注的不是去建构庞大的体系,也不是去从事语言和逻辑的意义分析,而是满腔热情地从哲学上去探究人类在现实生活和实践各个领域所面临的各种问题及其解决办法。在杜威的全部论著中,关于政治、社会、文化、教育、道德、科学技术、审美和宗教等各个领域的具体问题的论述占了绝大部分。他的哲学的精粹和生命力大多是在这些论述中表现出来。正因为如此,杜威哲学对美国现实生活的许多重要领域都发生了深刻影响。也正因为杜威哲学直接面向现实生活的这种特色,当它传入中国后,对中国的现实影响也远远超出任何其他西方哲学。

二、杜威的实践的转向体现了西方现当代哲学的基本走向

杜威等人的实用主义是西方现当代哲学中最有代表性的派别,因为杜威等人对现实生活和实践的强调在西方哲学从近代到现当代的转向中具有较大的代表性,在一定程度上可以说它相当突出地体现了西方现当代哲学的基本走向。

在西方哲学史上,哲学的发展经历了大大小小众多的变更。后起的哲学家往往会对先行的理论作出某些新的变更或解释。研究这种变更和解释当然是有意义的。但是,最值得哲学家们关注的还是那些具有划时代意义的哲学思维方式的根本倾向上的转向,因为它们往往体现了社会历史时代及与之相应的政治、经济以及思想文化体制的转向。杜威等实用主义哲学家在哲学上的变更与他们的先行者相比,就具有重大的甚至是划时代的意义。这是因为他们的哲学都是以已经陷入困境和危机的西方近代哲学为主要背景,他们所要求建立的哲学是能在不同程度上克服这种困境和危机的哲学,是在一定程度上能体现新的时代要求的哲学。

要了解杜威等实用主义哲学家所要建立的哲学的划时代意义,首先就应当了解他们所要取代的近代哲学的时代背景以及近代哲学本身的是非成败的状况,特别是它们的内在矛盾和危机。关于这一点,我在 2001 年发表的《西方哲学现代转型的历史和理论分析》一文中作了较为详细的分析,在我往后发表的众多有关论著中有更多发挥,这里只简单提及。

作为实用主义等西方现代哲学的先行者的近代哲学,一般是指从笛卡尔(也可前推到文艺复兴)到黑格尔时代的哲学。这是从资本主义在封建社会内部孕育、产生、成长到走向衰落和危机的时代。在政治上是资产阶级从反封建、与封建势力妥协到与封建势力相勾结来反对无产阶级的时代,在经济上是由简单商品经济发展到较大规模的市场经济,并实现以工业革命为支撑的现代化,然后又陷入经济危机的时代。从哲学上说,这是在文艺复兴的口号下开展宗教改革和人文主义运动,由此以人所固有的理性代替神的启示作为哲学的中心,并通过所谓认识论的转向逐步建立以心物(主客、思有)分立为出发点,以基础主义、本质主义、主体性形而上学等为特征,以无所不包的体系哲学(思辨形而上学)为目标的时代。在这个时代,在理性主义的旗帜下,在哲学上出现过以 17 世纪英国特别是 18 世纪法国唯物主义以及 19 世纪德国更为进步的费尔巴哈的人本学唯物主义,出现过以德国古典哲学特别是黑格尔哲学为代表的辩证法思潮,至于把哲学和政治及科学等相结合、以反对宗教蒙昧主义和封建专制主义为主要目标的启蒙主义,在西方各国都有发生,推动了那里的革命和进步。但是,正如近代西方资本主义存在着在原有体制内不可克服的内在矛盾一样,近代西方哲学同样存在着在原有理论框架内不可克服的内在矛盾。非常巧合的是:正当19世纪30年代西方资本主义第一次爆发了空前的经济大危机时,作为集近代主体性形而上学、近代思辨形而上学之大成的黑格尔逝世了。黑格尔学派立即解体,它像多米诺骨牌一样推动整个西方近代哲学大厦从整体上趋向倒塌。一个由近代到现代哲学转向的时代到来了。

在从近代哲学到现代哲学的转向中,最具有标志意义的是马克思在哲学上的革命变更,这一点将在下面提及。这里先要指出的是:与马克思大致同一个时代,许多西方哲学家也在试图改变西方哲学发展的方向。早在黑格尔在世甚至其顶峰时期,叔本华、克尔凯郭尔、孔德等人就已在向以他为最高代表人物的近代哲学发动攻势了。他们攻击的不是近代哲学家的个别论点,而是近代哲学作为一种有较大普遍性的思维方式。至于与马克思同时或稍后的西方哲学家,对近代哲学思维方式的批判更是成了一种普遍风尚。叔本华以后的尼采、柏格森,孔德之后的密尔、斯宾塞等人无不向黑格尔发动进攻。即使是那些仍然与康德、黑格尔等有较多思想牵连的哲学家,也大都要用新的时代的精神去改造康德、黑格尔的理论,并由此而被人称为新康德主义、新黑格尔主义。这些人对近代哲学的批判有一个共同点,即不是凭借某种新的物质或精神实体,而主要是凭借生命、生活、意志、力量、活动、行动、趋势、进化、变化等来重新解释近代哲学所谈论的心物、主客、思有等一切事物及它们之间的一切关系。换言之,他们要用一种立足于活动、行动、变化、趋势等的哲学来克服有着二元论、独断论、怀疑论、绝对论等诸多弊端的传统哲学。他们并没有取消存在论、认识论、方法论、价值论等传统哲学研究过的问题,而只是要求改变研究这些问题的方式,而这就是他们所要求的哲学的转向。西方哲学家们对转向的解释各有不同,但是,由于他们所谓生命、生活、意志、力量、活动、行动、趋势、进化、变化都与实践相关,是实践的不同的表现形态。因此他们所要求实现的转向可以概括为实践的转向。

关于西方哲学家们19世纪中期以来在哲学上实现的转向有着各种不同的提法。其中影响最大的是语言分析哲学产生以后特别是罗蒂所编的

《语言的转向》一书出版(1967)以后广泛流行的语言的转向。由于不仅分析哲学家把哲学问题归结为语言问题,欧洲大陆现象学、存在哲学、阐释学、结构主义和解构主义等也在一定意义上把哲学问题归结为语言问题,因而把西方哲学的现当代转向称为语言的转向的倾向可以说已成了一种普遍的、占主导地位的倾向。

我并不否定语言的转向这种提法的意义。其实,语言问题也是杜威极为重视的问题。杜威所谓事物、自然、世界对人的意义,都是通过语言这个必不可少的工具得以存在的。思维、知识,这些人类的认识以及人类各种形式的实践,甚至人类的产生和延续存在的先决条件就是语言。"说话的发生使得哑巴动物……变成了有思维和有知识的动物,并从而建立了意义的领域,这是一件十分明白的事实。"①这里说的正是说话(语言)使人类成为现实的人类("有思维和有知识的动物")。"器具和应用、用具和使用总是跟指导、提议和记录联系着的,而指导、提议和记录之所以可能是由于有了语言,凡为人们所谈过的有关于工具作用的东西,都要服从语言所提供的一个条件,语言是工具的工具。"②杜威这些话都说明,他认为人类作为人类生存和活动都必须利用语言。从这种意义上说,语言在杜威哲学中似乎起决定作用。把他的哲学的转向说成是语言的转向具有一定根据。然而,杜威同时明确认为,语言不是什么终极的、最高的存在,也不是出于人的愿望,而是作为有机体的人的行为的产物。"语言、记号和含义的产生,不是由于谁的意旨和心愿,而是由于姿态和声音的扩展,是它们的副产品。关于语言的故事就是关于利用这些事情的故事。"③语言始于说话,而说话本身就是一种活动。语言是在利用语言这种人类实践的特殊形式中产生的。

总之,语言总是人在生活中所使用的语言,语言的使用既是人的生存和发展(而这实际上也是人的生活、行为、实践)的条件,又是人的生存和发展的产物。语言必然是与人的生活、行动、实践分不开的。因此语言的转向实际上没有超越实践的转向范围,也可以说二者是统一的。而且单纯地分析

---

① LW 1:133.
② LW 1:134.
③ LW 1:139.

语言并不能解决语言所表达的理论与实践、知识与信仰(道德、价值)等传统和现代哲学都必然要分析的问题,实际上也无法真正实现西方哲学从近代到现当代的转化。马克思在哲学上的革命变更是西方哲学从近代到现代的最有标志性的变革,这一点至少在信仰马克思主义的哲学家中是众所公认的。然而马克思却没有使用语言的转向这种提法或类似的提法。如果语言的转向果真是西方哲学从近代到现代的根本性的转向,马克思是不可能视而不见的。因此我认为,在谈论西方哲学从近代到现代的转向时,与其说它是语言的转向,不如说它是实践的转向,只有后者才符合马克思的观点。要说明的是:我把现当代哲学的转向概括为实践的转向并无排他意义。语言的转向等各种转向的提法都有其成立的理由。但它们都不能离开实践的转向,或者说都是实践的转向的某种独特的表现形式。

如果实践的转向这种概括的提法能够成立,那我就认为,在马克思主义以外,在现代西方哲学派别中最能体现这种转向的是以杜威为突出代表的实用主义。其他现当代西方哲学流派在这方面的提法往往还不是那么直截了当,甚至只有在归根到底的意义上是如此。而杜威等人非常明确地把实践的观点当作是他们哲学的根本观点。这点我们在上面已经简单阐释了。如果我的这种说法能够成立,那么我认为以杜威等人为代表的实用主义是西方现当代哲学中最有代表性的派别。

三、马克思主义和实用主义在实现实践转向上的异同

在从近代哲学到现代哲学的转向中,最具有标志意义的是马克思在哲学上的革命变更,这一变革的核心在于提出了科学的实践观,从根本上实现了西方哲学的实践转向。关于这一点,众多的马克思主义哲学论著已有相当详尽的论述。我个人近些年对此也多次发文作过具体阐释。此处仅简单提及。

马克思和恩格斯对近代哲学的超越突出地表现在他们摒弃了黑格尔的唯心主义和费尔巴哈的形而上学,分别批判地继承了他们的辩证法和唯物主义,并将二者统一成为唯物辩证法或者说辩证唯物主义。这种以往通行

的表述当然有理论根据,但还需要进一步追问:他们是怎样实现上述批判继承并将辩证法和唯物主义统一起来的? 现在大家都承认,这个变革的决定性环节在于他们批判地总结了近代哲学陷入困境和危机的教训,特别是在于深刻地分析了怎样才能使哲学适应无产阶级的革命实践,由此摆脱了抽象思维和感性直观、绝对理性主义和经验主义等的界限,强调了现实生活和实践在哲学中的决定性作用。他们对无产阶级的现实生活和实践的意义的深刻分析使他们对唯物主义和辩证法有了与以往哲学家根本不同的认识。这突出地表现在把唯物主义和辩证法都与人的"感性活动"、实践联系起来。

　　马克思的唯物主义不同于旧唯物主义的根本之点,在于他不是从纯粹的、抽象的物质出发,而是从人的现实生活和实践(人的感性活动)出发。相对于旧唯物主义之为自然主义的唯物主义而言,马克思的新唯物主义是一种实践的唯物主义。马克思的辩证法不同于黑格尔等以往辩证法的根本之点同样在于马克思是通过人的现实的感性活动即客观的实践来理解辩证法的,因而既能揭示主观的辩证法,又能揭示客观的辩证法,并在实践的基础上达到主客观辩证法的统一。正是这种统一使辩证法具有充分的现实性和具体性。在马克思哲学中,通过感性活动、实践对辩证法的揭示与通过感性活动、实践对物质的客观性和先在性的揭示是统一的。因此马克思的辩证法是唯物主义的辩证法,而他的唯物主义则是辩证法的唯物主义。总之,现实生活和实践的观点是整个经典马克思主义哲学的根本观点。它不仅因强调人的实践在认识中的决定作用而具有认识论意义,还因强调人的实践使物质、自然界从抽象的自在的存在转化为与人发生牵涉从而对人具有现实意义的存在,并由此具有存在论(生存论)意义。马克思的社会历史观、人民群众观、价值观、文化观等理论也都是由其科学实践观而获得合理的解释。因此,马克思通过把实践的观点当作其哲学的根本观点标志着他在哲学上实现了一次全面的、深刻的革命,这也正是他的实践的转向。

　　马克思在哲学上的实践的转向与上面谈到的杜威的实践的转向具有原则区别。这突出地表现在如下两点上。首先,马克思把物质生产劳动看作是实践的基本形式。物质生产劳动是使人类得以生存的基本前提,也是人类得以从事其他一切活动的基础。物质生产劳动既蕴含着对物质世界的先在性的肯定,从而肯定了唯物主义的意义;又蕴含着人对物质世界的改造,从而也肯定了人的主观能动性。人类的物质生产劳动必然是一种社会性的活动,蕴含着以生产关系为基础的人与人的各种社会关系,具有明显的社会性和历史性。马克思由此对人类实践作出了最科学的解释,是一种科学的实践观。其次,马克思的这种实践观与马克思主义哲学作为无产阶级和人类解放的意识形态是统一的。马克思一再明确指出旧哲学局限于解释世界,但更重要的是改造世界。马克思实践观所讲的改造世界既包括了对自然的改造,又包括了对社会的改造,后者正意味着无产阶级和人类的解放。

杜威的实践观也具有丰富的内涵,例如他也谈论人的社会性和历史性,甚至也谈论对自然和社会的改造。但他没有把物质生产劳动看作是人的实践的基本形式,而局限于把实践理解为人作为生物有机体的行为,他的实践观不是科学的实践观。更为重要的是,杜威虽然也谈到改造哲学以利于人的全面发展以及理想社会的建立,但作为资产阶级哲学家,他没有、也不可能把他的实践观与无产阶级和人类的解放统一起来。

但是,在划清杜威实用主义实践观与马克思的实践观的原则区别的同时,我们也应当看到,作为西方哲学近现代大转向时期的哲学,二者在把生活、行动和实践的观点当作全部哲学的根本观点,并以此来批判和超越近代哲学的种种局限性和片面性,实现由认识论的转向到实践的转向上有着重要的共同之处。正因为如此,这两种哲学能够产生任何其他哲学都无法比拟的实际影响。

关于马克思主义产生了比任何其他现代哲学学派更大的实际影响,可以见证于马克思主义产生以来一百多年出现的客观历史事实。马克思主义在发展中当然会遇到失败和挫折。但这不是马克思主义本身的失败和挫折,而是一些人背离了马克思主义的本来意义所必然受到的惩罚。但一旦拨乱反正,重新明确把实践当作是检验真理的唯一标准,就又能继续取得伟大胜利。因此只要能坚持马克思的实践标准,马克思主义就是无往不胜的。在这方面,国内外都有大量例证,此处不需要一一列举。

实用主义作为一个资产阶级哲学流派,其可能产生的影响当然不能与马克思主义哲学相提并论。但是我们不能因此否定它在资本主义的美国所产生的巨大作用。美国人民在不长的历史时期内几乎从空地上把美国建设成世界上唯一的超级大国,其主要思想支柱正是实用主义。实用主义是美国最有代表性的哲学。现代欧洲各国哲学大都曾传入美国,并在美国占有一席之地,有的(例如分析哲学)在特定时期甚至可能在美国哲学讲坛占有支配地位。但它们几乎都毫无例外地被实用主义所同化,成为实用主义的组成部分。就实际影响来说,实用主义在美国哲学中始终占有优势。桑塔亚那等一些美国著名哲学家也承认,美国人不管其口头上拥护的是什么样的哲学,但骨子里相信的仍然是实用主义。只有实用主义才是美国建国以来长期形成的一种民族精神的体现。而实用主义的最大特色就是使哲学从玄虚的抽象王国转向人所面对的现实生活世界。实用主义的主旨就在于指引人们如何去面对现实生活世界,解决他们所面临的各种疑虑和困扰。实用主义当然具有各种局限性,人们也可以从各种角度去批判,但正是实用主义使美国能在许多方面取得成功,这大概是一个不争的事实。

在美国以外,实用主义也能产生广泛而长远的影响。这在中国可以说是最突出的了。自从实用主义传入中国以来,它的关注现实生活和实践的根本特征使它产生的影响远远超出马克思主义以外的任何其他哲学流派。关于这方面的情况,我在其他地方已一再阐释。在此仅指出,实用主义超越纯思辨领域而关注现实问题的特征,使它更多地卷入了现代中国社会的政治和文化冲突中。它长期与马克思主义处于对立的地位,必然受到在中国占意识形态主导地位的马克思主义者的批判。然而这种涉及政治和文化等领域的现实问题的批判反过来又使这些领域受到实用主义的影响。实用主义所主张的解决现实问题的方法与马克思主义所主张的方法有时会发生重叠,以致人们有时难以明察它们之间的区别。毕竟人们在面对现实问题时,除了应当关注一般原则外,还应当关注甚至首先应当关注解决问题的方法,探究如何使问题的解决既能符合社会和公众发展的利益,又能保障个人的合理要求。例如,在向市场经济体制转向时,应当首先关注的是如何发展市场经济,至于"姓社"、"姓资"的问题可以暂时搁置,放在市场经济建设的过程中去解决。而在探究解决问题的方法(例如建设市场经济的方法)方面,实用主义和马克思主义之间仿佛存在着一种张力:二者都把现实生活和实践放在首位,都主张一切从实际出发,都反对各种形式的教条主义和主观主义。我们既不能为了肯定这种张力而忽视二者的原则界限,也不能为了划清二者的原则界限而否定这种张力。

关于杜威的实用主义与马克思主义的关系问题是一个值得从各种不同角度和层面上来研究的重要问题。除了在上述实践标准问题上存在着某些共同之处外,在其他一些理论问题上也并非都只是针锋相对的。例如,杜威的经验自然主义所谈论的自然界在一定程度上可以说接近于马克思所强调的那个"人化的自然界";杜威在肯定自然界不以人的存在为转移而自在地存在的前提下提出的关于主客(有机体和环境)相互制约、主体的创造性和能动性的理论与马克思的相关理论也不直接抵触。又如,马克思主义的发展观是保障社会和个人的共同利益,而杜威从来不主张在损害社会、公众利益的条件下去维护个人私利。相反,他一直提倡私利要服从公益,个人和社会应当相得益彰。杜威的社会理想也并不是维护现存资本主义,而是建立一种能保障所有社会成员都具有民主和自由的权利、受到平等和公正的对待、获得全面发展的机会的"伟大共同体"(Great Community)。① 尽管杜威的这种理想社会在现存资本主义制度下并不能实现,但它仍能获得社会上许多阶层,特别是下层群众的同情;更重要的是,杜威一再主张要对现存资本主义制度进行改造,他也由此被认为是资本主义制度下的社会改革家、左派思想家。正因为如此,在中国,在不同程度上接受和利用实用主义的人,并不都是资产阶级庸人和鸡鸣狗盗之徒,也包括许多忧国忧民和务实求真之士。这也就是为什么实用主义在中国会有挥之不去的影响。这里的关键仍然是我们应当怎样看待马克思的哲学和杜威的实用主义哲学的根本意义。如果按照被教条化的马克思主义哲学论著的结构来理解马克思的哲学,按照近代哲学的眼光去看待杜威的哲学,则二者除了对立以外很难还有其他。但如果按照这两种哲学的根本意义去理解它们,那么作为体现同时代哲学发展趋势的哲学,它们之间在一些方面存在着一定的张力是一种客

---

① 参见 LW 2:315—350。

观存在的事实。

四、马克思主义与实用主义的对立统一
是当代哲学发展的主要趋势

苏东事变后,随着冷战的结束,世界形势发生了很大变化。这种变化在哲学上必然得到反映。马克思主义哲学在它过去的重要根据地苏联被公开抛弃,在跟随苏联的那些国家以及跟随苏联马克思主义哲学模式的马克思主义哲学家中也产生了多米诺效应,世界马克思主义运动由此落入低潮。但中国马克思主义者在中国共产党领导下,特别是在党的改革开放方针的指引下,不仅坚定地抵制住了这种效应,对苏联模式的马克思主义的失败作了必要的反思;同时还适应当代社会发展的新形势,对马克思主义在当代的发展道路,特别是使马克思主义中国化的道路进行了深入、全面和系统的探索,取得了极其重大的成果,使马克思主义哲学重新焕发出了其灿烂的光彩,特别是促进了中国特色社会主义建设实践的大发展,使中国在很短的历史时期内发展成了世界第二大经济体。其他国家的许多忠诚的马克思主义者同样在根据他们各自的社会政治和文化背景在探索有他们自己特色的马克思主义发展道路,同样取得了可喜的成果。因此,尽管出现过低潮,马克思主义由于适应社会历史的发展规律,不仅不会衰落下去,反而会在新的形势下获得新的发展。改革开放以来,中国马克思主义发展所取得的重大成就以及国外马克思主义者在更为困难的条件下所取得的成就都是最好的明证。随着科学技术的飞速发展和社会思想文化新变更的出现,马克思主义哲学必然要在某些方面改变自己的形态,但马克思主义哲学的根本精神不会改变。细察当前,展望未来,我们完全可以相信,马克思主义哲学仍是最能经得起各种考验和检验并持续获得发展的哲学,是最能体现当代时代精神精华的哲学。

至于现当代西方哲学,哲学界中大多数人也已不再像以往那样简单地用全盘否定的话语来形容。只要西方资本主义制度还能在较长时期内存在下去,与之相适应的西方哲学也仍然有存在的土壤。由于西方资本主义国家发展的不平衡性和不稳定性以及各种复杂的政治、经济和文化发展中的变故,各种具体的哲学流派的兴衰起落时有发生。但 19 世纪中期西方哲学的近现代转型发生以来一直存在的那些主要思潮还会以新的形态出现,因为它们除了与社会政治等易变的因素相关外,还与科学和人类认识的发展、文化传统特别是哲学本身的传统等因素相联系。例如存在哲学对存在的研究、语言哲学对语言的研究都有很大的持久性和现实性,不会随着一些易变因素的变化而迅速消失。至于最近几十年来出现的对政治哲学、心灵哲学、生态哲学等的研究更具有重要的现实意义。

自 19 世纪中期西方哲学出现具有划时代意义的哲学思维方式的转向以来,实际影响最为经久的哲学流派莫过于实用主义了。这是因为实用主义在众多的现当代西方哲学流派中最能体现西方哲学从近代到现代的转向,即我们在上面已论证的实践的转向。这里需要补充的是:杜威等美国实用主义影响的经久性还在于它的包容性和开放性。

美国建国的历史不长。它的哲学和文化特别是那些影响较大的哲学和文化大都是从欧洲传入的,但它们传入美国后又必然与美国本土哲学和文化特别是和实用主义这种在美国影响最大的哲学和文化融合起来。发源于欧洲的分析哲学、现象学、存在哲学、结构主义和解构主义(后现代主义)本来主要是在一部分上层知识分子中流传的,影响范围有限。但当它们传入美国并与在公众中广泛流行的实用主义融合后,很快也成了影响范围广大的哲学派别。与此相关,一批从事现象学、存在哲学、分析哲学研究的欧洲哲学家大都只有得到美国学界的认可后,才能成为真正享有世界声誉的哲学家,他们的哲学也才能产生较大的现实影响。这些都标志着美国事实上成了现当代西方哲学的大本营。这既与美国在政治、经济、军事、文化等方面成为西方世界的超级大国相关,也与美国实用主义能够包容各种不同哲学的开放性相关。

如果上述的论点能够成立,那么以杜威为最大代表的美国实用主义就成了当代西方世界流传最广、影响最深的哲学流派。马克思主义者与西方哲学的关系突出地表现为与实用主义的关系。这当然不是看轻现象学、存在哲学、分析哲学这些在西方上层哲学界的显学地位,更不是否定用马克思主义观点分析和研究这些哲学的必要性;而只是说这些哲学的影响只有传入美国并与美国实用主义相融合后才能成为影响范围更大的显学,用马克思主义观点对这些哲学流派进行分析和研究最好与对实用主义的分析和研究结合起来。在当今美国甚至西方世界,实际上只有实用主义才是广大范围的民众最易接受的哲学。马克思主义者无论是从划清与西方现当代哲学的界限并批判其消极影响来说,还是从批判地吸取它们可能包含的合理因素来说,最应当做的是深入持久地研究最能与众多西方哲学流派相融合的实用主义。

　　当今的世界是多极并存的世界。美国是最大的发达国家,中国是最大的发展中国家。中美关系在世界的多元格局中起着主导作用。在哲学上的表现大体上与此相适应。在中国得到创造性发展的马克思主义哲学与在美国继续发生最大实际影响的实用主义哲学的关系也是当代哲学发展中最突出、最值得关注和正确处理的关系。换言之,实用主义与发展着的马克思主义哲学的关系是当代资本主义与发展着的社会主义的关系在哲学理论上最集中的体现。在改革开放的时代,我们在经济、政治上仍然必须严格划清与美国的政治和经济体制的界限,坚定对社会主义的优越性的信念;但又要与我们的对方展开对话,寻找共同的空间,达成适当的协议,促进互利合作。与此相适应,在哲学等意识形态上,我们更必须严格划清马克思主义哲学与实用主义等资产阶级哲学的界限,坚定对马克思主义优越性的信念。但这不能是简单地去进行空洞的口号式的斗争,而是在真正把握马克思主义哲学的根本原则和深入研究对方的理论的基础上去和对方展开对话,既注意揭露和批判对方的错误和片面性,也注意发掘并批判地吸取对方理论中与现代科学和社会发展相适应的因素。应当看到,作为资本主义意识形态的实用主义和作为无产阶级意识形态的马克思主义哲学,必然存在根本性的对立;但二者作为同时代的哲学,它们之间在某些节点上毕竟可能存在着彼此相通的张力。因此我们应当学会善于把西方敌对势力对我们实行西化和自由化的企图与西方哲学中的确存在的积极因素严格区别开来,使我们在防范西方现当代哲学的消极作用的同时也看到其中可能与马克思主义哲学相通的因素,借鉴后者对我们建设中国特色社会主义和实现"中国梦"能起到一定的促进作用。这意味着马克思主义哲学与实用主义等西方哲学流派的关系是既根本对立又存在着一定的统一的关系。在这种对立统一中,马克思主义哲学占有主导地位,它将取得越来越大的优势。这正是当代世界哲学发展的主要趋势。

当代美国实用主义哲学[①]

江 怡

北京师范大学哲学与社会学学院

对我来说,2015 年似乎是一个有着特殊意义的年份:我在这一年的许多工作都与实用主义有密切的联系。年初收到《学术月刊》杂志的邀请,为其实用主义专栏撰写了《论珀斯与分析哲学的关系》,发表在 2015 年第 7 期上;8 月份参加了在复旦大学举行的"杜威与实用主义"国际研讨会,见证了《杜威全集》中文版的全部出版;9 月份参加了在法国巴黎举行的"第二届欧洲实用主义大会",在"中国的实用主义"专场上介绍了实用主义在中国的情况;受邀为这本新创刊的《实用主义研究》集刊撰文。其实,我对实用主义哲学的关注和研究已经有 20 多年的历史了。早在 1994 年,我曾发表《实用与实用主义》一文,对人们通常在实用主义理解上的混乱做了理论上的澄清。2000 年,我发表了《透视世纪末的美国哲学》,对实用主义在美国哲学未来发展中的作用作了一些展望。2004 年,我发表了《美国实用主义哲学现状及其分析》,对实用主义在美国的历史和现状作了一些初步的分析。2013 年,我发表了《实用主义如何作为一种方法》,提出了我对实用主义哲学的一种理解。2014 年,我在意大利出版的英文版《欧洲美国哲学与实用主义杂志》上发表了《21 世纪中国的实用主义研究》,对中国哲学界在 21 世纪中的实用主义哲学研究所取得的成果给予了分析。同年 7 月,我

[①] 该文最初为我于 2015 年 7 月在北京师范大学所做讲座的初稿。后经修订补充,现予以正式刊发。感谢我的学生对该讲座的记录整理,感谢陈亚军教授同意刊用本文。

在丹麦出版的《珀斯：五个问题》一书中专门谈到我对自己研究实用主义哲学的兴趣和成果的介绍。2014年7月，我参加了在美国麻省举行的纪念珀斯逝世百年的国际会议，并在会议上介绍了珀斯研究在中国的情况。所有这些都使得我对美国实用主义哲学有了较为全面系统的了解和研究。在本文中，我将从历史和现状方面分析美国实用主义哲学的主要特征，特别是新老实用主义之间的区别。

一、实用主义在中国的发展概况

我们知道，20世纪初，实用主义是较早传入中国的一种西方思潮，所以中国和西方思想的交流在某种意义上与美国实用主义的发展是同步的。珀斯1878年发表一篇重要的关于实用主义的文章，詹姆斯1890年发表了《心理学原理》，20世纪20年代杜威来中国访问，这段时间也恰恰是美国实用主义刚刚兴起和发展的阶段，中国的学术界和思想界紧随美国哲学思想发展的脉络，两者之间几乎同步。新中国成立以后，特别是"文化大革命"期间，我们对美国实用主义的态度和看法都有了重大的转变，把实用主义当作意识形态上的一种坏的东西，称之为资产阶级庸俗哲学，并加以批判。实用主义作为一种方法以及理论观点在中国不再有市场。在这种情况下，实用主义思想理论本身没有得到应有重视，我们对实用主义的研究只能在学术研究的范围之内，无法进入公众话语领域。在"文化大革命"期间，国内出版了一些关于当代美国哲学研究的资料，比如翻译了詹姆斯和杜威的一些新资料，但是这些资料是作为内部资料发行的，而不是公开出版物，在"文化大革命"之后作为资产阶级哲学研究资料在商务印书馆出版，公开发行。这段历史说明，我们对实用主义的理解和把握出现了重大的偏差，同时期实用主义在美国蓬勃发展，而国内却对之大加鞭挞，这种状况一直持续到改革开放初期才有所好转。

1988年，中国现代外国哲学学会在四川成都召开了第一次全国性的关于实用主义的会议。实际上，在这之前就有很多讨论和研究实用主义的文章在杂志上发表，其中特别重要的一篇文章是复旦大学刘放桐教授发表的文章——《重新评价实用主义》,引起了很大的反响,使国内又开始重新重视美国实用主义的研究。当然,这种变化与当时的社会背景有关,国内的意识形态和政治格局都发生了巨大变化,因而实用主义才在学术和思想的层面重新受到重视,进入普通大众和学术视域。成都会议的论文集于2001年出版。这本书记载了美国实用主义在中国传播和发展的历程,以及中国的马克思主义者和实用主义者之间交锋的历史,记载了80年代末中国学术界对实用主义最新的研究成果。

这是美国实用主义传入中国的一个大致概况,现在中国的思想界和学术界对实用主义的关注有增无减,在某种意义上势头正旺。20世纪90年代之后,包括罗蒂、伯恩斯坦等哲学家在美国大力鼓吹实用主义,再加上蒯因的逻辑实用主义在美国的根深蒂固,实用主义在美国哲学界和学术界成为一种哲学主流。今天,我们重新了解美国当今的实用主义,某种意义上是使中国学术界重新回到和美国实用主义同步发展的轨道上。

不仅如此,我们对实用主义的研究更是为了交流和对话。通过研究,我们发现,实用主义哲学与马克思主义以及中国传统儒家的思想有很多共同之处。任何一个理论在一个国度和文化环境中生存下来,主要的原因之一就是这种文化都包含着可以接收、包容外来文化的基础,所以从这个意义上来讲,中国儒家思想的很多观点与实用主义有契合的地方,马克思主义同样如此。

二、美国实用主义发展概况

我们知道,实用主义的发展经过了三个历史阶段。第一个阶段为第一代实用主义,主要包括珀斯①、詹姆斯、杜威三位哲学家,他们被统称为"第一代实用主义者",也称作"老的实用主义者"。珀斯作为实用主义创始人,特别强调以理论的实际效果作为检验理论真理性的标准。在他那里,主要

---

① Sander C.Perice,通常译为"皮尔士"。但这个译名完全无法与原词相符,为了更好交流和符合翻译通行原则,我建议把该名称译为"珀斯"。

是分析概念的有效性,提出了实用主义的一条基本原则,称之为"珀斯原则":"一个概念的真就在于它能取得预期的效果"。珀斯的思想非常复杂,不仅包括真理观,还包括整套的认识论甚至形而上学。我们过去对他的研究,主要集中在认识论也就是真理观上面,很少研究他的形而上学,更少关注他在形式逻辑或者说符号逻辑方面的成就。这在美国也同样存在,在20世纪60年代甚至70年代之前,美国哲学界对珀斯思想的研究也是非常少的。尽管大家都知道他是实用主义的创始人,但是并没有针对他的思想进行系统深入的研究,而是关注实用主义后来的发展,如詹姆斯、杜威等人。60年代8卷本《珀斯文集》出版之后,他的思想才真正引起关注,到了90年代以后对于他的研究才成为美国学术界研究的热点。关注的内容主要有两个方面,一方面是珀斯的形而上学,另外一个方面就是他的符号学。2001年,美国哲学家代表团访问中国,有不少哲学家在会议的学术报告中专门分析珀斯的符号学。2005年,珀斯基金会与北京师范大学联合举行了中美哲学家关于珀斯符号学的研讨会,这说明美国学术界对珀斯思想的独创方面给予了更多的关注,而不仅仅是他的实用主义思想。在2014年举行的珀斯逝世百年大会上,来自世界各地的近300名学者对珀斯思想的各个方面都给予了更多关注。珀斯思想的确对后来的实用主义产生了深远影响,以至于詹姆斯把他称为实用主义创始人。但是詹姆斯对珀斯哲学的解释却受到了珀斯的质疑,他认为詹姆斯的阐释庸俗化了自己的观点。所以他不愿意把自己的思想称为"实用主义",而更愿意叫作"实效主义"(pragmaticism)。这个词是珀斯生造的,原来英文单词里是没有的,用他自己的话说,他故意用这个丑陋的词来区别时下流行的实用主义。

那么,詹姆斯的实用主义在哪些方面发展了珀斯的思想呢?他主要是以心理分析为基础来发展和阐述珀斯的思想,把珀斯提出的以实际效果作为检验理论真理性的标准推而广之,不仅仅运用在科学方面,更是扩展到人类活动的所有方面,由此来说明人类的认识活动只有在取得预期效果的情况下才能被看作是真的,他把自己的观点概括成一句话,即"有用即是真理"。这句话后来成为实用主义反复遭到批评的口实,更是中国马克思主义者对实用主义批判的主要依据。实际上,根据普特南的分析,这句话并不是詹姆斯的真实思想。当他强调以实际效果来检验理论或者认识真理的时候，他强调的是人类认识的相对性，是在反对认识的绝对性这一点上来说"有用即是真理"的。詹姆斯的这个观点到现在还受到很多批评，但是由于他广泛地传播珀斯的思想，使得实用主义在 20 世纪 30 年代成为美国主流的思潮。

在他之后不久，杜威从社会理论出发，运用达尔文进化论的思想，把实用主义建立在社会哲学的框架之内，使其具有更强大的影响力，远远超出了学术界、认识领域和科学研究领域，进入人类社会的各个方面，这样就逐渐演变成一种美国精神。实用主义在珀斯那里仅仅是一种科学研究方法，到了杜威那里就成了美国人生活的基本态度和准则。关于这方面的情况，我国学者余怀彦教授 2015 年出版的《深层美国》一书就全面说明了实用主义哲学如何成为当今美国社会生活各方面主导思想的表现和原因。

实用主义第二代是以布里奇曼、刘易斯和莫里斯三位哲学家为代表。布里奇曼是美国著名物理学家，并获得了诺贝尔物理学奖，他从物理学角度去分析了物理理论和概念确切含义的标准，认为只能用操作（operation）来检验一种理论和概念的意义，因此被称作操作主义。与第一代实用主义者相比，第二代实用主义哲学家有一个突出的特点，就是他们强烈地受到分析哲学和逻辑经验主义的影响。维也纳学派自从 1936 年解散之后，绝大部分成员都移居到了美国，给美国哲学界带来了新的哲学风气，这种新的风气注重以逻辑分析手段处理传统的哲学概念，而老的实用主义者除了珀斯之外，詹姆斯、杜威更多强调用心理学、社会学的方式处理理论和概念。分析哲学给美国学术界带来了新生气或者说新的方法，使得哲学研究、理论概念的确认变得更为精确清楚。

第二代实用主义是在与分析哲学相互交融的过程中发展起来的，这段历史并不长，也就是 40 年代到 50 年代这十几年。现在刘易斯的概念论实用主义和莫里斯的符号学实用主义在当今美国哲学界的影响还比较大，而布里奇曼的操作主义影响则不大了。刘易斯思想的影响更多地限于学术界，而莫里斯的影响则不仅限于此。莫里斯 1970 年出版了《美国哲学中的实用主义运动》一书，总结概括了从珀斯到他的时代美国实用主义的基本发展历程,其影响之大,现在仍然被美国哲学家作为分析美国实用主义发展历史的经典著作。在该书中,莫里斯从其符号实用主义观点出发分析美国实用主义产生的历史背景以及实用主义的所谓语用符号学,实际上就是他的符号实用主义的基本观点,涉及的人物基本上是两代的实用主义哲学家。其中最有代表性的观点是,他提出了至今还被实用主义者津津乐道和默认的四大特征,即科学和科学的方法占主导地位、哲学中的经验主义、生物进化论和美国民族理念的形成。前三个特征主要指美国第一代实用主义者特别是詹姆斯、杜威的哲学特征。美国当今实用主义者仍然坚持着这几大特征,虽然其中生物进化论这个特征逐渐被人们淡忘了。莫里斯本人是一个符号论实用主义者,他强调从符号对人产生的作用方面来分析概念和语言的实际意义,也就是分析符号与人的相互作用。他把符号学分为三个方面:第一是语形学,就是分析符号的句法结构,符号与符号之间的形式关系;第二是语义学,关注的是符号与所知对象的关系;第三是语用学,分析人在使用符号过程中所产生的问题。他的这种划分已经成为美国符号学的基本组成部分,而且,这三个方面实际上包括了第一代实用主义者所关注的重点:珀斯关心的是语形学研究,詹姆斯关注的是语义学研究,而杜威则更加关注语用学研究。

第二代实用主义者受到分析哲学的影响,这使得实用主义发生了很大变化。这种变化就是,他们不再从心理学或者社会分析的角度来谈论概念的意义,而是转向了对语言的强烈关注,因此莫里斯的符号学才被看作是第二代实用主义的集大成者。这种变化在20世纪40—50年代成为美国哲学界的主导倾向,而50年代之后这种实用主义就被逐渐赶出了美国哲学的主坛。这时出现了一个重要人物蒯因(Quine),他被看作是新一代实用主义的创始人。他被称作是逻辑实用主义者,以表明他与传统实用主义的传承,但实际上他的哲学与第一代甚至第二代实用主义者有很大的区别。

作为第三代实用主义的重要代表,蒯因是美国哲学史上具有划时代意义的哲学家,主要原因在于他关注的哲学重点已经不再是社会进化、社会心理或者社会生活了,而是逻辑话语,关注的是我们的语言如何用逻辑方法来得以澄清。虽然他晚年强调他的经验主义与传统实用主义有密切关系,但他仍然坚信实用主义实际上代表着经验主义的重大转向,强调句子的意义而不是词的意义,把对句子的意义的分析作为语言分析的中心。随后他扩充为把整个科学体系作为分析的中心,认为在一种科学理论中,其中的一个语句被证明是假的并不足以推翻这个科学理论体系本身,我们可以不断根据经验校正单个语句,但不能完全推翻这个语句所在的理论体系,所以,他的哲学又被称作经验主义的整体论。

第三代实用主义的第二位重要代表人物是古德曼(N.Goodman),他几乎是与蒯因同时代的人。相比蒯因,他更加强调语言与实在之间的互动关系,他的哲学影响在很大程度上是与蒯因以及其他哲学家合作产生的。另外一个代表人物是戴维森(D.Davidson)。戴维森与蒯因有着许多相同之处,他强调我们行为的意义要根据当下的实际效果加以确认,他把"意义"看作句子成真的条件,也就是说,只有当一个句子在某种情况下真,这个句子才是有意义的。此外,在哲学圈之外更有影响的实用主义者是罗蒂。罗蒂毫不讳言他是一个实用主义者,并被看作是最不具有分析哲学传统的实用主义哲学家,他在1969年编辑出版的《语言的转向》一书中直接提出了对分析哲学的批评,在1979年《哲学与自然之镜》一书中更是把语言哲学看作是传统哲学,所以他对分析哲学一直是持批判和否定的态度,这与蒯因和戴维森很不一样。

三、新老实用主义的区别

虽然第三代实用主义者并没有共同的哲学纲领,甚至在许多重要观点上也存在明显差别,但我们仍然可以从整体上分析第三代实用主义与第一代和第二代实用主义的区别。在我看来,这些区别主要体现在以下四个方面:

第一,强调语言分析的重要性。第一代实用主义者詹姆斯和杜威并没有把对语言的分析放在重要地位,他们认为需要研究的是经验和意识活动,所以经验和意识是其思想的两个核心概念。在珀斯那里,他虽然注重语言分析,但更多的是针对概念而不是语词的分析。我们要知道,当一个哲学家在讲概念而不是语词的时候,他并不是在谈分析的问题;但是当他在谈语词而不是概念的时候,他才是在用分析哲学的方式处理语言。传统哲学家比较喜欢用"范畴",如康德、黑格尔对范畴的研究;到现代的时候,哲学家们更喜欢使用"概念",讨论概念的形成。从"范畴"到"概念"是思想上或者说研究方法上的一个变化。蒯因在《实用主义者在经验主义中的地位》中说,从"概念"到"语词"的转换表明了整个经验主义哲学发生了转折,亦即不再追问这个词背后隐含的意义,而是直接追问语词本身,也就是把这个词放在所出现的句子之中考察其意义,而不孤立地分析它的意义。当把"概念"转换成"语词"的时候,意义的基本单位就不是语词,而是句子,这就意味着对意义标准的判定发生了变化。现代哲学家更多的是进行语词的分析而不是概念的分析,从语词、句子然后到整个理论体系的分析,而传统哲学则是从概念到判断再到推理,这个思路反映的是人类认识活动的进程,而从语词到句子再到句子体系反映的则是人类表达方式的过程。分析传统的哲学家更强调对语言本身的分析。

第二,对传统哲学的回归以及对形而上学的重新研究。老一代实用主义者,如珀斯对形而上学的研究,是从反对笛卡尔的身心二元论开始的。经验主义发展的一个重要标志就是反对先验论,反对传统哲学中对超验之物的研究。实用主义者认为,关于实在本质问题并不是更要紧的问题,更重要的是,实在如何在经验层面上呈现,而这种变化多端的经验背后是否有个实在的支撑并不重要。所以老一代实用主义者更多地把经验建立在当下的感觉上,包括詹姆斯和杜威。第三代实用主义者虽然也不把对超验之物的研究作为哲学的基础,但是他们认为我们不能完全排斥和放弃这种研究。蒯因提出的"本体论的相对性"就是认为,当一种理论在谈论实体的时候,我们可以认为它在承诺这种实体是存在的。例如,物理学中的原子或其他最小组成部分,虽然我们观察不到它们,但当我们谈论它们的时候,我们已经假设它们的存在了。所以,本体论的承诺是我们谈论一切对象的基础,也就是最终的根据。对象存在问题一直是很伤脑筋的事情,无数哲学家和逻辑学家都费尽心力讨论对象的存在如何在逻辑上加以证明。蒯因的"本体论承诺"就是要避免这样的对象问题。根据本体论承诺,我们完全可以假设对象是存在的,而不需要证明其是否真实存在,在这个意义上存在问题就变得不重要了。那是在什么意义上说实用主义回归形而上学呢？一方面,他们用实用主义态度对待形而上学;另一方面,他们认为,我们所理解的存在并不是隐藏在经验之后的看不到的东西,而是我们看得见、摸得着的当下感觉,所以当把存在拉回到当下感觉时,就是在告诉我们,这就是我们所认识的实在,不需要追问经验之后的东西或者是否有某个东西存在。

戴维森并不研究形而上学问题,不强调超验的实在,但他把重点放到人类认识活动的根本结构上。我们知道蒯因反对两个教条,而戴维森提出了反对第三个教条,就是所谓的概念图式。这种教条认为,我们所有的认识活动都有先天的概念图式,这种概念图式决定了认识活动的性质、范围和特征。人类之所以能够相互交流,就是因为我们有着统一的认识模式。这种观点在语言学界和哲学界都是颇为流行的,很多著名哲学家都同意这个观点,而实用主义者却反对这种看法。在实用主义者看来,如果有先天统一的模式,就没办法解释文化的差异性,也没办法解释人类认识进步的可能性。所以,蒯因提出"翻译的不确定性",戴维森提出"彻底翻译的不可能性",认为我们的一切认识都是来自经验的,是在感受自然和社会的经验中积累起来的,我们可以把这种结果作为一个框架来统摄后来的认识活动,但是不能把结构本身当作先天的,它也是经验形成的。

由此,我认为,任何一种文化都无法用另外一种文化加以彻底翻译。中国文化为何在西方引不起重视,得不到理解,并不是说我们的宣传不够或者语言文化不行,而是文化差异的问题。同样,国外的汉学家来中国演讲,他们所讲的中国文化和我们自己感受的中国文化差别就很大。所以,我们不能期望一种文化能完全理解另外一种文化,这样才有了交流和对话的必要性。交流是为了更深入地相互理解,但这种理解只能是越来越好,而不可能有终结。不同的文化之间并不存在一个所谓的共同理性,我们对于另外一种文化的理解都是基于自身的文化。要彻底了解另一种文化,只有融入其中,成为它的一分子。戴维森所要反对的第三个教条就是这种共同的概念图式。从这个意义上来说,第三代实用主义者对形而上学问题的关注更多是从语言和现实的角度。

第三,相对主义倾向。这是实用主义很重要的一个特点,我们可以从莫里斯提出的实用主义四大特征中感受到。罗蒂把相对主义这个问题讲得比较透彻。他认为,一个理论的真与假,不取决于我们对理论本身的评价,而在于这个理论所处的文化共同体是否接受认可该理论,所以,文化共同体以及其中的同伴就是评判这种理论是否为真的标准。这是一种相当彻底的相对主义。

相对主义与实用主义的宽容精神有着密切关系。在罗蒂看来,我们可以用一种宽容的态度接受另一种文化,但是要从我们自身文化角度去评判和理解另一种文化则是不可能的。不能理解并不能成为评判这种文化真实性和有效性的标准,但是我们往往容易这样去做,把不理解的东西看作是有害的。相对主义在实用主义的认识论上有明显表现,而认识论上的相对主义通常导致哲学上的怀疑论。第三代实用主义者干脆就直接宣称自己是相对主义者。

第四,更加强调方法论的重要性。詹姆斯一直把实用主义当作一种方法。他有一个很有意思的比喻。他说,哲学就像是一座大厦,大厦里的不同房间里有各种观点的哲学家在沉思,房间与房间之间有通道,而实用主义者就站在通道上给大家指路。所以,实用主义是一种获取知识的方法。实用主义者不追问实在为什么呈现,不问实在背后的理由,而是追问实在是怎么呈现的,它是如何进入认识领域的,这个过程、通道和方法是实用主义的中心话题。用今天的话来说,我们不追问事物的性质,而是追问事物如何变成这个样子的,事物变成这个样子的过程就决定了它的性质。用哲学的话说,就是不要追问是什么,而要追问如何是,这就是强调方法的重要性。

上面所讲的新老实用主义之间的这四个方面的区别还比较粗糙,不够完整,但这几个方面的归纳,对我们学习把握实用主义还是很有用的。

四、新实用主义者对老实用主义者的评价

就像儒家、道家思想是中国的传统文化一样,实用主义就是美国的传统文化,它深入到美国的哲学、思想、文化和社会生活的各个层面。所以,对实

用主义的评价是了解新实用主义的一个开端。那么,新实用主义代表人物蒯因、罗蒂、普特南对老实用主义者又是如何评价的呢? 总体上说,他们各自侧重的方面不一样。

蒯因比较强调珀斯的作用,他在《实用主义者在经验主义中的地位》一文中明确把珀斯的哲学看作是经验主义发展的重要转折点。他认为,经验主义发展的历史中有五个转折点,珀斯是其中之一,即把意义的单位从语词转向了句子。他认为珀斯哲学主要有以下的贡献:一是以句子为中心来确定意义;二是行为主义倾向;三是意义的证实原则。我们知道,"意义的证实原则"是维也纳学派提出的一个重要观点,也就是命题的意义在于证实它的方法,这个原则是作为检验意义的标准。蒯因认为珀斯也提出了证实原则,那就是用可以期望的实际效果来加以证实,其实这种把效果作为标准与上述把方法作为标准是有异曲同工之处的,因为这种效果并非就是实际效果而是指可以预期的效果,这就包含了一种证实的可能性。四是人类中心论的观点。这是整个实用主义非常重要的观点,正是以人类为中心,以人的实际活动与经验为中心,才可以判定人类认识活动的真与有效性。蒯因认为,这直接导致了以后实用主义把真理与人的活动密切联系起来的倾向。在实用主义者看来,强调实践就是强调效果,也就是强调用实践的最终结果来检验真理。蒯因除了对珀斯哲学给予了评价,还对实用主义的一般特征作了描述,提出了四点:一,自然主义,认为一切理论都可以用科学的方法加以观察和研究;二,可谬主义,认为人类的认识是在不断纠错中发展的;三,行为主义;四,人造真理观。

普特南在 1995 年的《实用主义》一书中侧重讨论詹姆斯哲学,认为詹姆斯的哲学具有永恒性。这种永恒性体现在三个方面:第一,整体论,就是强调事实与价值之间的相互渗透。休谟提出的"是"与"应当"的问题引发了西方哲学史上对于事实与价值两分的争论。詹姆斯认为,事实与价值不是孤立和截然对立的,我们谈到事实的时候就包含了价值判断,没有纯粹孤立的事实;同样,我们在谈及价值的时候也是对事实的评判,也没有纯粹的价值,认为事实与价值之间是不能分开的,用普特南的话说,就是一种整体论的思想。第二,直接的实在论。关于实在与经验的关系一直是争论不休的问题。在实用主义者看来,实在论是我们一切认识的基础,这种实在论通常被称作"常识实在论"。这种实在论相信,我们的常识和当下感觉,如天是蓝的、树是存在的等,都是实在的,它们不过是我们对外在世界的认识和感觉。这种认识和感觉不是私人的,而是建立在公共的可以观察的基础上。这就是常识的、直接的实在论。第三,真理观。詹姆斯的"有用即真理"给他带来了很多批评,实际上他强调的真理是经验上的可确实性。他认为,真理是最后取得的意见,是一种对思想的把握,不是局部的、有限的意见或者某些人的意见。要对思想进行把握就要对实在有所反映,这个实在就是经验实在。詹姆斯曾说过,实在的唯一客观标准就是对思想的强制性,"真"不是与"有用"而是与"实在"联系起来讲的。所以,詹姆斯的真理观不是庸俗的"有用即真理",而是实用主义意义上的反映论,是对实在的关注。

最后是关于罗蒂对早期实用主义的评价,他比较重视杜威,在《建设我们的国家》一书中把杜威看作是美国哲学和精神的代表,连同诗人惠特曼,他们都追求美好的人类生活方式。罗蒂强调杜威的民主主义思想。杜威是民主主义者、社会活动家,在推进美国的民主进程中起了非常重要的作用。罗蒂认为,杜威哲学的最大特征就是把所有事情都变得具有了时间性,不承认存在完全确定的东西。所以,杜威哲学最大的成就就是把"真的"或者是"对的"看作是满意地表达了发现解决问题的方法,也就是说,只要你有解决问题的方法就是对的就是好的,而这种满意的方法有可能被其他更满意的方法替代,这样人类社会就得以不停地进步。因此,在实用主义哲学家那里没有最好,只有更好。

顺便提一下,杜威因为其哲学思想与中国传统思想有相通之处,又来中国讲过学,所以美国很多学者关心实用主义在中国的发展。美国夏威夷大学安乐哲很注意研究杜威哲学与中国思想的关系,曾于 2002 年在哈佛开了一个专题讨论会,但是却受到了两方面的批评。一方面是美国研究杜威思想的哲学家认为他错误理解了杜威的思想;另一方面,新儒家的代表人物杜维明认为他在讲儒家思想的时候没讲到位。虽然我们说一种文化不可能彻底了解另外一种文化,但是这样的交流却是唯一的相互理解的路径。罗蒂对杜威民主思想的关注是很有现实意义的,他很重视如何建设一个民主法治的国家。他在复旦大学的一次演讲中提到"在原子弹发明后的今天,人类仍然能生活在地球上纯粹是一种侥幸",因为一旦核武器落到恐怖分子或者独裁者手里将带来比自然灾害严重得多的后果。必须靠制度来遏制人性恶的方面的发展,而不是依靠德性道德、品质来约束,只有民主制度的建设才能使人类社会得到真正的保障。罗蒂对杜威民主思想的重视用意在此。

伦理学与美学：
从实用主义到身体美学和生活艺术

Richard Shusterman

Florida Atlantic University

一

　　维特根斯坦在他的《逻辑哲学论》中大胆直接地主张(没有进一步的论证或阐明)"伦理学和美学是同一的"①。当然,这一主张的真理性还未明晰。甚至这一主张的句法还明确地展现出这一术语的二元性。因此主张同一性并不是去报道一个事实,而是去推翻关于公然相异的推断。在维特根斯坦和我们的时代,大部分的知识分子不仅仅是把伦理的东西和审美的东西区分开来,而且经常把它们置于相互对立的位置。伦理学和美学被认为是指示了一般价值领域中的两个独立的领域,它们被一些完全不同的目标、方法和标准所主导,甚至表现在一些相互竞争和冲突的固定模式中:没有道德的审美者和没有审美品位的庸俗道德者。伦理态度关注的是行动和它的现实目的以及实践的结果,而审美态度是由占主导地位的后康德传统来定义的,它与实践态度截然相对,并且被认为是完全无目的的、非功利的观照。当然,正是康德关键性地通过与实践功能性相反的非功利性和无目的的目的性来规定审美的。

---

　　①　路德维希·维特根斯坦:《逻辑哲学论》,伦敦,劳特里奇1963年版,第147页。对维特根斯坦评论的进一步阐释,参见理查德·舒斯特曼:《实用主义美学》(牛津,布莱克韦尔出版社1992年第2版;纽约,罗曼 & 里特菲尔德出版社2000年版),中文版第9页。

　　作为一位实用主义美学的拥护者,我赞赏艺术和审美经验中丰富多样的和多元重要的功能性,我反对将伦理和审美之间视为对立的常规立场。尽管维特根斯坦关于它们同一性的直率而又隐晦的论断富有启发性,但它并没有把我们带得很远。因此,在《实用主义美学》和之后的一些著作(如《实践哲学》和《生活即审美》)中,我已经尝试着展现它们的联结,不仅通过阐述伦理因素和政治因素是如何有效地整合进我们对艺术作品的反应中,而且通过呈现一种对民主的审美辩护和通过阐明哲学作为一种生活的伦理—审美艺术的观点。① 在此我并不是以总结的形式来重述所有的论证,而是想通过另一种方式来挑战对伦理学和美学之间过于简单化对立的假定。通过以非常简明而广泛的方式来探究一些伦理学与美学联结的历史时期,我们将会发现简单地规定两者之间的任一关系(无论相互矛盾或相互同一)而产生的一个问题是,两者的概念在它们漫长的使用史中被赋予了不同的意义或解释。

　　尽管实用主义为人所知的是被威廉·詹姆斯定义为一种朝前看的哲学,他和其他实用主义者都认识到哲学的问题和概念承载着人类历史的印记,因此能够通过考察它们错综复杂的历史根源来让它们更加明晰地呈现(虽然也会更加的复杂)。谱系学的分析无法让伦理学与美学之间的交流困难变得简洁明了。不过因无法厘清这些术语间的不同历史意义和关系而产生的一些令人沮丧和容易搞混的困难,是能够避免的,因而伦理学和美学之间的对立不是在概念上的必然对立,不会导致所有艺术家(和思想家)试图统一两者的勇敢且成功的尝试看上去像实现方的圆那样荒唐。

二

　　伦理学和哲学一样历史悠久,可能在某种意义上更为悠久。因为伦理学的内容不仅包括关于善、正义和美德的性质,而且是关于指导生活的最好

---

① 参见拙著《实用主义美学》和《实践哲学:实用主义与哲学生活》(纽约,劳特里奇1997年版),以及《生活即审美:艺术目的的审美选择》(伊萨卡,康奈尔大学出版社2000年版)。

规则的话语式的哲学探讨。它也暗示着一种生活的普遍类型或方式[源于希腊的风俗(ethos)——习俗或习惯的概念],这可能不会以一种特别的话语方式来表达(甚至即使表达出来),可能也不会成为哲学讨论的正式主题。不仅如此,尽管前面的句子把善、正义和美德这三个概念放在一起,但是正如约翰·杜威所说的,这三个概念实际上在道德判断中是独立的变量,它们具有不同的来源,而且一者绝对不能简化为另一者。① 像善(good)这一概念原则上是处理我们的"欲望和目的"(如幸福、快乐和自我实现)的满足,所以正义(right)这一概念表达的是"被社会赋予和支持"的相互权利和义务这一对法律的观念,而对于美德(virtuous)这一概念的内容则是基于"普遍认可"或赞同的情感,这超越了欲望满足的简单积累和社会强制性的责任。在展现美德方面,圣人和英雄的所为的确胜于那种仅仅是善的行为,或者那种我们有权要求负责的行为。

杜威区分"这三种元素"为"独立的变量"的论点,并不是否认它们在实际的道德情境中是相互交织在一起的,而是坚持主张这三者不可简化为某种至高的伦理价值或层级,并认为它们在自己所暗示的道德判断中经常发生冲突。因此在道德情境中这三者的共存与冲突,不可能机械地从某种被设置好的单一的、至高的伦理标准或一致性中获得某一理性答案。在某种情境或某个时刻,某些道德因素似乎要优先于其他道德因素,但是对于哪种因素应该优先考量却是时常引起争议的。这种复杂性是使得道德抉择经常变得很困难的原因之一。我认为这些基本因素的多元性,由于在不同的语境和问题情境中发生重心转移,也使得道德判断和论证非常类似于美学中的批评性判断和论证。在这两种领域中人们不能要求以一种简单的标准或一套固定的规则,机械式地规定一种唯一的正确意见。而是人们必须去使用自己感知的洞察力、想象和关于什么是适当的实际品位。同时伦理学中基本因素的多元性由于使伦理学概念变得更复杂,也使得伦理学和美学的比较也变得更复杂。

① 参见约翰·杜威:《道德的三种独立要素》,引自《约翰·杜威:晚期著作》第5卷(卡本代尔,南伊利诺伊大学出版社1984年版),第286—287页。

美学展现了相似的复杂性。审美判断并不是由单一的美的标准所主导。不仅在审美判断中存在着许多起作用的审美品质，比如崇高、强烈或生动，它们不能被简单地称为美，而且在艺术判断中也有诸多标准，它们不是基于纯粹的知觉属性，所以在此意义上它们完全不是纯粹的审美属性。如此重要的标准如新颖性和创造性，很明显是基于历史因素，而非基于单独的知觉因素。意义的复杂性和伦理学与美学的标准，这两者在一定程度上是这些领域的一种评价性功能，以鼓励对相互竞争的定义、用法和标准提出争议和论点。不过这也是这些学科在漫长历史中的产物，也是它们在不同时期和不同文化中所扮演不同角色的结果。推翻后康德传统对伦理学和美学之间基本对立的假定，其方式之一就是回溯至古希腊文化和中国传统文化中。

三

尽管美学在 17 世纪 50 年代才被正式设立为一门哲学学科，但是这门学科的绝对大部分主题和问题在古代就已经讨论过了。在很大程度上这是因为艺术像宗教与修辞学一样，都是哲学必须要取而代之的竞争对手之一，从而使哲学获得作为智慧、幸福和合适的生活向导的最高源泉的文化霸权。不过另一原因是希腊人认识到美和艺术能够对人类的品格和伦理行为发挥非常强大的塑造性影响。由于苏格拉底和柏拉图经常强烈地批评艺术作品和艺术家的无知，导致我们时常忘记了美和艺术对他们的伦理思想和随后的伦理理论是多么的重要。虽然柏拉图在《理想国》的第十卷中广泛地谴责他那个时代的摹仿的艺术，他之所以这样做的真正原因是他肯定了在伦理学和美学之间存在着一种非常深和强的关联，这种关联在美、和谐、相称和有序之中可以感觉得到。柏拉图认为那些摹仿的艺术败坏了人的品格，因为它们利用假象和感觉主义来诱惑我们心灵的最低级部分和唤起激情，这打乱了灵魂的平衡秩序，很可能会败坏品格和激起不道德的行为。

不过在《理想国》的前面部分中，柏拉图坚持主张美和艺术在产生出作为正义而必要的伦理品质方面起着关键的作用。柏拉图认为正义是一种基本的心灵美德，它是由人类灵魂中适当的秩序所统治，接着他把这种正确统治秩序的观点投射到城邦的公共秩序之上。一个正义的城邦，就是当它由一种管理着不同阶层的公民的适当秩序所统治时，每一个群体都在为整个共同体的更好发展而尽善尽责，哲学家是居于最高统治地位的保卫者，他教化和统治着城邦的保卫者。不过柏拉图为了确保对保卫者的合适的教育和在心灵中建立普遍适当的秩序，后者构成了个体的正义美德，他认为我们必须要重视美学问题。不仅要求我们的理智而且要求我们的情感和欲望必须被训练来识别和欣赏正确的秩序，以便我们渴求和喜爱它。因此，美的和谐在这种教育中被提倡为关键的手段①。美作为好秩序的范例，它是值得渴求和爱的，它并不是由严格的机械的规则所固定，它不仅为教导人们去欣赏和识别好的秩序提供一种绝佳的手段，而且可以为好的政治秩序提供一种模式，这种秩序不能简化为严格规定我们所有行为的不变律法或指令。因此这完全符合柏拉图对他的理想政体是"kallipolis"（意为"美好城邦"）的描绘，也符合苏格拉底在概述城邦保卫者的品质和教育时被赞誉为"雕塑家"的描绘，他制作出了"在美中的完美统治者的雕像"②。

美学和伦理学之间的重要关联还在柏拉图的另一观点中得到确认，即哲学的人生是追求伦理审美的完美，其激励模式就是美。在《会饮篇》③，柏拉图赞扬把对美的追求作为哲学之源，并且他极好地描绘了哲学的人生就是一种持续不断地对更高的美的追求，这既在道德上使哲学家高贵，又在审美上使他们愉悦。此种追求不仅仅是去观赏和占有美的事物，而且是去创造和产生出美的事物："美妙的和精彩的演讲和思想"和"美的追求与实践"，这些为我们追求不朽提供基本的生命动力（正如生育和养育优秀的孩子那样），并在我们死后成为保存有关我们人生的美丽纪念。英雄们已甘

---

① 参见柏拉图：《柏拉图全集》（第二卷），王晓朝译，人民出版社 2003 年版，第 368 页。
② 参见柏拉图：《柏拉图全集》（第二卷），王晓朝译，人民出版社 2003 年版，第 527、544 页。
③ 参见柏拉图：《柏拉图全集》（第二卷），王晓朝译，人民出版社 2003 年版，第 237—256 页。

愿牺牲自己的生命去获得"美德的不朽记忆"。而哲学家的道德追求有着更多目标,他们还追求关于美本身的完美形式的一种持久视野,它不仅能提供关于美的最大乐趣,而且能带来持续"产生真实美德"的完美知识,而不是只产生美德的美丽印象和偶然记忆。①

因此,美学在爱美的希腊人的伦理思想和生活中扮演着非常关键的角色。一种美德生活的范例被认为是一种美的生活,并且美德之美被当作是一个关于美德生活之所以值得追求和有价值的重要原因。美德之所以值得我们去钦慕和仿效,这是因为它的吸引力,而不是因为道德规则凭借一套固定指令所带来的强迫,这种固定指令规定了对不服从的义务和惩罚。所以希腊人并没有明确地把美与伦理之善截然分开,正如我们所看到的那样,这不仅从他们对复合术语"kalon-kai-agathon"("美与善")的一般使用中看到,而且可以从他们频繁地使用"kalon"中看到,此特殊术语指"美",也指向伦理之善。我认为我们的伦理和美学词汇在某种程度上始终表现出它们之间的重要交汇或重叠。我们在道德上说某事是"正确的"、"正义的"、"公平的"或"恰当的",但是所有这些用语都有明显的美学含义和用法,正如"平衡"这一概念,我们经常用来判断什么是正确的、正义的、公平的或恰当的。柏拉图把"秩序"这一概念看作是正义的基础,此概念同样明显具有和统一价值相联的审美含义。在我们的美学话语中,典型的伦理学谓词"好的"的使用频率(比如在描述文学作品、戏剧和绘画),与标准的美学术语"美的"一样多,甚至有时前者更多些。

如果我们把目光从柏拉图和欧洲转向广泛地影响了亚洲伦理思想的儒家传统,我们会看到一种相似的甚至更强的对伦理学与美学之间联结的强调。在《论语》②中,孔子坚持"和为贵"的伦理重要性,而不是仅仅遵从固定的道德法则或命令,同样地,他也强调审美实践如音乐和仪式是产生和保持和谐的重要方式(1.12)。君子是被当作在道德行为上的楷模,因此他必

---

① 参见 W.D.劳斯翻译的《与柏拉图的重要对话》,纽约,明导出版社 1956 年版,第 103、105、106 页。

② 参见安乐哲、罗思文译:《论语》,纽约,巴兰坦出版社 1998 年版,编号指章与节,而非页码。

须通过完善自己的品格来审美地自我塑造(成己),而这是基于"乐节礼乐"(16.5)。不过儒家通过强调"动容貌"、"正颜色"和"出辞气"来进一步强化美德与审美现象的联结,这些强调的内容应该是美德的展现,并且有助于达到和谐(8.4)。因此整部《论语》都致力于描绘某种展现美德的身体姿态、面部表情和着装打扮。

孔子强调君子的美德发挥其作用不是通过道德命令、威胁和惩罚,而是通过鼓励效仿和爱慕。"君子以文会友,以友辅仁"(12.24)、"君子喻于义",并且由于他们的吸引力,会有人因为同样的德行而努力"见贤思齐焉,见不贤而内自省也"(4.16—4.17)。同样,荀子也主张音乐和礼仪的审美—道德的力量对塑造一个人的品格和行为的作用,这种力量转变为一种更加成功的和谐形式,会有助于广大的社会群体之间的和谐。荀子清楚地阐释了礼的审美活动是如何结合"情与文"的"养也"之后获得"养体和养目",并逐步获得秩序之理与"中道"的知识(19.2c、19.2d);礼不仅滋养情感使其得到必要的表达,而且在形式上让情感表达得更加得体、平稳,在道德上和社会意义上让它更适当和美丽。所以礼改善自身内在品格的同时,也影响着他人的行为朝更和谐的方向前进,因此荀子称它为"强固之本"(15.4)。对于音乐,荀子也类似地认为它是必要的和令人愉悦的,因为它来源于人类不可分割的情感本性。"夫乐者乐也,人情之所必不免也。"但是音乐不仅表达人直接的自然情感,它会升华这种情感,并且更普遍地让人的性情更好、更吸引人和更适度地表达,这都是为了"中道"的统一、和谐、有序和认知。由于音乐"足以感动人之善心",所以"故乐者、天下之大齐也,中和之纪也,人情之所必不免也"。由此音乐具有非常重要的伦理的、社会的和政治的重要性。①

生命,即感觉的身体是我们所有审美情感和审美愉悦的中心。尽管大部分西方哲学家(被我们占主导地位的观念论传统所引导)已经忽视了身体在审美经验中的作用,我已经通过发展一门称为"身体美学"的学科来努力使它成为中心,这门学科也远不止关注身体的外在形式。对于这项事业,

---

① 参见荀子:《荀子》,安小兰译注,中华书局 2007 年版,第 196、198 页。

中国的儒家传统(也包括道家学说)一直给予很多启迪。由于儒家传统在中国思想中依然处于非常重要的地位,所以我想强调伦理学与美学的有力联结对于现代中国哲学家来说应该是自然而然的事情。现代中国哲学家不会考虑把这些观念看作是相互矛盾之事,因为他们意识到若不能理解儒家伦理的审美维度就无法真正地理解儒家伦理思想。所以美学在现代中国是学院哲学中一门非常核心的学科,它是伦理理论和实践的重要思想外源。不幸的是,在当今中国这种理论信念并没有超出学院而充分地变成人们的日常实践活动。最后,正如我从一些与中国舞者的谈论中所获知的那样,对于舞者身体在追求表演的审美需求时,无法做到充分的道德考量。所以我也不想称赞现代中国是一个异域的乌托邦,也从来没有打算诅咒西方人今天的所作所为。相反,我的目的是高扬古代中国思想的价值,以便能帮助我们重建美学与伦理学之间的联结。

四

在现代西方文化中,美学与伦理学的联结已经被认为是有问题的,因为希腊美德伦理学的审美维度很大程度上已经被一种道德观所取代了,即道德是一个由法则、权利和义务组成的并指导恰当行为的综合体系。尽管这一体系现在大部分是用一些纯哲学术语来解释和辩护,但是它还是历史性地立足于绝对上帝的观念(属于犹太基督教传统),绝对上帝创造了宇宙和宇宙的价值,它一直根据绝对的自然法和道德法来统治宇宙。"伦理"和"道德"这两个术语经常被当成同义词来使用,并且两者都源于习惯或习俗这一相同的观念(希腊传统中叫 ethos,拉丁传统中叫 mores)。不过现代的哲学家经常用不同的术语来区分伦理概念和道德概念,前者是关于价值和如何生活的一般问题,后者是指一种关于义务、强制法和权利的明确、条理和综合的体系,它应该规定恰当的行为。

非常有必要提及康德,他不仅为基于义务的道德概念作出了最有影响力的表述,而且最为关键的是把审美领域与伦理道德的实践领域区分开来,这一区分是基于细致地把(伦理道德意义上的)善的概念,与审美意义上的美的概念区分开来。康德认为对美的审美判断是建立在主观的愉快经验之上的，它没有任何的实践兴趣、功利或目的，也不依赖任何的概念，但它与善的判断一样可以获得某种普通认同，后者（善的判断）是基于客观的兴趣和目的，也依赖于概念。[①] 当然，康德也意识到伦理和审美存在某种联结。最为出名的是他提到美作为道德的象征，并告诉我们通过摆脱个人兴趣和功利来鉴赏事物以此为道德做准备，正如他承认的那样，审美经验本质上是依赖于我们认知上的想象力和知性能力。不过康德审美理论的重大突破是为了给审美领域留下自主的空间，这是通过明确地把审美从伦理和认知领域区分开来实现的。康德谨慎地把审美从伦理或实践领域和纯粹认知或科学领域区分开来（这反映在他的三部著作：《纯粹理论批判》、《实践理性批判》和《判断力批判》），这不仅仅是因为他明确地区分理智能力和天才地描绘对差异的分析的结果。这也表达出现代性更为广泛的文化力量和文化专业化的逻辑。

马克斯·韦伯用文化的理性化、世俗化和特殊化来描绘这种逻辑，这是对传统西方统一的基督教世界观的去魅，并把它有组织化的领域分割成三个独立自主的世俗文化领域，即科学、艺术和道德，每一者分别由它们自身的理论判断、审美判断和道德实践判断的内在逻辑所主宰。在现代性中把美学从伦理学中截然分立开来，这对于推动艺术自治的观念是非常重要的，也因此把艺术从服务于基督教和政治权力的意识形态的传统角色中解放出来。纯粹美学自治的观念可以在"为了艺术而艺术"的这一最强有力的信条中发现，这在现代艺术的发展中已经具有历史性的价值。但是，认为艺术和审美判断应该被视为完全不考虑伦理因素和社会政治因素的观念，已经不再非常有效和可信了。太多的现代艺术十分清楚地表达着伦理关怀，甚至把政治上的抗议置于表现内容的中心位置，毫无疑问，一些特定的规约艺术生产与接受的制度（如博物馆、画廊、专门展览、艺术杂志和艺术院校等）已经嵌入道德义务和政治义务的网络中了，这都反映在他们的美学活动中。

[①] 对于更详细地批判性分析康德美学理论中隐藏的兴趣和社会伦理因素，参见理查德·舒斯特曼，《关于鉴赏的瑕疵：休谟和康德美学理论中作为自然的社会特权》，引自《表面与深度：批判与文化的辩证法》（伊萨卡，康奈尔大学出版社2002年版）。

甚至像 T.S.艾略特这种坚定的现代主义者也逐渐意识到，一种作者和读者都摆脱了道德和社会考量的"'纯粹'的艺术鉴赏"是"虚幻的"、"抽象的"或"臆想的"。①

在这一部分我已经用了很多的艺术术语来谈论美学，这有一种把美学等同于艺术哲学或艺术理论的倾向了。不过这从历史角度来说是站不住脚的。美学学科在现代是由亚历山大·鲍姆加登在18世纪中期首次建立的，它是关于感官知觉的一般理论。它的名字源于希腊词"aisthesis"，鲍姆加登把美学定义为"感官知觉的科学"，且它的目的是"完善感官知觉本身"。这一定义并不限于艺术。那时美学是作为逻辑学的补充，这两者一起提供一种综合的知识理论，鲍姆加登称之为生成论（Gnoseology）。尽管他认为感官知觉是一种低于概念思维的官能，但是整个美学计划是为了展示感官知觉（尤其经过系统训练）是如何有力地助益于知识的，是如何更普遍地改进我们的思维和生活的。鲍姆加登最初的哲学美学计划至少在两种意义上是实践的。首先，这一学科的目的不仅仅是一种为了真理自身的描述性真理，而且涉及改进感官知觉的向善目标，它不仅为科学和"自由的艺术"提供"优良的素材"或"扎实的基础"，而且让我们"在日常生活的实践行动中"更容易获得成功。更好的感官知觉能够让我们对他人的需求和遭遇更加敏感（对于我们欲求的需要和方向也是一样），而且以这种方式让我们成为更有效的道德行动者。总之，美学被当作一项规范性的事业，这意味着它的应用超出了自己的实践，也超出了美的艺术领域。其次，美学不只是包含理论活动，它还包括训练被改进的感官知觉的实践练习，鲍姆加登把它描述为苦行僧般的或勤学苦练式的审美活动。除了沉思冥想，美学还意味着行动。非常不幸的是，尽管鲍姆加登承认美学不仅关注感官知觉，而且也涉及实践事务，但是他把身体从他的美学理论中排除出去了，这是在追随笛卡尔的理性主义传统，他把所有的知觉和任意动作看作是与理智活动一样，并且假如身体不是道德脆弱的危险来源的话，他把身体只看作是一架机器或一套机

① 参见 T.S.艾略特：《使用诗歌与使用批判》（伦敦，费伯出版社1964年版），第98、99页，对艾略特立场更详尽的阐述，参见理查德·舒斯特曼：《T.S.艾略特与批判哲学》，纽约，哥伦比亚大学出版社1988年版。

械装置。因此,我的身体美学计划是很有必要的,它不仅把美学带回它原初更广泛和更实际的方向,而且把身体引入实用主义美学的知觉层面,这一美学是为了生活的伦理艺术,而不仅仅是为了纯粹的艺术。①

把美学当成一般的知觉理论的观念并没有持续很长的时间。康德重新把美学当成基本的鉴赏理论。尽管鉴赏很显然是一种知觉形式,但是康德理论的焦点是为了使审美的鉴赏判断根本不同于单单的感觉的感官鉴赏,并且它的首要目的是为这种鉴赏判断提供出一种主观的标准或模式。不过鲍姆加登也认为美学的范围要比艺术的范围宽广得多。康德也认同这一点;事实上,自然为康德的纯粹审美判断提供了范例,无论这种判断是聚焦于美还是崇高。但是对于黑格尔来说,美学是极其纯粹的和抽象的。在他极富影响的美学导论讲座开篇,黑格尔就指出:"美学"这一术语是"如此的不适宜"和"令人失望",它无法指称所研究的领域,"这门科学最合适的表述是'艺术哲学',或者更精确地来讲,是'美的艺术的哲学'"。接着黑格尔主张美的艺术所涉的内容(因此也是美学和纯粹艺术哲学的内容)不是对艺术形式的感官知觉,也不是享受艺术所带来的愉悦,而是纯粹艺术所表达的理念。理念和概念是同一个东西,它们带来的不是对某个特定知觉的清晰意识,而是对"最综合的心灵真理"的明确意识。因此,黑格尔把美学从知觉中抽离出来而朝着概念前进;使美学脱离具体的实践和生活的经验,而以概念真理作为自身的方向;他坚称美学是"通过思想的手段来思考艺术,目的并不是为了刺激艺术创作,而是为了科学地探究艺术何为"②。

作为19世纪里程碑式的人物,黑格尔对20世纪美学产生了持久的影响力,并且他视美学与美的艺术同一的观念,依然主导着今天许多理论,同样影响今天美学理论的还有悠久的柏拉图和亚里士多德传统,即让艺术与生活分离,把制作与实践分开。由于柏拉图批评艺术过于远离现实,所以亚里士多德只把艺术定义为制作(在希腊语中称为 poiesis),与生活的道德实

---

① 实际上身体美学的构思是通过对实用主义美学的研究和通过研究哲学作为具体的生活方式或生活艺术形成的。参见拙著《实用主义美学》与《实践哲学:实用主义与哲学生活》,纽约,劳特里奇出版社1997年版。

② 黑格尔:《美学》(第一卷),朱光潜译,商务印书馆1979年版,第142页。

践形成对比。柏拉图除了拒绝艺术,认为它体现了欺骗性的非现实性,他也担心艺术的力量会渗透和玷污人的灵魂,因此会败坏恰当的行动。柏拉图认为艺术创作和艺术鉴赏都是非理性的形式,艺术家和观众在一种神性中联结,它来源于缪斯。亚里士多德对此反应式的防卫是把艺术从品格和行动中分离出来,这不仅表现在他的“卡塔西斯”(catharsis)的理论中,还基于他把艺术当作一种外在构造的理性活动,即制作。作诗活动是通过一些生产性技巧来制作一种与众不同的对象,因而与较高级的伦理活动和实践行动形成鲜明的对比。根据亚里士多德的观点,这种实践行动是源于行动者的内在品格,并且反过来帮助塑造这种品格。艺术制作的目的是外在于艺术自身和制作者的(它的目的和价值存在于被制作出来的作品中),而行动的目的在行动自身和行动者中,受如何行动的方式所影响,而不受制作的结果的影响①。

　　把艺术从生活中分离出来的根深蒂固的传统观念,已经被现代主义的艺术自治的信条所强化,也包括康德关于审美与实践的对立观念。肯定艺术从习俗道德中获得审美自主权,这给予了现代艺术家更多的创造自由。但是我们关于艺术—生活二元论的偏见,以及由此带来的将艺术视为制作手工艺品,而不是在提炼人类主体性的观点,导致了对艺术作品的迷恋,却忽视了它们在鉴赏经验中的实际使用。这会让我们无视艺术对创作者的生活与性格,以及对观赏者的品格所产生的不容否认的作用。这会导致为了片面追求表现出引人注目的作品而滥用艺术家的身体和灵魂,没有对由表现需求所带来的痛苦、压力、伤害和着迷的狭隘投入表达出伦理关怀。表演艺术家仅成为表现的工具。但为什么不把他们看作是目的呢? 这一目的是为了丰富提炼主体性的艺术而形成的。艺术在伦理的生活艺术中作为一种实践的形式和自我提升的手段,这种理念是东亚艺术概念的基础。艺术过程重要的不是艺术家创作的作品及其表演,而是艺术过程对艺术家和他的自我理解的提升与自我转变的方式,由此他能成为一个更完善和自明之人。

---

　　①　参见亚里士多德:《尼各马可伦理学》,邓安庆译,人民出版社 2010 年版,第 211—214 页。

日本中古时期的能剧(No theatre)大师世阿弥元清(Zeami Motokiyo)被认为是日本杰出的能剧作家和理论家,他说:"我们艺术的根基在于精神。精神通过艺术展现了一种真正的启示,因此……倘若一位表演者真正想成为一位大师,他不能仅仅依靠舞蹈和姿势的技巧(这些只不过是"外在技巧")。他的精通得建立在自我理解的状态上。"①同样地,世阿弥元清阐释了自我理解的一个方面,就是要认识到艺术家依赖于广阔的自然环境的力量,引用一组俳句来说明这一点,也是在说明属于自然的美的造物:

> 睁眼看这樱桃树,
>
> 并仔细瞧上一番。
>
> 花儿已不见踪影。
>
> 因为花期已结束,
>
> 在这春季的天空。

仅靠树自身的内在力量并不会让花开;花会开是因为树与周围的自然能量和周围空间(比如春季的天空)的交互作用,花能够在这空间中绽放它的美,因为(用世阿弥元清的话来说)"自然世界是生发万物的大容器"②。世阿弥元清认为技艺精湛的能剧表演者必须对周围的氛围(如季节、背景等)和观众的情绪很敏感,以便能够把这些因素和表演融合在一起。所以,表演的美学涉及一种对环境的伦理—生态的敏感性。

在为伦理和美学之间的深厚联结做论证的同时,我并没有主张区分两者都是无理的,也不认为不存在某个点或层面上可以让两者进行对比。我只是警告在某种语境中进行一种非常功用性的区分和对比,这种区分和对比会转变成一种本质的二元论和对立。在某种语境中,把艺术作品中的美学技巧和作品表达的道德信息区分开来是应该被考虑的,比如当我们赞扬前者而反对后者(或者反之亦然)。在此我想说的是当艺术作品使用某种形式在美学上是值得称赞的,而在道德上是被指责的(或反之亦然)。但是根据某种特殊语境中进行对比的合法性,并不能得出在伦理和美学之间存

---

① 世阿弥元清:《论能剧的艺术》,普林斯顿大学出版社1984年版,第90页。
② 世阿弥元清:《论能剧的艺术》,普林斯顿大学出版社1984年版,第119页。

在着普遍的对比和基本的对立的结论,这一结论可以看作是指向两种基本不同和基本对立的属性或价值。

思想家们经常进行错误的区分,区分在某种特殊的语境中是很有用的,然后把这种区分具体运用于一些相反本质的普遍意义上对比,并且进一步把这种对立带回现象中来理解。不过实用主义告诫我们不要把在某些语境中的、有一定作用的区分,僵化为绝对的、毫无益处的二元论。通常我们首先是在一个统一的价值整体中,经验到高尚行为的价值以及代表性艺术作品的价值,这一统一的价值整体没有对这一高尚行为的伦理维度和美学维度进行区别、分离和对立。当我们在欣赏莎士比亚的悲剧或亨利·詹姆斯的小说时,我们不会首先把他们的艺术技巧和道德理智作为独立的部分进行欣赏而后又把它们连接起来。相反,我们是经验到一种显而易见的统一综合,在这种综合中伦理因素和美学因素交织在一起,以至于只有提炼后的分析抽象才能把它们区分开来。虽然这种抽象有时很有效(比如对风格进行技术式分析的工作),但是它不能用来解释伦理与美学之间的区别到底是一种根植于价值本体论,还是源于实际价值经验的基本对照。理智主义者的谬误是常见的,也是顽固的,因为我们经常迷恋于用这种区分来解释我们的经验,以至于我们把它当作经验和世界的基本结构的固有内容。

这种逻辑的谬误用一些其他的概念比用伦理和美学这两个概念可能会更加让人明了。例如,想想两个对我的身体美学计划非常重要的概念。①在某种情境或为了某些目的,我们能有效地区分甚至对比健康与健硕或幸福与快乐。但是很明显这不必认为健康与健硕(或幸福与快乐)是两种基本对立和冲突的价值,也无须认为当我们遇到它们时,我们应该在一种差异和紧张中才经验到它们。我们可以对我之前所提及的对伦理与道德的哲学区分获得一种类似的结论。人们可以拥护这种区分的实用层面,而不用得出结论说道德基本上是与伦理对立的,以及那种道德考量在伦理生活中是不会被明确地和有效地考虑在内的。

---

① 对身体美学的系统论述,参见理查德·舒斯特曼:《身体意识:关于正念与身体美学的哲学》,剑桥大学出版社 2008 年版。

一旦我们认知到伦理与美学之间的严重分裂并不是人类经验和价值本体论的基本特征，而主要是西方现代性文化的一个短暂的历史片段，这种文化关注着把艺术从制度化的道德审查的束缚中解放出来，那么就很容易理解这样一种生活艺术的哲学理念，即生活艺术融合了伦理与美学。我在拙著《实践哲学：实用主义与哲学生活》中阐发了这一理念。

<h1 style="text-align:center">五</h1>

尽管实用主义最早鼓励我去批判艺术与生活之间的分裂，这一分裂构成了美学与伦理之间令人不快的二元论的基础，但是我同样受到东亚思想的鼓舞去努力弥合这一裂痕，东亚思想重视哲学作为一种具体的生活方式，并且它对身体训练的理智层面和精神层面的重视，形成了我的身体美学计划和伦理学作为生活艺术的观念。根据这一观念，一个人的行为不能仅由已建立的伦理规则和道德义务来指导（或评判），而是一个人要通过不断精进的自我反省、自我养成和自我风格来尽力让自己的行为和性格达到一种吸引人的状态。当然，这不仅包括一个人的身体层面，而且还要求意识到这种自我改善总是在关注我们社会和自然环境中的他人他物，他们反过来会塑造自我，为自我提供意义、发展和愉悦的可能。

如果生活艺术的理念是指一种我过去用来弥合艺术与生活和美学与伦理之间对立的方式，现在就让我来简单地呈现另一种我最近还在实验的方式：通过由身体美学所激发的现代艺术中的表演工作。我经常被一些艺术家问及身体美学与现代艺术的联结问题，我的回答是有一种很明显的联结方式就是把我们活生生的身体放入艺术工作中。通过与巴黎艺术家晏·托马（Yann Toma）的合作，我已经完成了一系列摄影和影片，内容关于我穿上金色的莱卡（lycra）紧身衣裤后的即兴姿势和即兴表演。我穿上这种服装后最初引来的是目瞪口呆的注视（在我们初次合作的罗亚曼修道院），并封我为"L'homme en Or"（"金色的男人"）。这一新的人物形象在我和晏·托马之间的合作中标示了一种真正的转变，把我们最初的摄影实验转变为一系列延伸的表演片段，在其中我让自己从一个单纯的摄影主体变成了一个熟练的艺术合作者,我移动摄影背景,决定如何摆弄姿势,甚至让类型从静止的摄影转向移动的摄像。我们决定继续进行这项合作,我们在巴黎和其他风景胜地进行夜间的户外拍摄,比如城市、城墙、喀他赫纳的海岸(哥伦比亚)和佛罗里达的南部海滩,在静态的摄影和动态的摄像中产生出了一种特异的身体流动(somaflux)的风格,这一风格可以在欧洲和南美的画廊中发现,也可以在印刷品和网络媒体中看到。

正如我在其他地方所阐述的那样,身体流动系列作品的意义远超出这些映像所呈现的。① 它们涉及一种合作式的表演过程的复杂艺术,涉及一种直观交流(能量、情感和目的)的不断发展的舞蹈,涉及互相协作的即兴创作,虽然这种即兴创作最终会在照片打印和录像中展现,但是它自身不仅在共享的审美经验中是极其丰富的,而且在体现互相负责和互相关照的伦理向度的人际交流中也是极其丰富的。就像舞者和杂技演员所展现的合作,晏·托马和我都需要信任对方和关照对方。对于把哲学看作是一种具身的生活艺术的理念,我的身体美学所要探寻的是什么东西让我艺术式地转变为"金色的男人",这种东西产生出了这个"金色男人"所现身的艺术世界的作品。反过来讲,那种艺术式的转变也帮助我转变成一个哲学家,这是基于提供给我新的视角来看待艺术创作的表现过程和审美经验,我在之后出版的理论著作中把它表述出来了,这也是通过发展我的自我认同的意识实现的,从一个关注生活艺术的实验身体哲学家转变为一个集金色、自由精神和审美于一身的"阿凡达"。这种自我认同的延伸已超出了狭隘的哲学意义;通过把我置入一种新的角色、新的环境和新的挑战中,它在道德上考验和发展自我,追问自我,拓展自我和加深自我认识。"金色的男人"不仅仅是一种为制造艺术形象的装扮,它在隐藏和伪装我真正的自我认同;他更像是一个关于真实又复杂且易变的自我认同(一直在进行)的形象设计,一种混合的延展进一步帮助塑造、丰富和转变自我认同,这种工作构成了自我

---

① 参见理查德·舒斯特曼:《一位黑暗与光明中的哲学家》,引自安玛丽·妮娜克丝(编辑):《自明性,自我观察》,蒙特利尔自我摄影 2011 年版;《摄影作为行动过程》,参见期刊《美学与艺术批评》2012 年第 70 期;更详尽的阐述,参见《通过身体思考:身体美学论文集》,剑桥大学出版社 2012 年版,中文版第 11 页。

道德修养的关键层面。通过我的作品如《金色的男人》，我不仅专注于一些重要的被禁止之事；我也在游戏中重新发现了一种愉悦的天真，重新获得了在孩童时了解的且已失去的动作和姿势。

如果要我公开地展现"金色的男人"，这会有被指控为表现狂的风险，它实际上是通过把自己揭示给他人，来服务于哲学中的自我认识的传统伦理工作（为了自我提升）。难道我们没有自我表现就不能有很好的自我认识吗？为了发现自己的盲点和为了更全面地了解自己，我们需要他人对自己的看法。因此苏格拉底向亚西比德解释道，自我为了恰当地观看自己需要一个爱人，正像一个人对自己脸庞的观看反映在爱人的眼中。如果艺术表演能够提供那种反映的互动，凭借这种互动一个人通过自我表现能够观察和转变自己，如果这种艺术的自我表现能够吸引他人的目光，他人的反应能够进一步让哲学家更好地了解和提升自己，那么为什么不去拥护这种实验和不去承认艺术表演能够服务于伦理目的和美学目的的呢？我把这一问题留给你们，也把我在即兴表演中所尝试探索的一些意象留给你们。

（肖根牛 翻译；陈佳 校对）

Pragmatism and Scepticism

Anton Leist

University of Zurich

I   Peircian beginnings

One way to characterize the movement of pragmatism is by its struggle to overcome the philosophy of consciousness or, in historical terms, the philosophy initiated by Descartes. Many see pragmatism as a counter – movement to this period of modern philosophy, and as being engaged up to the present with building an alternative inside of or (as suggested by Rorty) even outside of philosophy. This way of framing pragmatism might sound implausible as the philosophy of consciousness, and Descartes' philosophy especially, is currently no longer considered as ' state of the art ' . During the 20th century the terminology of consciousness and its cognates have been well laid to rest, to the advantage of a Kantian and linguistic conceptualism. Yet, the perspective introduced by Descartes is not narrowly wedded to a psychology of consciousness. If we frame this introduction more generally by way of ' epistemology ' , it will sound more plausible that core elements of its original thrust are still with us today, positively as well as negatively.

Peirce was quite aware of the epochal importance of Descartes and he began his published writings with a fundamental critique of the latter's classical tracts. (The way he paradoxically held Descartes dear reminds a bit of the *Com-*

munist Manifesto 's praise of capitalism. Again, the same goes for present admirers of Descartes.) The new philosophy of Descartes shows, according to Peirce, the individual need for foundation and thereby its distance to the faith-based scholasticism of the Middle Ages.① This new and critical achievement Peirce wanted to preserve. But he also thought that the philosophy of consciousness has, important though its motives were, gone awry in its own development. According to Peirce, philosophy after Descartes, and largely due to him, has lost sight of science and has worked itself into a largely scholastic discipline again. Peirce's alternative at this time of his writing was to substitute the iconoclastic language-game of philosophers with a sort of science-oriented reflection.② But for this Descartes' method of doubt as the entry into the faulted language game had to be attacked effectively, and this was what early Peirce set out to do.

It is quite obvious that in his early articles Peirce took the 'method of doubt' as a troubled origin of epistemology.③ But Peirce also saw something historically new and positive in the need for foundations, and this ambiguous attitude toward doubt is a source of unrest in epistemology to this day. Undertaking the task of distinguishing between *relevant* and *irrelevant* (or even meaningless) *doubt* is one way to see a series of philosophers still at work in reformulating epistemology. During the 'linguistic turn' in the middle of the last century Cartesian doubt seemed to have been laid to rest for good.④ But, as shortly thereafter, a less enthusiastic and more sober view towards the linguistic approach became possible, the sceptic reawakened and – it seems – became

---

① Peirce, Incapacities, 28.

② By introducing the 'end-of-inquiry idea' of truth in a later article of this period this changes towards an ideal view of science, opposed to the blunt reference to manifest science in the earlier article.

③ The 'early' articles which set pragmatism on its rails include the following especially: *Faculties* (1868), *Incapacities* (1868), *Fixation* (1877), *Ideas* (1878).

④ Even Rorty's 1979, for example, was little interested in Descartes and took the internal development of linguistic philosophy itself as the proper terrain of its critique, which was meant as a critique of epistemology in its most actual (Kantian) manifestation.

again an irrepressible figure within philosophers' disputes.

I see the cause for this in two conundrums in particular. First, how to judge the role of doubt for theories of knowledge has – to this day – not been answered clearly, despite several centuries of attempts. This is not too surprising if one takes the sceptical challenge as representing the more general task of administering epistemology its right place within our human endeavours. What sort of questions should epistemology (and connected with it, philosophy in general) be thought to answer?① Secondly, Descartes' epochal philosophical task-setting by looking for individual certainty chimes increasingly well with just what Peirce thought to be the crucial difference between the Middle Ages and the present: a growing need for individual self – understanding. What early on was practiced among aloof philosophers became more and more standard behavior of worldly individuals.②How to answer the sceptic thereby becomes a real *cultural* topic with wide-spread social consequences. 'Common sense' is no longer clearly the 'other side' of scepticism, as it seems to have been for Moore.③

Given the second of these diagnoses pragmatists nowadays face a sort of paradox. On the one hand, following Peirce, they want to lead philosophy out of its self-enclosure, into which it has been thrown (among other motives) by radical doubt. Pragmatists want knowledge to be 'in contact' with social reality and function by improving society. On the other hand the method of doubt has become a deeply entrenched part of the social culture itself, and whether or not to the extent of radical doubt nobody knows exactly.④Due to this paradox of how to deal

---

① The response to doubt is not, as sometimes suggested by Rorty, the only or perhaps even the most important task epistemology devotes itself to. But Rorty is right that historically scepticism ushered in epistemology, and—thinking of 'brains–in–a–vat' – still does.

② I wonder whether Moore's famous strategy of Here is one hand and here is another to answer doubt in the external world would ring convincing for the 'common man' today, as it seems to have done in 1925.

③ Philosophers today who are aware of this are Rorty (1989) and Cavell (1996).

④ One could think of popular films like *The Matrix*.

with doubt, how to think of scepticism has itself become relevant for our present cultural situation. And how to think of scepticism *within* philosophy may be of help for such a diagnosis: perhaps philosophy's discourse in this case is a blue-print for cultural developments in a wider sense.

II How Peirce began

We would not talk about scepticism today if Peirce's critique in his early works had been a success. Peirce was effective in suggesting a shift of epistemology to another level, and he introduced several ways of how to counterpose presuppositions and dogmas in Cartesianism. Most of these ways have been re-enacted more extensively in the hands of creative linguistic philosophers during the 20th century.[①] But Peirce hardly did more than gesturing at another level, and, furthermore, did so in a highly ambiguous or contradictory manner. With Kuhn in mind one might think that such paradigm – shifts cannot be motivated by argument and that Peirce could not have done better in any case. But in order to undergo the shift (if it is a shift at all) one had to lay bare the increasing number of epicycles in the old model first, and this is where Peirce has not been too convincing. The same goes for James and Dewey on occasions where they stepped into his footsteps.

Here is how (roughly) Peirce argues against 'Cartesian doubt' in his early articles.

(1) *Real doubt thesis* : Real (local) doubt should be substituted for universal (Cartesian) doubt.

(2) *Consensus thesis* : Rational consensus should be substituted for truth.

---

① See, for example, Bernstein 2010, ch.1, pointing to several of them.

1 is a thesis critical of Descartes' radical doubt, offering what one could call a 'practical shift' of doubting. 2 is a thesis critical of aiming at 'certainty' and is suggesting the famous 'end of inquiry' — criterion of truth. Peirce adds several other pairs of conceptual juxtapositions, but I will concentrate on these two.①I will call them the '*real-doubt thesis*' and the '*consensus thesis*'.

The real — doubt thesis holds that universal doubt is impossible and that doubt is necessarily connected to a practical context of doubt, which is always particular and local. Peirce's objection to radical doubt is by way of contrast with doubting something in everyday life or in science (such as looking for a specific sum of money in one's purse or the outcome of an experiment).

His reasons against universal doubt seem to be these:

(1a) Doubt is necessarily a "living doubt", doubt really felt, and such a doubt needs to play an active role within processes of inquiry (Incapacities, 29 ("doubt in our hearts"); Fixation, 115).

(1b) Universal doubt would depend on self-deception (Incapacities, 29).

(1c) Universal doubt is not answerable (Fixation, 115).

In the following I will address only 1a, which I think in the end to be right, even if not having been made convincing by Peirce himself. A strange argument amongst these three seems to be 1c, which Peirce does not discuss at any length. Why should doubt be meaningless if it is not answerable — something that just is what the radical sceptic states? In a simple version of 1c it would be presupposed what has to be argued for. 1c has to be combined with, or backed up by, other arguments.

---

① Other Cartesian vs. pragmatist pairs are 'belief as consciousness' vs. 'belief as habit', 'certainty as intuition' vs. 'cognition as derived', 'thinking without signs' vs. 'thinking with signs', etc. See Incapacities 31.

Is universal doubt connected to self – deception, as 1b says? Lesley Friedman (1999,740f.) agrees that in order do universally doubt one has to deceive oneself about one's believing in the normal sense. The argument holds: as it is not possible to doubt universally in a literate way one has to deceive oneself about what one is doubting. This argument again presupposes a restricted definition of what it is to doubt. Again it has to be backed up by argument for such a definition. Overall, it seems that 1a might be the one argument against radical doubt Peirce has brought forward. But how is one to read 1a?

1a suffers from two problems. Firstly, an argument against universal doubt should not depend merely on a definition of 'doubt' which is contestable. It is not obvious that for doubt to be possible and respectable, an accompanying felt need of doubt is necessary. Doubt can be a part of reflection only, accompanied by a feeling or not. The same goes for many emotions: one may *know* that one hates, loves, fears (etc.) someone else, without – at a certain moment – *feeling* this state of emotion. It is not too different with doubt: one may be in a state where one realizes one's reason for doubt (of a told story, of a political dogma, etc.) without at this moment actually feeling the doubt.

Secondly, more important is a distinction which Meyers (1967) pointed out. Universal doubt is not a doubt concerning specific facts but a doubt concerning *the status* of our knowledge of facts.

"Descartes is not really looking for new factual knowledge; he is seeking to place his present knowledge on what he takes an acceptable basis." (Meyers 1967,21)

This makes the kind of doubt Descartes suggests crucially different from the doubt about concrete facts in everyday life and in science. Peirce should have taken this difference into consideration and should have argued against the possibility of such a status–of–knowledge–doubt.

Could Peirce simply have *presupposed* that a distinction between questioning the content of knowledge (looking for facts) and the status of knowledge does not make sense? Not at all, as he extensively discusses different methods of the 'fixation of beliefs' (those of tenacity, authority, a priori and science). From this he clearly engages in the kind of meta-inquiry which is typical for epistemology. Alternatively, is it obviously meaningless to ask for the truth of the *whole* of knowledge? Peirce certainly thought such a question was misguided and could not be the object of a judgment as to truth or falsity. This is where the consensus-thesis comes into play.

A first part of the consensus-thesis is established in section 4 of *Fixation* (1877). Here Peirce is clearly setting out a path of inquiry which is meant 'to work' instead of being 'true'.

"The irritation of doubt is the only immediate motive for the struggle to attain belief. It is certainly best for us that our beliefs should be such as may truly guide our actions so as to satisfy our desires; and this reflection will make us reject any belief which does not seem to have been so formed as to insure this result... Hence, the sole object of inquiry is the settlement of opinion. We may fancy that this is not enough for us, and that we seek not merely an opinion, but a true opinion. But put this fancy to test, and it proves groundless; for as soon as a firm belief is reached we are entirely satisfied, whether the belief be true or false... The most that can be maintained is, that we seek for a belief that we shall *think* to be true. But we think each one of our beliefs to be true, and, indeed, it is mere tautology to say so." (Fixation, 114-5)

What Peirce says here in part is certainly mistaken. We do *not* "think each one of our beliefs to be true". We combine with most of our beliefs a presumption of truth, but we also are very hesitant towards some of our beliefs. And a further argument would be needed to include a presumption of truth within every belief, something Davidson tried to provide more recently. With his remarks above, Peirce seems to refer simply to actual science, basing this step either on a definition or some hidden insight. It may 'be best for us' that truth is guiding our actions, but why should we reduce truth solely to its 'guiding function'? Is truth not something essentially different (i.e. correspondence) which, as one of its consequences, has a guiding function? Further argument here is needed and missing.

Only a bit later does Peirce add his famous criterion that truth is something to be achieved at the end of an inquiry in form of a full consensus among all inquirers.①This of course is a radical break with all earlier remarks referring to actual scientific practice and use. By this Peirce adds an *ideal* of consensus to the realistic consensus–making in actual science. What Peirce is foreshadowing with this ideal consensus – thesis is an argument which was developed later by Davidson and taken up and radicalized by Rorty. The corresponding thesis these two philosophers defended also serves the purpose of distancing scepticism.

For the following I will formulate this additional thesis as follows:

(3) *Holism – of – knowledge – and – meaning thesis* : Because of the inter–translatability of all languages, knowledge is necessarily part of the whole of knowledge; and the whole of knowledge cannot be wrong.

3 puts an end to universal doubt to the same extent, even if not by the same method, as was meant by Peirce's consensus–thesis. The truth of the whole is compatible with the falsity of each singular belief. Also, there is always some partial and local doubt within the whole, something coinciding with Peirce's fallibilism: every piece of knowledge is fallible, i.e. could be wrong. This is not true of the whole – according to 3.

Again, an argument for this still has to be provided. There is an ongoing dispute whether 3 definitely knocks out scepticism.②I will come back to this later.

---

① "The opinion which is fated to be ultimately agreed to by all who investigate, is what we mean by the truth, and the object represented in this opinion is the real. That is the way I would explain reality." (Ideas, 139)

② See Davidson 1983 for and Nagel 1999 and Stroud 1999 against. (I will deal more explicitly with Davidson in section 5.)

But even if it does,3 does not clearly claim to be a version of pragmatism.What is missing in 3 is early Peirce's strong emphasis on 'real doubt',practical relevance and science as an experimental project.The experimental aspect is part of the real—doubt thesis.Peirce backs it up most strongly with his examples of a dispositional theory of meaning,put forward in *Ideas* .It is not at all clear,in other words,how 1a (which I take to be an original and necessary ingredient of pragmatism) and 3 go together.

It seems that at this point we need a confirmation of how to understand 'pragmatism' in order to find some insight into its relation to scepticism.

III　The pragmatist's circularity problem

Pulling together suggestions from Peirce's pointing to processes of inquiry, natural science,scientific experiments and the dispositional theory of meaning, 'being relevant from a (real) practical point of view' seems to belong to the core idea of pragmatism.A practical point of view,understood realistically,is illustrated by experimental,technical action as well as by social communication and discourse.To make things easier,let us start by paradigmatically thinking of an experiment,like putting a piece of gold into a specific acid.Will it dissolve or not?

From this we could characterize pragmatism somehow like this:

(P) 'Pragmatism' is a kind of philosophical critique which addresses arguments and statements referring to the whole of knowledge by bringing to bear some elementary facts of human practical activities.

If one were to answer radical doubt by help of P,however,one would be struck by a crucial difference in levels of concreteness.Radical doubt is directed at the *whole* of knowledge, and is meant to be answered by a piece of knowledge, albeit one connected with practical activities. If 'common sense' were not an ambiguous term, one could also say that a common – sensical justifying reference is involved in P, whereas radical doubt would be juxtaposing common sense.①

There are, of course, different candidates for 'practical activities' in P. The usual candidates called up in pragmatists' texts are 'experimental inquiry', 'instrumental action', 'coping', 'achieving consensus', 'activities with beneficial or harmful consequences' etc. All of these descriptions of practical activities seem to presuppose some sort of reality, either the reality of common sense or of science. But *if* such a presupposition is made, then stressing the practical aspect in order to oppose transcendental statements is an idle detour – the presupposed reality alone is standing against the transcendental aim, be it a reality (that is subject to doubt) or a positive transcendental aim, as for example absolute certainty.

The problem of incoherence is a serious one, as knowledge and action, 'theoretical' and 'practical' reasons or judgments do not fall apart into fully different spheres. Practical reasons as well as actions, *human* actions at least, are in need of some piece of knowledge. In typical human action besides desires, beliefs have to be involved. Reference to actions therefore cannot come to the aid of all–encompassing questioning of knowledge, as if they ensue from some 'other side' of knowledge. Rather, if problems of knowledge were of an all–encompassing kind, actions and practical reasons would already form an integral part of these problems and could not also constitute extraneous help. To put it in simpler terms: if foundationalism (constructing knowledge from an absolute bottom seems

---

① 'Common sense' is a term which is best to be avoided in philosophical disputes as its possible function strongly depends on a sociological diagnosis: to which extent are common sense beliefs right or wrong? I will come back to this issue later. For the present it may be enough to equate it to widespread beliefs and attach a question mark concerning the legitimacy of these beliefs.

problematic, the perspective of action cannot be of assistance as action itself is making use of knowledge. It cannot be of help as it itself forms part of the very problem of foundationalism.

Given all this, the diagnosis seems unavoidable that whatever the difficulties of epistemology, actions and reference to practical activities appear not to be of help, either critical or constructive. Radical reflection on knowledge and action seem simply not to meet each other conceptually on the site of epistemology and radical doubt!

This tendency of incoherence was already noticeable in relation to my discussion of Peirce. The real-doubt-thesis does not address the Cartesian doubt concerning the whole of knowledge at all. At best, it could suggest real doubt to be 'more relevant' practically. But this is not an argument against the sceptic. The consensus thesis too could either be meant realistically or ideally, ideally in form of a consent at the fictitious 'end of inquiry'. In the first case it again misses universal doubt, in the second it answers it, but in an analogously transcendental way. That there is or will be an ideal consent determining 'reality' *is* meeting the sceptic, but is not offering an argument against him. The sceptic *is* of course also doubting that such an ideal consent will say anything about truth and knowledge here and now.

What are the alternatives leading out of this impasse, the pragmatist's '*circularity problem*'? One alternative would be to reject that practical action needs knowledge in order to be effective. Another one would be to think of 'practical relevance' as being put into force not directly but indirectly. The first alternative could be called the '*primitive action*' alternative. According to this alternative action would be primitive to the degree of not involving knowledge, i.e. a knowing subject who also is the agent. The second alternative could be called the '*indirect pragmatism*' alternative, due to its postulation of an indirect argument to the advantage of practical relevance.

To my mind the incoherence problem has not been stated explicitly enough within pragmatist epistemology, neither has there been an overview of how different pragmatists try to avoid the incoherence/circularity arising out of the core pragmatist idea (of practical relevance). Roughly, one perhaps could say that the Darwinian line of argument present in Dewey and partly in Rorty hints at the primitive action way out. Alternatively, there are indirect strategies in Davidson, Wittgenstein and also in Rorty. I will restrict myself to Rorty.

In the end I do believe that the indirect pragmatism alternative would do the job. In order to see more clearly how it might be posited, let me give a more specific version of P:

(P*) 'Pragmatism' is a kind of philosophical critique which addresses arguments and statements referring to the whole of knowledge by forwarding a '*practical context*' *view* of knowledge through a critique of two alternatives. These alternatives are either the metaphysical or the scepticist answer. Criticizing both leads to the practical context view.

I am calling the circularity problem inherent in P the 'pragmatist' circularity problem, because it is connected with any conceptualization of 'practical', and thereby unavoidable for pragmatists. It is of course important for pragmatists to avoid it. But it is also important to be aware of its role in the context of transcendental arguments. It is one of the elements leading out of such arguments and into the right direction of an alternative, which will contain the element of practice.

IV   Rorty and knowledge as non–representational

To start with Rorty is promising from a pragmatist's point of view for two reasons: first, Rorty more than any other recent philosopher renewed the Peircean diagnosis of a close, even constitutive link between (philosophy as) epistemology and radical doubt. Similar to Peirce he thinks that giving some space to the sceptic shows *per se* the involvement of a basically wrong model of knowledge.①I will give a sketch of his argument below. Stirred by Rorty a stream of philosophers who would not consider themselves pragmatists became very conscious of the inherent problem, and even the inherent diagnostic relevance of scepticism for epistemology.②

Second, Rorty is also very much aware of the prevalence of sceptical attitudes in our common Western culture, something addressed by him under the term of 'irony' (Rorty 1989). But this raises the problem of how these two levels of argument fit together: the cultural diagnosis and the epistemic attempt to overcome scepticism, without contradicting themselves (something also demanded by Williams 2003).

Here is, to begin with, Rorty's argument for the role of scepticism in a nutshell:

(1) Radical (universal, transcendental, global) doubt is a symptom of a specific concept of knowledge.

(2) Radical doubt is to be refuted indirectly by criticizing the attached concept of knowledge.

(3) Knowledge as representational is a flawed concept of knowledge.

(4) Alternatively, knowledge is to be reconstructed as non-representational. As such it is neither a form of idealism, nor the possible object of radical doubt.

---

① Such a diagnosis is given early on in Rorty 1979, chs.3 & 5, and in many statements later. See especially 1979, 229. Early Rorty preferred the term 'epistemological behaviourism' to 'pragmatism', but soon substituted the latter term. To my knowledge Rorty himself never linked his diagnosis closely to Peirce's early articles. He thought throughout that Peirce was too inconsistent a philosopher to be honestly called a pragmatist.

② The philosophers to be mentioned include T. Nagel, B. Williams, D. Davidson, M. Williams, B. Ramberg, R. Brandom, J. McDowell, and others. There are others like B. Stroud who are strongly motivated by Hume and are free of Rorty's intentions. How to deal with the sceptic is somehow or other a topic for all of these.

As can be seen easily, the burden of the argument rests on (3) and (4), and on (3) more than (4). If knowledge could be perfectly understood in the representational mode, an alternative in non-representational form would not be an option from the beginning. On the other hand, if (3) can be backed up by argument, (4) would add to this and help towards a shift from one conception of knowledge to the other.

Unfortunately, all arguments Rorty makes in favour are to be classified under (4) and not easily under (3). There are two points he wants to set out to the advantage of (4): one resting on the idea of (as mentioned) 'primitive action', and one I will call the 'coherence-cum-causality' concept of knowledge. Whereas the first argument results from Dewey and the larger pragmatist tradition, the second originates from Sellars' critique of the myth of the given and Davidson's theory of triangulation (itself inspired by Sellars). In contrast, Rorty has little to say concerning (3), if one disregards remarks such as that (3) leads to radical scepticism. As scepticism is not yet *per se* fatal, that would not be an argument. We just want to know why scepticism is fatal.

I will try to suggest an argument for (3) which Rorty might hold and which I consider correct. A problematic tendency in Rorty's overall argument, however, comes from drawing the wrong conclusion from (3), once (3) is accepted. The problem in representational theories of knowledge, mentioned in (3), arises from a transcendental use of 'representation', whereas normal or local uses are acceptable. But Rorty's two arguments (primitive action, coherence – cum – causality) in favour of (4) are also of a transcendental kind. As will be seen, these arguments are not at all convincing. Instead, I will conclude that practical relevance in a non-transcendental, everyday sense is decisive for the control, meaning and truth of knowledge. So far an overall comment on what is to follow:

A classical objection towards knowledge as representation is that this concept is *circular*. If you want to answer in which sense knowledge is 'representative', the only one meaningful answer would be, because what is represented in knowledge answers (corresponds to , matches , pictures , etc.) its representation. At best , that is , the answer as to what representation is draws from the assertoric sentence used in the statement or belief. This sentence is doing the ' representational job '. What is missing is its correspondent in reality − that is its correspondent save its being a content of a sentence , statement or belief. There are two readings of this correspondence , one *internal* and one *transcendental* . The internal one sees no problem in this fact : representation needs language and is always bound to it. The object of representation is ' out there ' , but ' out there ' in the way it is represented. The transcendental way of stating the same relation however creates a problem : to explain (understand) representation one would need a grip on content *independent of* language , sentence , statement , belief , consciousness , etc. This is impossible and in *this sense* there is a flaw in representational knowledge. (3) would be right , if understood transcendentally.

Rorty latches onto this transcendental reading and follows it up with two further arguments for (4) , whilst retaining the transcendental mode of argument. Non−representative knowledge again is a transcendental concept − a concept explaining the *whole* of knowledge. The primitive action argument suggests that knowledge is understood as an instrumental relation towards the world , similar to using a tool. Instead of representing something through language , we are ' coping ' with the environment , our concepts and everything done with them is like ' tool−using behaviour '. [1] Thinking , believing and asser-

---

[1] See Rorty 1989 , xiv : "... we could begin to think of the relation between writers on autonomy and writers on justice as being like the relation between two kinds of tools − as little in need of synthesis as are paintbrushes and crowbars." "The proper analogy is with the invention of new tools to take place of old tools. To come up with such a vocabulary is more like discarding the lever and the chock because one has envisaged the pully , or like discarding gesso and tempera because one has now figured out how to size canvas properly." (12) Dewey 1920 , 83 : " (C) onceptions , theories and systems of thought... are tools. As in the case of all tools , their value resides not in themselves but in the capacity to work , as shown in the consequences of their use."

ting should be seen as a tool−using activity and not as one of picturing or representing.

The problem with this suggestion is its becoming incoherent along the lines described in the last section. Our normal understanding of 'tools' is connected with cognitive representation, and if we try to free instrumental acting from all cognitive elements, nothing like *acting* remains. This can easily be seen if we put 'success' at the place of 'justified belief' or 'truth'. For a human action to be successful it has to be judged as successful (otherwise attempts to achieve something would not come to an end). And then this action is dependent on the judgment, which was meant to be explained by non−representative action. Perhaps the whole manoeuvre was not intended anyhow, as it often is said that concepts or statements themselves are tools.[1] But what is that meant to say? If they are tools which cannot be applied and judged to be successful, in which sense are they tools? The analogy becomes meaningless.

Rorty mentions the tool−analogy only at certain moments in giving a sketchy summary of the non − representational view. Perhaps one should, therefore, not press the primitive action idea too much. It may not be meant as an argument on its own but only as an offer for pragmatist window dressing. This also is suggested by the second argument, as coherence − cum − causality is itself hardly coherent with primitive action. In a way action can be put into the causality−relation between the perceiver and the perceived, but if that causality runs through human actions (and not through other materials) then it becomes irrelevant. All that counts are lines of causality, however they run. So, I think the tool− and primitive action analogy often used by Dewey and sometimes by Rorty is to be put aside if one favours the second argument.

---

[1] Not so in Rorty, as he is aware of the unusual use of 'tool', which he comments: "I shall, for the moment, ignore this disanalogy." (1989,13) He seems to think that his (Davidsonian) theory of metaphor answers the problem, but it is not clear that it does.

V Coherence and causality

The idea of this argument, basically, is this:

(CcC) Knowledge is given within the coherence of beliefs, manifesting thereby causal impacts from the world, without having (conceptual, rational) control over these causal impacts.

The idea can also be expressed as follows:

(CcC') Knowledge is a coherence of beliefs combined with causal *content agnosticism*. Causal content agnosticism is agnosticism concerning the explicit law-likeness of causal effects on knowledge, save the knowing of causality in general.

CcC seems to have several advantages. First, it is not a representational position, and therefore avoids the meaninglessness/circularity problem. Second, it is not a form of idealism (and therefore metaphysics), as it accepts causal effects behind our beliefs. The beliefs are not 'floating free' of the world, as in idealism. Third, it also is not a form of reductive naturalism, because agnosticism concerns causal content. Reductive naturalism tries to explain beliefs as causal effects, something CcC thinks to be impossible. (Reductive naturalism is one version of realism, and thereby again one form of metaphysics.) Fourth, and last, CcC is also meant to eliminate scepticism. By this it fits into the overall analysis which thinks that realism, idealism and scepticism are analogously open to the problematic of participating in the representation idea. The elimination of scepticism has most cogently been stated by Davidson, and is implied in the logic of coherence. I mentioned this already earlier and refer back to it:

Holism-of-knowledge-and-meaning thesis : Because of the inter-translat-ability of all languages, knowledge is necessarily part of the whole of knowledge; and the whole of knowledge cannot be wrong.

The whole of knowledge cannot be wrong, because due to coherence-rela-tions of meaning every doubt has to presuppose some beliefs as meaningful, and thereby as true. If some parts in the whole are true, the whole cannot be fully wrong.①

Rorty accepted CcC for quite some time, and holds on to it in all his later writings. What has to be made clear is that CcC does not mention anything 'practical' at all, and thereby is no longer 'pragmatist' in the original Peircean sense which meant to oppose scepticism by practical activities and practical rele-vance. Davidson as the most explicit defender of CcC did not classify himself as a pragmatist (though he did, at times, accept similarities with Mead's ideas of so-cial communication). Davidson's theory of action can be included under the am-bit of CcC's overall statement, thus avoiding a theoretical/practical gap; but CcC does not depend in any way on statements concerning action itself. So it remains unclear whether CcC lays to rest pragmatism rather than transforming it. This might also be the way how Davidson himself would have understood it. But as Rorty calls himself a pragmatist, he seems to need the primitive action argument, something Davidson never touched.

Could, perhaps, Davidson too be forced to accept something like practical rel-evance (even if not primitive action) in his more detailed explication of CcC? This is, I think, just the case if we focus more closely on his theory of 'triangula-tion'.②Here is a summarized definition of what triangulation is meant to achieve:

---

① The point seems to have been made first in Davidson 1983. There are several formulations of the same thesis to be found in Davidson, even if of different depth. For discussion see Stroud 1999, 145.

② See Gluer 2011, ch.5. For a presentation and illustration of triangulation see the example of the adult-child communication in Davidson 1992.

(Tri) A perceptual sentence S referring to some visible object O becomes meaningful for speakers A and B if (i) A and B understand that not only they but also the mutual other is referring to O in his/her perception and they adapt their understanding to the one of the other, (ii) O causes the meaning of S if condition (i) is fulfilled; (iii) there is an agreement between A and B that O is the cause of the meaning of S.

Tri combines a social condition (reciprocal approach to each other's understanding) with a causal condition (causal basis in the object referred to) and thereby says something similar as CcC. If one starts with the causal condition another way to explain the role (and necessity) of the social condition is the following: What A perceives on a single occasion is indefinite for A and cannot become definite on physical terms alone. Therefore, the potentially multitude of perceptive content has to be restricted – by help of B's selective offer in meaning. And the same goes for B by help of A's selective offer. If agreeing on one meaning they both fix the perceptual content as well as the cause of the perception. If this were right, triangulation fulfilled two functions at once: it explains meaning to be necessarily social, and it explains meaning arising causally not only from a social agreement but also from the independent object referred to.

A crucial question in our context is whether the causal relationship in Tri is falling under a sort of 'content agnosticism' as introduced in CcC or not. I think it clearly does, as it is not a causal determination which binds the agreement on meaning between A and B, but it is the agreement on meaning between A and B which determines what the causal content is. If A and B agree on the meaning of 'dog' in commonly referring to a thing in view of them, they also agree that it is this thing in view of them, the dog, that is causing their seeing a dog.

Content agnosticism concerning the causal side leaves, however, quite a gap in the whole explanation of meaning, sentences, statements, beliefs, etc. The gap consists in that we cannot be sure that we share the same meaning once we cannot be sure about similarity of causal connections. What, for example, if the causal relations in A comes from the visual perception of a dog, and in B from the smell of the dog? Could nevertheless both mean the same with 'dog'? Ontological differences could be still quite vaster, as Quine made clear in his remarks on the 'indeterminacy of translation'.①We have the typical impasse here, which arises from general and transcendental attempts to explain. On the one side an explanation would be *circular* if the dog (as 'dog', i.e. a single animal) were to play a part in the causal relation, which itself is meant to corroborate that 'dog' means a specific single animal. On the other side, the causal part of the epistemic relation cannot be taken for granted if content agnosticism reigns. *Anything* in the background of what we mean to refer to could then be the cause of reference.

This dilemma can also be generalized like this: either a fully *general* explanation of knowledge (encompassing under 'knowledge' all linguistic and cognitive elements of knowledge) presupposes as existent what cannot be presupposed, as it too needs to be explained; or statements on the causal relation fully leave open the kind of relation, because of their openness concerning cause. Another way to restate the dilemma is as one of either metaphysics or scepticism. Either the 'real thing' has to be postulated without experience of it (metaphysics); or it is ever open whether and in which form it exists (scepticism). Is there a way out of this impasse?

The only one solution, I think, is to give up on the general and transcendental claim. This can be seen easily if the two parts in CcC, coherence and causality, are not understood as on a par, but the causal is seen as a given included under the umbrella of coherence. How the causal relation to the dog in view is to be thought of, becomes more explicit if it is not only a 'first' dog (for a child, say) outside of all beliefs of animals, but if it is looked at against the background of a set of beliefs. If B were to identify other animals and stuff in general primarily according to smells (for example, because B is blind), this would lead to other

---

① See Quine 1969.

differences where conflicts of different sets of beliefs would arise.

Davidson himself seems to favour a sort of equilibrium between the coherence and the causal level. But as suggested, such an equilibrium cannot exist if (and only if) the triangulation events are meant to build up, and in a way put a foundation to the meaning of concepts. For causality to make sense, then, the causal relation would have to cohere with the linguistic level and would thus be dependent on it. This opens the door either to a realistic metaphysics (strong naturalism) or to scepticism. Both are alternatives Davidson would like to avoid.

Is there an alternative to total particularism given this scenario? One would be what is often denoted as 'common sense'. Common sense would be paying tribute to the circularity problem and would build on common language and its offerings. This again would be another reading of CcC, putting causality fully under the control of a coherent identification of the causal relata. A and B do mean the dog by 'dog' because of their meaning being caused by perception of the dog. The causal relationship is playing some role here, even if not one in the determination of the meaning of 'dog', as 'dog' is already given as meaningful. The causal relation helps to distinguish between perception and hallucination, the use of 'dog' without having a dog in view. This is some function for the causal relation, but not the stronger one expected at the outset.

Are there alternatives? I think there is one especially I would like to call 'social naturalism' or 'contextual pragmatism'. This kind of naturalism is the attempt to strike a balance between classical pragmatism and causality as a single, linguistically undetermined relationship. It accepts the circularity problem hidden in P, and it gives up on the attempt to fix meaning by an undetermined causal relation. It strikes a balance between these two extremes, as it accepts that (avoiding circularity) some sort of reality has to be accepted as already given without being explained, and (avoiding indeterminacy) a practical context is the best way to fill what 'reality' means. Causality is to be made definite by introducing practical contexts in which it becomes concrete and explicit. In order to make the choice of contexts as explanative as possible the most general ones, action-type sort of contexts, have to be chosen.

P* has already been formulated to point into the direction of these remarks. But P* now can be put a bit more succinctly:

(P**) '*Contextual pragmatism*' is a solution of the dilemma between metaphysics and indeterminism. 'Contextual pragmatist' explanations of cognitive elements in knowledge are ones that avoid metaphysical and indeterminate explanations. For a contextual pragmatist explanation selects such a practical context which is the most general one without falling back into indeterminacy!

P** involves a methodological principle of selection between different explanations of knowledge in the pragmatist spirit, i.e. in taking note of practical relevance. P** is of course no longer a transcendental principle but a local one, even if on the highest possible level of generality.

How does P** differ from Rorty's idea of pragmatism? It differs in that it also strikes a middle ground between a representative *and* the non-representative account of knowledge. By accepting action contexts for the understanding of knowledge it also, on the back of action, accepts representation. On the other hand it also gives some admission to the non-representative account. It does this by *dissolving* what normally is called 'truth' into practical success criteria in a specific context. These criteria will be ones connected with a representational mode, but nevertheless tied to success under specific types of action.

To make P** more concrete I suggest that two types of practical contexts are chosen that — following early Habermas — I will call 'instrumental' and 'communicative' action.① The idea of these two types of action, clearly profiled

---

① See Habermas 1968.

by Habermas throughout his epistemological writings is that there are two different forms of success involved: *experimental success* in the sphere of instrumental action and *discursive success* in the sphere of communicative action. Habermas himself, and still more so Rorty, put experimental success *under* the overarching aim of discursive success, thereby achieving the model of only one type of success in the end, discursive success. I will *not* follow this conclusion and instead will keep the two contexts of experimental and discursive success not only apart, but also as *coequal* .

There is one reason especially why it seems necessary to do this: whereas experimental success is success in acting towards independent nature, communicative action is success in acting *towards and with* other agents (living in an independent world). Habermas himself put extreme importance on this difference, but hesitated to draw the conclusion that there are different types of success − or (as one also could say) types of *practical truth* . Keeping experimental and discursive success equi−important harmonizes with the standard distinction between 'theoretical' and 'practical rationality'. Norms and values are true according to discursive consent in a community, but empirical and theoretical beliefs are *not true* according merely to such consent, but according to experimental success.①

Keeping the two spheres of action distinct leads me to oppose perhaps Rorty's most important conclusion from his non−representational position: the *pluralism* of truth. Rorty thinks scientific truth, historical truth, aesthetic truth etc. not to be ordered in any way hierarchically, but to be fully distinct according to different practical spheres and aims. As all these part−languages are for him nothing else but different 'tools' aimed at different ends, they do not come in conflict

---

① Discourse theorists will be quick in replying that experimental success also is dependent on consent among language users or scientists, and this certainly is true. There is unavoidably interpretation involved in the natural sciences, as in everyday use. But (tacit) consent is only a necessary, not a sufficient condition, whereas in the communicative sphere consent is *the only and sufficient* criterion for truth − practical truth. Those ethical norms people consent on *are* the true ones. (Of course, spoken in a highly idealized way.)

with each other.It seems to me that Rorty could not even give a coherent explanation for administrators who have to decide on which discipline or institutions to
spend more money than on others.If the administrator were to allocate more resources to medicine than to operas, he would have to refer to good and bad consequences, and thereby would have to include *representations* – something to be
avoided at all costs in a total non–representational view.Total truth pluralism is
not an option here, contrary to what Rorty thinks.Rather we are in the usual, Hu-
mean sort of difference between the empirical (experimental) sphere and the
normative sphere.These two are different and have to interact in the way well
known in ethical theories.

VI   The role for scepticism

What does this leave us to say to the sceptic? There are two points to be addressed, especially.First, how does contextual pragmatism answer radical scepticism, if it does at all? And second, how does this ' philosophical ' role of scepticism cohere with what has been diagnosed as ' cultural scepticism ' or ' irony ' in
Rorty ' s words? Is there a reading which would make Rorty less inconsistent as it
first seems?

So far as the first point is concerned the exchange between Stroud and Davidson seems to me to lead to the best answer, which states : radical scepticism is
possible and not to be exorcised totally, but its relevance can be mitigated.(This
formulation can be read in a non–reductive pragmatist way, which does not presuppose a criterion of ' relevance ' and is not a form of *petitio* of the kind
looming large in Peirce ' s early articles.) The way in which radical scepticism is
not meaningless but ' makes sense ' has become more precise, but also less puz-
zling that it normally seems.

Stroud (1999) points out that triangulation theory explains that it would not
be possible for A and B, or a linguistic community, if they share an amount of

beliefs (something they required by coherence to have beliefs at all) *to have* largely erroneous beliefs – related to their belief-system as it were. The point can be made already with the paradoxical character of "I believe that it is raining and it is not raining" (1999, 156). ①In order to hold a set of beliefs they should not contradict each other. However, it is easily possible that unbeknownst to the believer his belief is wrong. And the holism-of-meaning-thesis does nothing to prevent this possibility from occurring even regarding the whole of beliefs of a person or a community. Unbeknownst to the knowledge community its beliefs *could be wrong*, either all singularly or all together and at once. But this means that radical scepticism is possible.

What could prevent this consequence? Stroud refers to Kant's transcendental idealism as the only method in principle to oppose scepticism. Kant thought to have a way of giving proof that the world believed is also the world itself. He thought so because he believed in the claim that certain conditions of knowledge are excepted from fallible knowledge, those *a priori*. These conditions make (empirical) knowledge possible but are not themselves forms of (empirical) knowledge. Davidson would need to suggest an analogue in his theory to this *a priori* statement of Kant's, something he wisely is not willing to do. He accepts that it is impossible to disprove scepticism logically (Davidson 1999, 163), but nevertheless thinks to have good empirical reasons for the causal condition in Tri to overcome radical sceptical doubt.

In a way this can be read as accepting the sceptical attack, even if downplaying its relevance. Radical doubt is not to be ruled out ('logically'), but it also is not to be taken seriously. Here Davidson seems to agree with Stroud who sees it as one of the advantages of holism that it softens its relevance. That, given our belief-system, its content has to be largely true (in *our* system) saves us

---

① Note that the second part-sentence is *not* within the range of the propositional attitude, but somehow in the perspective of the speaker.

from the possible *experience* that it is largely false. Such a possibility is excluded because it would produce contradictions within our system of beliefs – the system would break down and with it the 'new' and 'true' beliefs. (Whether the insight that we are all brains in a vat would be such a case is another question. That depends on how the 'real' world is made up.) Stroud and Davidson seem to agree, even if voicing the result differently. According to Stroud the possibility of all of our beliefs being wrong "is not actual" (1999, 157), and therefore not something that throws up disturbances within our regular thinking.

This diagnosis can be taken over, it seems to me, by contextual pragmatism. But it would split up the diagnosis according to different spheres of action. Scepticism must play a different role in the empirical and the normative sphere. We are invited to such a view by Hume: Hume's radical scepticism was one concerning empirical reality, not one on practical norms. And his reason was, simply, that practical norms are based on creation, whereas empirical reality is based on reality, or on nature. Once we have a nature/social creation division (something Rorty of course wants to avoid), scepticism loses its radical sting in the practical part – and so would, to my mind, become irony. There is still, however, the sting of scepticism concerning reality. Here the answer is a little, but only a little different to Hume's total unanswerability of the sceptic. Here we have Stroud's answer: what comes out of our experiments may not be true in the end, but we never will be able to know it, because knowledge is always already an integral component of our experiments. Another way to make the same point, it seems, is Peirce's admonition that all beliefs are fallible. Not one of them, including all together, is known as true. All might be wrong. This is what fallibility means.①

Rorty defines the ironist as someone who has "radical and continuing doubts about the final vocabulary it currently uses" (Rorty 1989, 73). This very

---

① Davidson sometimes says that all beliefs could not be true. But that is wrong.

much seems to make all people into philosophers, or even philosophical scepti-cists. Non-philosophers hardly ever have some clarity concerning their 'final vo-cabulary', and if they have some it is rather in the normative sphere than in the empirical. Non-philosophers may not be simply on the 'other side' of philoso-phers, as Hume suggested in his 'inside study'/'outside study' distinction of the force of doubt, but they are more so in the empirical than the normative sphere. Given my distinction of spheres, which harmonizes partly with Hume's, there is an explanation for this.

For doubt in the theoretical sphere to be motivating it would need an aware-ness of epistemological problems, something hardly on the everyday agenda of the public – save some special cases involved in religious belief, as the existence of God itself, or creationism, or similar topics. On the other hand, doubt in the norm-ative sphere *is* an everyday affair in all parts of society, be it individual self-i-dentity, private social relations, national, social and/or political norms, interna-tional relations. In all of these there is, obviously, great doubt that practical aims can be fulfilled, or in more abstract language, of what is 'right' or 'true'. But this kind of doubt is not one of the existence of 'right' independent of our knowledge, but one of our abilities to bring 'the right' about. As wide-spread practical thinking is quite burdened with normative realism, this analysis might not seem true on the surface. But if practical truth can only be a kind of consen-sus, as pragmatism suggests, doubt about it has to be explained as doubt in the human ability to *achieve* such a consensus. This obviously is a kind of local and not transcendental doubt.

My suggestion in conclusion would be this: irony as a cultural state of doubt is doubt directed primarily at practical matters, the different spheres of practical social life. Whether this kind of doubt is unanswerable, whether it is endless or not, is a practical matter: namely how to achieve consent on the norms in these spheres and whether it proves possible in the end.

Literature

Bernstein, R. (2010) , The Pragmatic Turn, Cambridge.

Cavell, S. (1996) , The Avoidance of Love, in: S. Mulhall (ed.) , *The Cavell Reader*, Oxford.

Davidson, D. (1983) , "A Coherence Theory of Truth and Knowledge", in: *Davidson, Subjective, Intersubjective, Objective*, Oxford 2001.

—(1992) , " The Second Person ", in: *Davidson, Subjective, Intersubjective, Objective*, Oxford 2001.

—(1999) , "Reply to Stroud", in: L. E. Hahn (ed.) , *The Philosophy of Donald Davidson*, Chicago.

Dewey, J. (1920) , *Reconstruction in Philosophy*, New York 2004 (also: The Middle Works vol.12, Carbondale 1982).

Friedman, L. (1999) , "Doubt & Inquiry: Peirce and Descartes Revisited", in: *Transactions of the Charles S. Peirce Society* 35, 724–746.

Glüer, K. (2011) , *Donald Davidson. A Short Introduction*, Oxford.

Habermas, J. (1968) , Erkenntnis und Interesse, Frankfurt; engl. *Knowledge and Human Interests*, Beacon Press 1972.

Meyers, R. G. (1967) , "Peirce on Cartesian Doubt", in: *Transactions of the Charles S. Peirce Society* 3, 13–23.

Nagel, Th. (1999) , " Davidson ' s New Cogito ", in: L. E. Hahn (ed.) , *The Philosophy of Donald Davidson*, Chicago.

Peirce, Ch. S. (1886) , "Questions Concerning Certain Faculties Claimed for Man " (Faculties) – *The Essential Peirce*, Vol. 1, N. Houser/C. Kloesel (eds.) , Bloomington 1992.

—(1886) , "Some Consequences of Four Incapacities" (Incapacities).

—(1877) , "The Fixation of Belief" (Fixation).

—(1878) , "How to Make our Ideas Clear" (Ideas).

Quine, W. v. O. (1969) , " Ontological Relativity ", in: *Ontological Relativity and Other Essays*, New York.

Rorty, R. (1979), *Philosophy and the Mirror of Nature*, Princeton-Oxford.

—(1989), *Contingency, Irony and Solidarity*, Cambridge.

Stroud, B. (1999), "Radical Interpretation and Philosophical Scepticism", in: L. E. Hahn (ed.), *The Philosophy of Donald Davidson*, Chicago.

—(2003), "Ostension and the Social Character of Thought", in: *Philosophy and Phenomenological Research* 67(3), 667-674.

Williams, M. (2003), "Rorty on Knowledge and Truth", in: Ch. Guignon/D. R. Hiley (eds.), *Richard Rorty*, Cambridge.

Pragmatism's Two Sources
of Social Philosophy

Roberto Frega

French National Centre for Scientific Research

I Competing traditions in social philosophy

The resurgence of pragmatism in political philosophy which has taken place in the last thirty years has been dominated by two main intellectual strategies, the first consisting in reclaiming it as part of the liberal tradition, the second consisting in inscribing it within the broad camp of critical theories. Prominent in this second perspective have been the contributions of scholars which to a greater or lesser degree are affiliated with the Frankfurt School of Critical Theory. It was first Jürgen Habermas who, in the early Nineties, relied on John Dewey's theory of publics to develop his theory of deliberative democracy, and one can easily see the profound influence of Dewey's theory of democracy in shaping Habermas' interpretation of the public sphere and of civil society as well as his proceduralist views. Axel Honneth has improved on this first stage by drawing on Dewey in his conception of social freedom as well as in his most recent proposal for a theory of democratic ethos. More recently, Rahel Jaeggi has resorted to Dewey's theory of inquiry to propose a reactualized theory of immanent critique in the classical style of the Frankfurt School (Jaeggi, 2014), and publications exploring the connections between pragmatism and critical theory are now proliferating at a high pace.

Overcoming a past history of conflictual relations between pragmatism and critical theory, these works have rightly emphasized the important theoretical affinities between the two traditions, showing the potential contribution of pragmatism to a critical program in social and political philosophy. Resisting the established practice of inscribing pragmatism within a classical liberal understanding of politics, and avoiding equally mainstream temptations of reducing pragmatism to a mere set of new tools for renewing the justificatory program of ideal theory, scholars coming from the tradition of critical theory have rightly noted the potential of pragmatism – notably Dewey's – for an approach to politics which emphasizes the critical dimension of theory, and which focuses on phenomena such as the exploitative character of modern society, the alienating impact of mass media, and the pathology – inducing effects of capitalism. These works have had the indisputable merit of putting an end to the shallow and ungrounded series of critiques of acquiescence to *status quo* that several generations of scholars have raised against pragmatism (MacGilvray, 2000). In so doing, they have contributed in a definitive way to firmly locating pragmatism in the camp of 'nonideal theory' and shown its potential for a program in political philosophy which is not dominated by justificatory concerns and which is directly oriented toward concrete aspects of social, political, and economic renewal.

Their respective merits notwithstanding, each of these strategies has succeeded in its attempt at resurrecting pragmatism as a political philosophy only at the high price of forcing it into an alien theoretical mould, as if pragmatism could legitimately enter the field of political theory only at the price of heavy conceptual reductions to the theoretical frameworks of other and better established traditions. It is the claim of this paper that this strategy produces also unhappy consequences, as it fails to fully appreciate the original contributions pragmatism can offer to contemporary debates in political theory.

How should these limitations be overcome, how could we apprehend pragmatism as a political philosophy on its own terms? It is my contention that in order to do this, a newer look at historical texts is needed, and one which is not encumbered by theoretical questions and interpretative frameworks developed by other traditions. This is a longer route, and in this paper I will be able only to provide some hints at the potential benefit it could be able to deliver, if followed in a more thorough way. To do this, in the following sections I will reconstruct the basic tenets of John Dewey's social philosophy, conceived as a set of meta–theoretical assumptions concerning the nature and task of our intellectual undertakings in the social and political domain. This historical detour will bring home two major theoretical conclusions: the first is that a self–aware pragmatist social and political philosophy will be closer to the tradition of critical theory than to that of Anglo–American liberalism. The second is that such a social philosophy will nevertheless differ from critical theory on some major points which the debate has tended to obscure. As a conclusion I will claim not only that pragmatism has developed a genuine program of its own in social philosophy which is worthwhile pursuing today, but also that this program can be adequately understood and then further developed only under the condition that we preserve its original two theoretical inspirations – the critical emancipatory social thought of the continental tradition and the empiricist liberal reformism of 19th century British philosophy. My contention is that pragmatist social philosophy can be adequately understood only under the condition that these apparently diverging and incompatible strands of social thought are reconciled, precisely in the manner John Dewey, George H. Mead, Jane Addams, Mary P. Follett and other pragmatist political thinkers and activists have tried to do. This seems to be a challenging task, precisely because contemporary social and political philosophy is built on the assumption of an irreducible divergence among these two sources. Yet we will not be able to hear the distinctive pragmatist voice unless we understand how, according to the pragmatist, the reconciliation of these-for us irreconcilable, for them complementary – sources need to be achieved.

Starting from these premises, this paper will bring these conclusions home through a close scrutiny of textual evidence for social philosophy in Dewey's works (Section 2) aimed at retracing these 'two sources' and at showing how he combined them in a consistent way. Section 3 will draw some theoretical implications from the evidence gathered in the previous section before bringing the paper to a close.

II   Pragmatism's social philosophy

Readers acquainted with the tradition of Critical Theory may be surprised to discover that Dewey was developing a research program in social philosophy close to that of the not yet born Frankfurt school some decades before Max Horkheimer took the lead of the *Institut für Sozialforschung*. But they would be equally surprised by discovering that for Dewey such a program in social critique was to be understood as a radicalization of the liberal tradition rather than its overcoming. As readers of Dewey's *Liberalism and Social Action* know, what he was calling for was indeed a new and more radical form of liberalism, something that was closer to Commons' "reasonable capitalism" than to the critical project of an overthrown of the capitalist society advocated by the first generation of the Frankfurt School.

To understand how these apparently conflicting statements can coexist within Dewey's philosophy, a fruitful strategy consists in examining the evolution of his own understanding of 'social philosophy', considered as a set of general assumptions about the content, nature, and tasks of normative disciplines. One of the rare formal definitions Dewey gave of social philosophy comes from an unpublished syllabus dated 1923: 'Social philosophy is concerned with the valuation of social phenomena. The latter include all the customs, institutions, arrangements, purposes and policies that depend upon human association, or the living together of men' (MW 15:231). Dewey proposes to conceive social philosophy as the critical task consisting of formulating normative standards for assessing social phenomena starting from an immanent examination of these social phenomena themselves.Accordingly,the task of social philosophy is to carry further.

> the process of reflective valuation which is found as an integral part of social phenomena,apart from general theorizing.[...]Social philosophy is a technique for clarifying the judgments which are constantly passed of necessity upon social customs,institutions,laws,arrangements,actual and projected.Its subject – matter involves a study (1) of the influence of distinct types of social grouping upon the generation of beliefs and standards as to right and wrong, good and bad; and (2) of the reflex reaction of these beliefs and standards,upon other social forces with special regard to their effect upon the production of goods and bads by these social forces.Its purpose is to render the social criticism and projection of policies which is always going on more enlightened and effective (MW 15:231–232).

In the same years,the expression 'social philosophy' is repeatedly used by Dewey in *Reconstruction in Philosophy*,a text consisting of the lectures Dewey gave in Japan the same year of his China lectures and that he published shortly after his return to the United States.In *Individualism Old and New*,published in 1930 and in *Liberalism and Social Action*,published in 1935,the expression 'social philosophy' is used to single out his approach to politics from the competing paradigms of classical liberalism and Marxism.From these uses,the reader gets a clear sense of a research program that fuses together the main themes of social philosophy:a concern for a direct engagement with present social ills,an orientation toward nonideal theory, the search for criteria for validating specific normative claims,a sense of the relevance of the social and historical circumstance in fixing the ends and means of social reform,the rejection of a purely political approach to socio–political issues.It gives,also,the clear idea that when it came to formulating his most basic assumptions, Dewey was consistently firm in rejecting Marxism and more interested in adopting a liberal view, although a pretty unorthodox 'social' one.

A look at the ensemble of Dewey's works may however give the impression that the expression 'social philosophy' is not used by Dewey in a consistent way. It occurs some 65 times within the totality of his *Works*, and seldom as an object of distinct concern. We need therefore to look carefully into these manifold usages to distill his specific understanding of social philosophy. This reading will prove the existence of two normative projects which from the perspective of contemporary theory may appear to be incompatible, whereas in a pragmatist perspective they need to be kept together: a project of radical critique of capitalist American society, and a project of progressive reform through educational, social, and other means of political action meant at actualizing and renewing the liberal tradition. For the sake of the present analysis, I propose to group Dewey's remarks on social philosophy into four chronologically organized phases.

In the first phase that goes from Dewey's first writings till 1901, there is no single occurrence of this expression in his published works. Dewey's interest in political philosophy during the first phase of his career is limited but well attested, however it displays no concern for the social dimension. In (Dewey, 1888), certainly the most important political text of the period, there is no trace of a social approach, and democracy is meant to refer to a political regime and to a moral ideal. The lack of references to the social as the central dimension of human life and hence of politics is not surprising in this first phase of his thought, dominated by idealist assumptions which drove his interest either toward the psychological or the moral dimension of experience.

A second phase occurs between 1901 and 1919, when the term is seldom used, generally in three ways all revealing about how Dewey began to conceive the task of social and political theory. The first way refers to education, the second to the works of the British philosophers of the 19th century, and the third to his own view of social life. It is in particular in educational texts that the expression appears, generally with the aim of emphasizing that pedagogy must take social factors into account rather than confine itself to the study of the individual. Indeed, throughout these texts Dewey emphasizes the social dimension of education, depicts the school as a 'social institution', which is to say an institution essentially involved in the progress and functioning of the whole social body. By this Dewey means that education is appraised in the perspective of its contribution to the functioning of society rather than to the psychical development of children. According to this view, which is inspired by a reformist attitude toward educational matters, 'an educational reform is but one phase of a general social modification' (Dewey, 1901). Here Dewey pits 'the reformist' against 'the conservative' and describes them as two competing social philosophies, meaning by this two competing general views about the role education should have in mediating the relationships between individuals and society, and as is known, he sides uncompromisingly with the reformist view. In other texts the same critique is applied by Dewey to revolutionary philosophies, which are criticized similarly to conservatives for their incapacity to provide clear indications about how to make the world a better world.

This treatment of social philosophy shows that for Dewey the kind of normative work required from philosophy and similar intellectual professions consists first and foremost in providing practical and concrete indications about both the means and ends of social reform. On the one hand, with reference to education, it needs to provide normative standards to define the place of education within the larger picture of social life. On the other hand, it must describe the steps to be undertaken to reach these goals as well as the methods – organizational and educational – which this undertaking requires. Given the internal connection between means and ends, the theoretical discussion about ends is not complete till means, processes, and procedures are taken into account. Dewey insists on the 'impossibility of separating either the theoretical discussion of the course of study, or the problem of its practical efficiency, from intellectual and social conditions which at first sight are far removed; it is enough if we recognize that the question of the course of study is a question in the organization of knowledge, in the organization of life, in the organization of society' (Dewey, 1901). At the same time, and inseparably, he argues that social philosophy should be concerned with the study of the means by which these ends can be achieved, and should orient a process of transformation of these very means, perceived as the conditions by which the ends are achieved. In educational matters as well as in political reflection, Dewey sees critique as being merely an intermediate step toward what is for him the highest and most important normative undertaking: the reconstruction of society which takes place through the formulation of experimental hypothesis conceived as guidelines for political reform. Hence, the constant mingling of philosophical and pedagogical considerations in Dewey's texts in the philosophy of education.

The distinguishing mark of a social approach is the positive acknowledgment of the entanglement of means and ends, which implies in turn that social philosophy should proceed through the analysis, critique and reform of existing social conditions. A social philosophy intended as a form of reflection limited to final ends and values is rejected as incomplete. Moreover, for Dewey there is an internal connection between social philosophy and reformism because social philosophy should indicate means, steps, stages, and paths to be pursued in order to reach the normative goals it sets. This articulation of means to be employed, of things to be done, of practical steps in a feasible roadmap is as important as the evaluation of final ends to reach. Hence, for example, in addressing himself to teachers and administrators in school, Dewey is not merely pointing to them the function of the school in achieving the good society, nor is he merely unveiling the ills of the present situation: he is discussing with them local improvements, projects of reforms, suggestions for updating the curricula, and so on and so forth. This explains the priority a pragmatist like Dewey would give to empirical investigation and local intervention over what, with disdain, he used to call "theory at large". Dewey's emphasis on terms such as 'direction' and 'control' to define the normative task of social theory is to be understood precisely in this sense: a social philosophy must help orient the social process, a process which Dewey sees as being always in change, always in the making, and hence always in need to be oriented, controlled, directed through what he usually terms 'intelligence', or social inquiry. Dewey's social philosophy is to this extent progressive rather than revolutionary: Dewey never tired of criticizing the revolutionary project for its incapacity to articulate experimentally how the transformational process should unfold, to devise concrete means to bring society step by step from its present circumstances to better ones.

A second use of the expression 'social philosophy' typical of this phase is historical, as Dewey often refers to the social philosophy of Modern thinkers, specifically those of the British tradition from Hobbes to Spencer, in order to denote philosophical theories that have a reformist orientation, i.e. theories which address social issues such as poverty, exclusion, oppression, and equality *through specific projects of reform.* In all these occurrences, the use of the term 'social philosophy' is rather loose, and never employed by Dewey to describe his own work. Yet they point consistently towards a social–reformist understanding of the task of philosophy. Discussing Herbert Spencer's philosophy, Dewey defines social philosophy as 'a theory of conduct which, being more than individual, serves as a principle of criticism and reform in corporate affairs and community welfare' (Dewey, 1904). Spencer's social philosophy is criticized for being 'speculative' or 'romantic', by which Dewey meant 'couched merely in terms of a program of criticism and reconstruction' (ibid.). This 'merely' points polemically towards the lack of a direct engagements with social and material circumstances in connecting means to ends. A third and less prominent use typical of this second phase refers to the generic meaning of social philosophy as a theoretical undertaking having society as its object and emphasizing the inescapably social dimension of phenomena such as individual life, politics, education.

We enter into a third phase in 1919 with the unpublished 'Syllabus of Eight Lectures on Philosophical Reconstruction', that will be the basis for his conference series in Japan the same year. In the syllabus as well as in the published lectures the expression social philosophy appears explicitly in the title of the last lecture: 'Reconstruction as Affecting Social Philosophy', in a way that clearly shows Dewey's willingness to endorse as he never did before 'social philosophy' as an accurate description of his own intellectual work. In the same year Dewey delivered a series of conferences in China titled 'Social and Political Philosophy'. All these texts emphasize the same methodological point which is the critique of 'sweeping generalizations', under the assumption that 'general answers supposed to have a universal meaning that covers and dominates all particulars [...] do not assist inquiry. They close it. They are not instrumentalities to be employed and tested in clarifying concrete social difficulties' (Dewey, 1920). Here Dewey's critical target is invariably German philosophy from Hegel to Marx, and the central argument is that social philosophy, in contrast with other methods, denotes a form of inquiry on specific social problems having in view solutions to be put to test and implemented through controlled methods.

Dewey insists here on the fact that social philosophers should not engage in general – his preferred words are 'sweeping' and 'at large' – enterprises such as the critique of capitalism, of modernity, of bureaucratic rationality which in the end do not tell much concerning how to act here and now: they should rather concern themselves with helping 'men solve problems in the concrete by supplying them hypotheses to be used and tested in projects of reform' (Dewey, 1920). What needs to be stressed here, besides the emphasis on the problem-driven orientation of inquiry, is the clear subordination of the task of generalized critique to that of science-led projects in social reform and reconstruction. To be noted here is the recurrence of the same methodological stance: the social theorist develops tools and forges hypothesis to be used by social actors, which are also entitled with the responsibility of fixing their own goals and assessing the success of their undertakings. This attitude toward a context based, reformist, and progressive social theory is perfectly consistent with Dewey particularism in ethics, with his proceduralism in politics, and with his agnosticism when it comes about discussing final values. This is the radical immanence of Dewey. This point strikes a sharp contrast with the tradition of critical theory, for which the diagnosis of large scale social trends provides the necessary theoretical base from which to engage in normative practices of critique.

We enter a fourth and last phase around 1924. Starting from that year Dewey drops the term, that in the following three decades will be used only seldom and practically never again to define his own philosophical project. At the same time, Dewey's concern for social issues will constantly increase, as it can be seen from his interest for the social as a general philosophical category (Dewey, 1928) and for social phenomena, social reform, social problems, social control, social movements, social revolution, social life, and so on and so forth. From this time on the social dimension became so entrenched in all aspects of Dewey's thought that he felt no need to explicitly describe his political philosophy as social. All major political texts of the time emphasize the failure of purely political conceptions of democracy. After 1923 the most consistent and extensive use of the term can be found in Dewey's several essays devoted to liberalism, where he defines and analyzes liberalism as a distinctive social philosophy, meaning by that a philosophy with a distinctive conception of the individual and of his place in society, and to which he opposes a different social philosophy, one that rejects the individualist standpoint of liberalism.

III   Reclaiming pragmatism as social philosophy

As this short reconstruction shows, the double – British and German – intellectual genesis of pragmatist political philosophy reflects itself in a double edged conception of social philosophy: on the one hand, a critique of the American society of his day, which echoes themes from the Marxian and left Hegelian tradition. Dewey's writings of the 20's and especially the 30's are filled with sharp critiques of the existing state of western civilization. His remarks on liberalism having become 'a house divided against itself' (Dewey, 1930b), his criticism of the division of society into a leisure class and a labor class (Dewey, 1916), his criticism of corporate capitalism with the ensuing call for a socialization of industry (Dewey, 1935), his criticism of the psychological and social damages produced by large scale unemployment (Dewey, 1930b), his criticism of the ideological power taken by the media and of the reiterate failures of the educative system at coping with social needs (Dewey, 1939), his diagnosis of the rise of the 'impersonal forces' (Dewey, 1939) and of the 'machine age' (Dewey, 1927), all point toward a model of social critique which resonate positively with the manifold critiques of the malaise of civilization that Sigmund Freud, Max Horkheimer, Karl Mannheim, Max Weber, Walter Benjamin, and others were developing in the same years.

On the other hand, these texts clearly betray a reformist conception inspired by Bentham and Mill and based on a scientific program of social direction and control which relied on the empirical examination of consequences produced by acting according to experimental hypotheses. Indeed, Dewey saw social philosophy as the prolongation of Bentham and Mill's programs in social reform (Dewey, 1918). What Dewey called the 'method of intelligence' was neither a mere appeal to deliberation nor an anticipation of communicative rationality. Dewey's conception of democracy as method cannot be reduced to a defense of deliberative democracy. Rather, his call for the diffusion of the scientific method in dealing with social problems was meant literally: it was an appeal to experimental, observational, empirical research as the most reliable way for dealing with social problems, in line with the teachings of the Chicago School of sociology and committed to the progressivist program of social reform. Of social philosophy, he believed that its function was 'to aid in creation of methods such that experimentation may go on less blindly, less at the mercy of accident, more intelligently, so that men may learn from their errors and profit by their successes' (Dewey, 1927). Its priority was not to work out a critical theory of society, but rather to develop what a few decades later Harold Lasswell, reclaiming Dewey's heritage, will define the "policy sciences". As he wrote in the last chapter of *Reconstruction in philosophy*, devoted to social philosophy, "in the question of methods concerned with reconstruction of special situations rather than in any refinements in the general concepts of institution, individuality, state, freedom, law, order, progress, etc., lies the true impact of philosophical reconstruction". The radical empiricist stance stands here clearly in opposition to the more speculative and generalizing theory of society in the tradition of the Frankfurt School.

Dewey's constant interest in direction and social control, the call for a systematic application of science to social and political problems, the reformist orientation, the reliance on rationality as the best tool for solving social problems, the faith in technology and the genuine interest for corporate life as potential sources of social good, and the constant focus on means–ends connections can be understood only through reference to the British tradition in social philosophy: like Mill and Bentham before him, Dewey was persuaded that the most important task at hand was the systematic scrutiny of present situated social problems in the search for working solutions through the application of the scientific method. The movement of Chicago sociology to which he actively participated in his Chicago years was heading in this same direction. On these and similar points he could not be further from the sweeping critique of rationality, rationalization, technology, the media, and capitalism that we find in the German tradition of social theory spanning from Marx to at least Theodor Adorno. And we could not be closer to the social philosophy of Bentham and Mill and to their idea that through science 'mankind are directed to the only true track of investigation which can afford instruction or hope of rational agreement, the track of experiment and observation' (Bentham, 2002).

Dewey struggled his entire life with these partially diverging understandings of social philosophy, in the same way in which he struggled to reconcile two competing conceptions of freedom, the classical liberal view based on the idea of free will and autonomy and a social conception based upon the idea of power to act. Equally unhappy with Marx's class struggle and with Bentham's naive utilitarianism, Dewey sought to open up an alternative paradigm of social philosophy, one which, while incorporating elements from both, displayed nevertheless irreducible features. Dewey's reconstructed conception of social liberalism is to this extent instructive: particularly in (Dewey, 1935) and (Dewey, 1939) but also elsewhere, Dewey has made clear that his political views steer clear of the Locke—Smith liberal tradition as well as of that which was directly inspired by the German tradition of Marx.

In his own reconstruction, pride of place is given to a conception of democracy shaped by the science—based reformist tradition of Bentham and Mill but mediated through the critique of individualism to be found in the Hegelianism of T. H. Green. From Bentham and Mill, among other things, Dewey retained the awareness that science was to be considered the best ally of social reform, that a purely political conception of democracy was unable to deliver the goods promised by classical liberalism, and that a thoroughgoing program of social and economic reform was badly needed so as to counter the ' vested interests ' that stand in the way of social progress and individual emancipation. Indeed, for Dewey the work of Bentham and Mill ' is proof that liberalism can be a power in bringing about radical social changes ' (Dewey, 1935). From Green he retained the idea that the liberal ideal of freedom could be preserved while getting rid of its fragile individualistic metaphysics, and that the task of social philosophy was precisely to show how this could be possible. Dewey learned from Green that it was possible to argue for the responsibility of the state in providing for social institutions and reforms without having to accept an organic theory of the state in the Hegelian manner. He then criticized liberals because, 'in identifying the extension of liberty in all of its modes with extension of their particular brand of economic liberty, they completely failed to anticipate the bearing of private control of the means of production and distribution upon the effective liberty of the masses in industry as well as in cultural goods' (Dewey, 1935). But he equally criticized Marxists because their materialistic determinism and social organicism denied the very possibility of individual freedom and its emancipatory potential. He defended a conception of social freedom, according to which 'effective liberty is a function of the social conditions existing at any time' (Dewey, 1935), so that it cannot be *a priori* restricted to the merely political sphere. The idea that freedom and the other political values can neither be defined nor implemented through a vision which restricts its focus to the functioning of political institutions need be at the basis of a pragmatist social philosophy which is not forgetful of its own history.

IV   Conclusion

This paper set out to show that a closer look at Dewey's statements about social philosophy reveals a balanced concern for reformist-liberal and for critical-radical themes. This conclusion has not only historical interest but also theoretical relevance. Indeed, the theoretical upshot of this historical reconstruction was to show where pragmatism stands in relation to mainstream contemporary traditions in political philosophy once we set it on its proper terms rather than reducing it to one or the other of its constitutive dimensions. Far from leading to contradictory demands, the reformist–liberal and the critical–radical projects in social philosophy merge fruitfully in the pragmatist tradition, for whom the critical sting – what Dewey termed *criticism* rather than critique – is always pressed for the sake of concrete and situated reform. In that sense, the priority of the normative attitude of reconstruction forces critique into a subordinate position. Indeed, criticism denotes for Dewey – in a way not dissimilar from Wittgenstein – the negative and preliminary task of liberating potentialities in view of constructive formulation of hypothesis to be tested through concrete social action in specifiable social circumstances, and which had to be focused and problem – driven rather than general and speculative. To that effect, Dewey used to criticize classical liberalism and Marxism for the same reason, which is to say their weakness 'for purposes of constructive social direction' (Dewey, 1917).

As a social philosopher, Dewey was more interested in *criticism* as a constructive and creative activity exercised in ordinary circumstances by ordinary agents and aimed at opening up new possibilities from within social experience (Dewey, 1930a) than in *critique* as an academic enterprise aimed at unmasking and unveiling structural pathologies in the style of the grand social theorizing which has spanned the critical tradition from Marx to today, with its panoply of concepts such as alienation, reification, social pathology, iron cage, malaise of civilization, rationalization, ideology, etc. It seems indeed an inescapable feature of this tradition, that critical theory should proceed from an overall diagnosis taking the form of a general theory of society in which a negative philosophy of history is often embedded, and which is called for to explain the kind of structural pathologies which are said to affect contemporary life and whose unmasking defines the goal of social theory itself. Contrary to this way of proceeding, pragmatism has traditionally avoided engaging in such large scale theorizing, always preferring to rely on more contextually situated forms of analysis, considered to be better suited to engage present historical circumstances in processes of social transformation. To this extent, Dewey's approach to education should be considered as a paradigmatic instantiation of how social philosophy should proceed, once the thesis of the end-means continuum is taken seriously. In this sense, his detailed and often technical concern for the methodological, organizational, financial, political aspects of the educational process should not be considered mere chapters of his pedagogy, but rather as necessary ingredients of a complete and consistent process of social inquiry. What the textual evidence shows is precisely that whenever it comes to social philosophy, the reformist, practically oriented attitude takes over the critical – diagnostical one, and the Millian – benthamite heritage takes over the Marxian.

This reformist attitude, as said at the beginning, did not prevent Dewey from engaging in harsh criticisms of what he saw as dangerous drifts in the organization of modern mass societies. But he never consumed his intellectual resources in the development of sophisticated conceptual apparatuses for grounding projects of critique, preferring to devote them to the task of devising working solutions, formulating guidelines, trying to understand how society could be changed from within by relying on existing social forces, liberating the energies that he saw as being imprisoned in the repressed creativity of millions of individuals participating in the large scale transformations of the 20th century. In that sense, his interest was not in criticizing reason, technology, corporate life, capitalism, or industry 'at large', but in trying to understand *how* the extraordinary potential they were unleashing could be put to use in the interest of the greatest number of human beings. Hence to the negative vocabulary of the critical tradition, Dewey preferred the positive vocabulary of reconstruction, transformation, direction, control, reform, education, experimentation, learning, intelligence, and democracy. These terms, taken together, compose the positive and constructive side which is essential to any pragmatist social philosophy. They circumscribe the perimeter of pragmatism's 'democratic experimentalism' and define its lasting normative project, a project whose ethical foundation, in Dewey's word, was the faith in human capacities.

In conclusion, as I hope to have shown, while the differences between pragmatism and critical theory may to a certain extent boil down to the level of a family quarrel, they are nevertheless differences that matter, and that should not be neglected if we want to liberate the whole theoretical potential of pragmatism in contemporary social and political thought.

References

Bentham, J. 2002, *Rights, Representation, and Reform: Nonsense Upon Stilts' and Other Writings for the French Revolution*, Clarendon Press, Oxford.

Decker, K.S. 2012, "Perspectives and Ideologies: a Pragmatic Use for Recognition Theory", *Philosophy & Social Criticism* 38(2), 215–226.

Dewey, J. 1888, *The Ethics of Democracy*, The Early Works, vol.1, Southern Illinois University Press, Carbondale, pp.227–250.

Dewey, J. 1901, *The Educational Situation*, The Middle Works, 1899–1924, vol.1, Southern Illinois University Press, Carbondale.

Dewey, J. 1904, *The Philosophical Work of Herbert Spencer*, The Middle Works, 1899–1924, vol.1, Southern Illinois University Press, Carbondale.

Dewey, J. 1916, *Democracy and Education*, The Middle Works, 1899–1924, vol.9, Southern Illinois University Press, Carbondale.

Dewey, J. 1917, *The Need for A Recovery of Philosophy*, The Middle Works, 1899–1924, vol.10, Southern Illinois University Press, Carbondale, pp.3–49.

Dewey, J. 1918, *The Motivation of Hobbes' political philosophy*, The Middle Works, 1899–1924, vol.11, Southern Illinois University Press, Carbondale, pp.18–41.

Dewey, J. 1920, *Reconstruction in Philosophy*, The Middle Works, 1899–1924, vol.12, Southern Illinois University Press, Carbondale.

Dewey, J. 1927, *The Public and Its Problems*, The Later Works, 1925–1953, vol.2, Southern Illinois University Press, Carbondale.

Dewey, J. 1928a, "Justice Holmes and the liberal mind", The Later Works, 1925–1953, vol.2, Southern Illinois University Press, Carbondale, pp.177–184.

Dewey, J. 1928b, "Philosophies of Freedom", The Later Works, 1925–1953, vol.3, Southern Illinois University Press, Carbondale.

Dewey, J. 1928c, "The Inclusive Philosophic Idea", The Later Works, 1925–1953, vol.3, Southern Illinois University Press, Carbondale.

Dewey, J. 1930a, "Construction and Criticism", The Later Works, 1925–1953, vol.5, Southern Illinois University Press, Carbondale, pp.125–145.

Dewey, J. 1930*b*, *Individualism Old and New*, The Later Works, 1925–1953, vol. 5, Southern Illinois University Press, Carbondale, pp. 42–124.

Dewey, J. 1935, *Liberalism and Social Action*, The Later Works, 1925–1953, vol. 11, Southern Illinois University Press, Carbondale, pp. 1–65.

Dewey, J. 1939, *Freedom and Culture*, The Later Works, 1925–1953, vol. 13, Southern Illinois University Press, Carbondale.

Dewey, J. 1944, "Challenge to Liberal Thought", The Later Works, 1925–1953, vol. 15, Southern Illinois University Press, Carbondale, pp. lw15.261–276.

Dewey, J. 1973, *Lectures in China* 1919–1920, The University Press of Hawaii, Honolulu.

Festenstein, M. 1997, *Pragmatism and Political Theory from Dewey to Rorty*, Polity Press, Cambridge.

Frega, R. 2013*a*, "Between Pragmatism and Critical Theory: Social Philosophy Today", *Human Studies*.

Frega, R. 2013*b*, "From Normative Spheres to Normative Practices: New Prospects for Normative Theory after Habermas", *International Journal of Philosophical Studies*.

Frega, R. 2015, "Beyond Morality and Ethical Life: Pragmatism and Critical Theory Cross Path", *Journal of Philosophical Research*.

Habermas, J. 1996, *Between Facts and Norms*, Polity Press, Cambridge.

Hetzel, A., Kertscher, J. Rölli, M., eds 2008, *Pragmatismus-Philosophie der Zukunft?*, Velbrück, Weilerswist.

Hildreth, R. 2009, "Reconstructing Dewey on Power", *Political Theory* 37 (6), 780–807.

Hogan, B. 2015, "Pragmatic Hegemony: Questions and Convergence", *Journal of Speculative Philosophy* 29 (1).

Honneth, A. 1998, "Democracy as Reflexive Cooperation", *Political Theory* 26 (6), 763–783.

Honneth, A. 2011, *Das Recht der Freiheit: Grundriss einer demokratischen Sittlichkeit*, Suhrkamp, Frankfurt am Main.

Jaeggi, R. 2014, *Kritik von Lebensformen*, Suhrkamp, Frankfurt am Main.

Kadlec, A.2006, "Reconstructing Dewey: The Philosophy of Critical Pragmatism", *Polity* 38(4), 519–542.

Kloppenberg, J.T.1986, *Uncertain Victory. Social Democracy and Progressivism in European and American Thought*, 1870–1920, Oxford University Press, Oxford.

MacGilvray, E. 2000, "Five Myths about Pragmatism, or, Against a Second Pragmatic Acquiescence", *Political theory* 28(4), 480–508.

Markell, P.2007, The Potential and the Actual: Mead, Honneth, and the I, *in* D.O. Bert van den Brink, ed., "Recognition and Power. Axel Honneth and the Tradition of Critical Social Theory", Cambridge University Press, Cambridge.

Midtgarden, T.2012, "Critical Pragmatism: Dewey's Social Philosophy Revisited", *European Journal of Social Theory*, pp.1–17.

Owen, D.2007, "Self-Government and Democracy as Reflexive Co-operation". Reflections on Honneth's Social and Political Ideal, *in* D.Owen van den Brink Bert, eds, "Recognition and Power. Axel Honneth and the Tradition of Critical Social Theory", Cambrdge University Press.

Ray, L. 2004, "Pragmatism and Critical Theory", *European Journal of Social Theory* 7(3), 307–321.

Renault, E.2013, "Dewey, Hook et Mao: quelques affinités entre marxisme et pragmatisme", *Actuel Marx* 54(2), 138–157.

Ryan, A.1995, *John Dewey and the High Tide of American Liberalism*, WW Norton & Company, New York.

Särkelä, A.2013, "Ein drama in drei akten", *Deutsche Zeitschrift für Philosophie* 61(5–6), 681–696.

Shalin, D.1992, "Critical Theory and the Pragmatist Challenge", *American Journal of Sociology* 98(2), 237–279.

Stears, M.2002, *Progressives, Pluralists, and the Problems of the State: Ideologies of Reform in the United States and Britain*, 1909–1926, Oxford University Press, Oxford.

Talisse, R.B.2005, *Democracy after Liberalism: Pragmatism and Deliberative Politics*, Routledge, New York.

White, S.K.2004, "The very idea of a critical social science: the pragmatist turn", *in* F. Rush, ed., *The Cambridge Companion to Critical Theory*, Cambridge University Press, Cambridge.

Zimmermann, B. 2006, "Pragmatism and the Capability Approach: Challenges in Social Theory and Empirical Research", *European Journal of Social Theory* 9 (4), 467–484.

杜威研究

Propositions and Other Instruments
in Dewey's Later Thought[1]

Larry A.Hickman

Director Emeritus, Center for Dewey Studies

Southern Illinois University Carbondale

Several years ago Phillip Deen, who I am happy to say is one of my former students, located an interesting set of manuscripts in the Dewey Papers collection in Morris Library at Southern Illinois University Carbondale. After careful examination, Deen concluded that they are advanced drafts of chapters for a book – length manuscript that went missing when Dewey returned from his summer place in Nova Scotia to his apartment in New York City in 1947. After painstakingly editing the material and writing an extensive introduction, Deen published it in 2012 under the title *Unmodern Philosophy and Modern Philosophy*. We could also refer to it as "Dewey's new book".

One of the central claims of Dewey's new book is that our cultural projects tend to be faulty because we have never been able to shake off the influences of pre–modern concerns, or the antique tools fashioned by what Dewey calls "the

---

① Standard references to John Dewey's work are to the critical (print) edition, *The Collected Works of John Dewey*, 1882 – 1953, edited by Jo Ann Boydston (Carbondale: Southern Illinois University Press, 1969 – 1991), published in three series as *The Early Works* (EW), *The Middle Works* (MW) and *The Later Works* (LW). "LW 5:270," for example, refers to *The Later Works*, volume 5, page 270.

medieval synthesis". In other words, to borrow Bruno Latour's felicitous phrase, Dewey was telling us that "we have never been modern".

When I was asked to write a review of Deen's book, I attempted to distill Dewey's critique of modern philosophy as follows: "the failure of modernity (the reason why 'we have never been modern') is...due to a series of bad choices: doubt and skepticism over experimentalism; substance over process; structure over function; intuition①and revelation over cosmological and methodological naturalism; the soliloquy of an individual, internal consciousness over the observable behavior of social inquiry; preference for a mind/ body split over organic holism and acceptance of mind as 'extended and embodied'; ruptures over continuity; the unexamined values of custom over those that have been evaluated in relevant contexts; and studied and proud ignorance of context, especially in the field of inquiry. Each of these failures can be characterized as a failure of nerve: on one side of the coin of modernity we find the problem of skepticism; on its obverse, the quest for certainty"②.

In his new book Dewey expanded on his 1896 "Reflex Arc" essay and his 1925 *Experience and Nature* by taking on one of the central tenets of "modern" philosophy, viz. that the brain is the center of knowing in the broad sense and thus also the center of adaptive behavior. Here is Dewey:

> The idea that the commotion and excitement, the driving urge to be doing something with and to surrounding conditions can be anyway given a primary location in the brain or central nervous system has no scientific support. On its face it seems laughably absurd. The nervous seat of the emotional is the autonomic nervous system, both anatomically and physiological-

----

① This is of course intuition taken as unquestioned "insight" rather than as material for further inquiry.

② Larry A. Hickman, "John Dewey's Critique of our Unmodern Philosophy." *European Journal of Pragmatism and American Philosophy*, vol.5, no.1, 2013, pp.124–125.

ly, and the connections of this system are with such vital functions as circula-tion, breathing, digestion, secretion, ejective or eliminative bodily apparatus and the act, and accompanying motor steadiness...The sound of a church-bell or of a locomotive-whistle is experienced in virtue of certain active adaptations of the motor mechanism of auditory apparatus...Every event and object has a figure, *eidos*, form; its qualities are patterns and the patterning is deter-mined by the sequential pattern of our adaptive behavior.①

This material is especially interesting when read side by side with Mark Johnson's book *The Meaning of the Body*.Johnson emphasizes the central role of "visceral processes performed by the respiratory, digestive, cardiovascular, uro-genital, and endocrine systems," all of which recede, unfelt, into the background of the drama of the higher levels of adaptive behavior associated with the brain.② In his trenchant expansion of the work of Dewey (and others) , Johnson builds a case that the dualities that lie and the heart of the Western philosophical tradition – mind/body, thought/feeling, fact/value, and so on – lead us away from a proper understanding of the role of the body in generating meaning.Dewey and Johnson are on the same page regarding the consequences of these misun-derstandings for the teaching of philosophy as well as for wider social issues.

Johnson convincingly argues, for example, that the conceptual-propositional theory of meaning advanced by the likes of Fodor, Davidson, Searle, *et alia*, is defective because propositions are not, as has been claimed, the basic units of human meaning.His example is so simple and straightforward that one wonders how the giants of linguistic philosophy could have ever missed its point: *it seems clear that babies learn the meanings of things and events without formulating*

---

①　John Dewey.*Unmodern Philosophy and Modern Philosophy*, edited by Phillip Dean, Carbon-dale and Edwardsville: Southern Illinois University Press, 2012.pp.196-197.

②　Mark Johnson.*The Meaning of the Body*.Chicago: University of Chicago Press, 2007.p.6.

propositions.①Beyond that, of course, there are good reasons to look askance at a theory of meaning that implicitly denies appropriate engagement with meanings to visual and plastic artists, to say nothing of musicians, practitioners of yoga, and even lovers, on the basis that the meanings with which they work are not sufficiently linguistic.

For his part, Dewey was quite clear. In *How We Think* he reminded us that "When it is said, however, that thinking is impossible without language, we must recall that language includes much more than oral and written speech. Gestures, pictures, monuments, visual images, finger movements—anything consciously employed as a sign is, logically, language." (MW 6:314) In his 1938 *Logic: The Theory of Inquiry* he stressed that although language includes oral and written speech, it also includes "not only gestures but rites, ceremonies, monuments and the products of industrial and fine arts. A tool or machine, for example, is not simply a simple or complex physical object having its own physical properties and effects, but is also a mode of language. For it says something, to those who understand it, about operations of use and their consequences. To the members of a primitive community a loom operated by steam or electricity says nothing. It is composed in a foreign language, and so with most of the mechanical devices of modern civilization. In the present cultural setting, these objects are so intimately bound up with interests, occupations and purposes that they have an eloquent voice." (LW 12:52)

Dewey thus undercut the standard analytic notion of propositions as unique carriers of meaning, and he denied that they are the kinds of things that can be true or false. He thought that they are simply proposals and as such are more properly characterized as relevant or irrelevant, effective or ineffective, economical or uneconomical, and so on. One of Dewey's most succinct discussions of propositions can be found in his mini-debate with Bertrand Russell regarding warranted assert-

---

① Johnson, 8.

ibility and truth. His wider point, however, which was generously expanded in his 1938 *Logic*, is that propositions are "means, instrumentalities, since they are the operational agencies by which *beliefs* that have adequate grounds for acceptance are reached as the *end* of inquiry". ①When coupled with his statement that art "may thus be defined as an esthetic perception together with an *operative* perception of the efficiencies of the esthetic object" (LW 1:281) and his statement that "art is a continuation, by means of intelligent selection and arrangement, of natural tendencies of natural events," (LW 1:291) Dewey's treatment of propositions bursts the bounds of the conceptual/propositional model. It is undeniable that propositions as proposals are among the abstract features of logic as a theory of inquiry. But they must also be understood to include non-linguistic proposals about how to treat the materials of the sculptor, the chef, the winemaker, the yoga practitioner, and the sailor (to say nothing of lovers), all of which involve non-linguistic meanings.

Dewey replaces the *conceptual-propositional* theory of meaning with a *continuity/context* theory of meaning. He understands propositions as tools, as he says, and thus as instrumental to the adaptive behavior of complex organisms (including, it is safe to conclude, babies, musicians, artists working in visual and plastic media, yoga practitioners, and even lovers). Meanings are generated by living organisms within the continuities (and discontinuities) of adjustive tensions. They are context sensitive, and they are even sexy: under the proper conditions they may, Dewey tells us, "copulate and breed new meanings." (LW 1: 152)

As Dewey reminds us in chapter four of *Experience and Nature*, "[W]hen things are defined as instruments, their value and validity reside in what proceeds from them; consequences not antecedents supply meaning and verity." (LW 1: 123) Propositions, then, in Dewey's sense, far from being the basic units of

---

① John Dewey. "Propositions, Warranted Assertibility, and Truth". LW14.175.

meaning, are provisional suggestions. They are by no means uniquely linguistic. One of Dewey's examples is a baseball pitcher making a "proposition" to a batter." ["As slang has it", he writes, "a pitched baseball is to the batter a ' proposition' ; it states, or makes explicit, what he has to deal with next amid all the surrounding and momentarily irrelevant circumstance. Every statement extracts and sets forth the net result of reflection up to date as a condition of subsequent reflection." (MW 10:356)] Propositions are conjectures. They invite experimental inquiry. They point forward to an indefinite future. They are among the tools we use for the resolution of situations that have become sufficiently irritating that they require further action. Babies do it. Sculptors and painters do it. Musicians do it. Yoga practitioners do it. Lovers do it. We all do it.

Now it might be objected that the manner in which Dewey understands propositions still leans too far toward a conceptual/propositional theory such as the one that Johnson criticizes. But three features of his position militate against this conclusion. *First*, as I have already suggested, there is the fact that even though propositions are for the most part linguistic, they are not uniquely so. They include what is visual, tactile, auditory, and olfactory and gustatory. (Every wine connoisseur knows this very well.)

Second, there is the matter of fitness, in the sense of the fitness of a tool to perform a task. Dewey thinks that propositions are tools marked by properties of fitness in the very sense in which "hammers, looms, chemical processes like dyeing, [and] reduction of ores, when used as means, are marked by properties of fitness and efficacy (and the opposite) rather than by the logical properties of truth-falsity...." (LW 14:176) [1] Dewey thus associates propositions with a series of objects and techniques that involve accommodation to and adaptation of the environing conditions of living organisms. Diligent readers of Dewey know that

---

[1] Axes are sometimes said to be true when they perform well, and it is also possible (and sometimes advisable) to true a bicycle wheel.

these two activities together—accommodation and adaptation—constitute what he calls *adjustment*. His reconstruction of the notion of propositions thus emphasizes process instead of structure, and technology instead of ontology.

Third, there is the matter of vagueness. Dewey's description of what he calls "first propositions" recalls the uncoordinated activities of infants, that is, activities that often tend to be too coarse and vague to be immediately effective. As an aside to those who may be new parents (or grandparents), I should add that it is by no means meant as an insult to you or your offspring when I report that Dewey's description of first propositions includes the words "clumsy", "un-economical", and "ineffective." (LW 14:177) (But of course this can also be quite charming). Those are in fact terms that we sometimes use to describe the learning behavior of infants. But they could also be used to describe the learning behavior of scientists and engineers, novelists and historians when those professionals undertake radically innovative projects.

The point of my remarks so far is that Dewey's discussion of propositions rejects the conceptual/propositional view as Johnson describes it. Further, when coupled with a theory of mind as extended or expanded, understanding "extended or expanded" in the sense that the skin–barrier between organism and what is relatively external to it is regarded as permeable and an instrument of continuity as well as separation, Dewey's use of the term "proposition" captures.

*   *   *

Although my allotted time is brief, I do want to make a final, related point. We know that Dewey's technological metaphors have at times been an offence to some of the traditions of European philosophy where the term "instrumental" is understood primarily as what Langdon Winner termed "straight–line instrumentalism" and employed in ways that are far removed from Dewey's own use of the term. Dewey recognized that difficulty, but refused to be deterred, noting that any term can be misunderstood. (In this connection the various misconstruals of the terms "pragmatism" and "satisfaction" come to mind.)

In *Unmodern Philosophy* Dewey offers his own definition of "instrumental," as designating "the intermediate position and function of the subject matter of knowledge in the inclusive complex of the transaction constituting human living as a going concern."①In other words, what is instrumental is what is transformative within sequences of inquiry that are concerned with the adjustment of the organism with respect to its environing conditions (including, it should be emphasized, those conditions that are social in nature).

It might be asked whether Dewey's organic metaphors, which are based on his appropriation of Darwin together with his commitment to methodological naturalism, are compatible with his technological metaphors. In other words, does his "ecological" talk of organic adjustment tend to clash with his "technological" talk of tools? This is an important question, since even in the work of a philosopher as important as Juergen Habermas we can find barriers between what is technical and technological, on one side, and the activities that are termed "communicative" and "emancipatory" on the other.②

Is there is a conflict in Dewey's work between his "*ecological*" metaphors, which have to do with situations and organic adjustments, and his *technological* ones, which have to do with tools and techniques? Is it the case, as one commentator has suggested, that Dewey's "ecological" language does not do justice to the "functions and relationships of different kinds of tools and artifacts in changes of activity nor supply satisfactory means of analyzing the historical, institutionalized and cultural dimensions of human activity?"

In order to probe more deeply into this matter, the following points may be relevant. First, Dewey was deeply involved with the social/cultural dimensions of

---

① Dewey.*Unmodern Philosophy*, 242, Hereinafter, numbers in parentheses in the text, other than *Collected Works* references, refer to page numbers in *Unmodern Philosophy*.

② Reijo Miettinen. "Pragmatism and Activity Theory: Is Dewey's Philosophy a Philosophy of Cultural Retooling", *Outlines*, no.2, 2006, 15.

tools and tool use. During 1916, in the introduction to *Essays in Experimental Logic*, *he was writing that the genesis of the objects of mathematic and logic was on all fours with the genesis of the tools and machines of farming*, *such as the self*-binding reaper, as well as other cultural tools such as the telephone. Also in 1916, in *Democracy and Education*, he was writing of atoms, molecules, and so on, as tools for the carrying out of science. (MW 9:230)

Second, Dewey generally distinguished between tools and signs only functionally, that is, as demanded by the context of a particular sequence of inquiry. He would probably have been reluctant, therefore, to have identified a sign (only) as a "psychological tool as a means of internal activity aimed at mastering oneself." In rejecting inner/outer dualism, Dewey argued for a continuum between the organic and the inorganic not only with respect to the historical genesis of tools and techniques, but also with respect to their current and prospective use. Here again we see Dewey's continuum/context theory at work. On this point Dewey is in the excellent company of Maurice Merleau – Ponty and Marshall McLuhan, among others.

Third, Dewey built on William James' metaphor of the continuity of the perches and flights of birds to undercut the duality of inner and outer. The various pairs we term "sensation and idea", "peripheral and central", and "stimulus and response", for example, are for James and Dewey just moments in a continuous process, individuated only in terms of their relation to one another within the processes of adjustment. Dewey was clear enough in his 1896 "Reflex Arc" article: apart from retrospective analysis, there is nothing within those processes that can be termed either stimulus or response. What there *is* is a change in a system of tensions that involves the organism – environment matrix, followed, in some cases but by no means all, by some sort of analysis that carves out particular moments as needed in order to advance the progress of inquiry.

So Dewey does utilize tool metaphors in his 1938 *Logic*, even if briefly, and this is even more prominent in his 1916 book *Essays in Experimental Logic* and his 1916 lecture "Logical Objects" (as well as chapter 17 of *Democracy and Education*, *which is replete with technological metaphors that carry over nicely into the* 1938 *Logic*.) I have already rehearsed some of the relevant passages in these works, and I hope that at this point it will suffice to say that one of the central points of both *Essays in Experimental Logic* and "Logical Objects", is that logical objects are neither (a) physical properties abstracted and grasped in "rational apprehension", nor (b) mental (i.e. psychical existences, nor c) "metaphysical'in one of the most commonly used senses of that word" (MW 10:89), but just tools that have been generated from inference and that we use to do abstract types of work in more or less the same sense that hammers and saws have been generated from other practical activities in order to do work of a more concrete variety. Talk of structure thus gives way to function, and talk of metaphysics is supplanted by talk of the requirements of practical technological activity, whether abstract or concrete in kind.

It seems relevant here to recur to Dewey's remark in *Unmodern Philosophy* that "knowing as it takes place in the sciences is a mode of technology." (242) It also seems relevant, given the question of whether Dewey thought his *Logic*, his theory of inquiry, could be the basis for cultural retooling, to quote a passage that follows on the heels of the one just cited.

> ...the significance of the [scientific] method is so far from being re-
> stricted to physical subject matters that, from the standpoint of philosophy,
> one of the main (if not *the* main) reasons for taking the art of knowing as it
> is exhibited in the method of scientific inquiry as the data for framing the
> theory of knowledge is that the resulting theory will be a powerful tool (if it
> is permitted to use the word) in getting rid of the obstructions which now
> stand in the way of employing the method in free formation of beliefs that
> have decisive influence in [the] conduct of social affairs and transactions.
> (243)

Continuing, he provides a sharp distinction between wide and narrow senses of technology.

The view that, philosophically speaking, knowledge is one form, a central form, of technology, does not mean that its subject matter and products are specifically similar to technologies exhibited in production of commonalities and services in the electrical industry or in transportation or application of bio−chemistry in agriculture. It means that knowledge is, first, a form of technology in the methods it employs in producing more knowledge and improving its own methods and, furthermore, is *capable* of being a technology in human social guidance of technologies now called such but whose human and social consequences are left a matter of pulling and hauling of conflicting customs and institutions which are hardly touched by effective use of the method of intelligence at work. (244)

I can't put the matter any better than Dewey does, so I will leave it at that.

Dewey's Pragmatist Philosophy
of Religion Revisited
Reconstructed and Reconsidered

Arild Pedersen

University of Oslo

I   Introduction

What follows will be only partially a contribution to the philological business
of Dewey–interpretations. Dewey himself was not much engaged in that kind of
activity related to other philosophers. Instead I will engage in the same kind of
activity as used by him when he developed his ideas on religion in the 1930ties.
At that time Dewey presented his three lectures on religion, published in a slim
tome under the name of *A Common Faith* , as a cross–boundary answer to an active cultural political debate in the US, rather than as an academic contribution
to the theoretical field of philosophy of religion. In other words, as a true pragmatist, not least according to Richard Rorty, who advised cultural politics rather
than metaphysics as a fitting task for 'we' or 'us' pragmatists. [1] Remember,
perhaps, that the infamous process concerning teaching about the theory of evolution had been held in Tennessee just seven years earlier, in 1925, later made into

---

[1]   Richard Rorty. *Philosophy as Cultural Politics*: *Philosophical Papers*, *Vol.* 4. Cambridge &
New York: Cambridge University Press. 2007.

a movie starring Spencer Tracy as hero of scientific rationality, fighting religious fundamentalism.①

That process was followed by much optimism concerning the ultimate triumph of secularism and rationality over religions and irrationality, although the optimism had some setbacks during the chaos of the World War II. And the state law prohibiting teaching of the theory of evolution in Tennessee was not abolished until 1967. Today, 80 years after the publication of *A Common Faith* , the brute fact is that many kinds of religion are as strong as ever. And some, like Islam, in so far as it inspires fundamentalist Islamists like al-Qaida or Boko Haram or ISIS, are even outright lethal. Thus my looking back at Dewey's contribution to this debate is supposed to be a very small or even tiny cultural political contribution of my own in such a contemporary debate.

To do this I shall first give an overview of some of Dewey's earlier views on religion with particular reference to him being influenced at that stage of protestant congregationalism and neo-Hegelianism. Then I shall present an interpretation of Dewey's view on experience as it is worked out, mostly, in *Art as Experience* 30–40 years later, in 1934. I take it that it is there we find, and in particular in the concept of consummatory experience, Dewey's most elaborately explicated theory of experience, still heavily influenced by Hegelianism, although in an 'inverted' form. Since Dewey in *A Common Faith*, published in the same year as *Art as Experience* , is adamant that what he depicts by means of the adjective ' religious' is not a particular kind of experience on its own, but an aspect of experience in general, an investigation of what this aspect is like should obviously be done on the background of his general theory of experience. Finally I shall critically evaluate whether Dewey's criticism of ordinary religions and his ideas of a reconstructed humanistic religion can be used today in a contemporary cultural political debate about the role of religion in society.

---

① Stanley Kramer. *Inherit the Wind.* 1960.

II　Organical Congregationalism and Hegelianism

It is probably hard for non-religious people to understand what it is like to be born and grow up in a specific religion, which is thus taken for granted, and in particular if this religion harbors fundamentalist views. Dewey did that, growing up under the maternalist care of a strong ambitious mother belonging to so - called emotional Congregational pietism, with a Calvinist ' partialist ' theology of believing that only a few select are destined for salvation. ① The good thing about this kind of protestant religion is that it does not profess to know, differently from other forms of Christianity and Islam, who this will be. Neither does it know about any direct relationship between virtuous deeds in this world and rewards in an otherworld. The other good thing, which most likely had a lasting effect on Dewey, was its stressing of the independence and unity of each church community, that it functioned as a congregation, which when translated into philosophy, became the kind of communitarianism that was a part of Dewey's pragmatism.

However, as emotional congregational pietism collided with the modern world, Dewey, like many other British and American philosophers at the end of the nineteenth century, found a rationalist substitute in Hegelianism, in particular the version taught by his tutor at Johns Hopkins, George Sylvester Morris. Thus he became infected with what he himself referred to as ' the Hegelian Bacillus ', an infection which was life-long, although the germ itself underwent some important mutations, turning his Hegelianism just as much 180 degrees around ("inverted") as that of Marx. ②

Here I shall restrain myself to summarize some of the most important features

---

① 　Robert B. Westbrook. *John Dewey and American Democracy*. Itacha and London: Cornell University Press. 1991. p.3.

② 　Robert B. Westbrook. *John Dewey and American Democracy*. 1991. p.13.

of the Hegelianism that influenced Dewey's perspective, first on experience, and then on religion: If we start reading Hegel's most dramatic presentation of his system, *The Phenomenology of Spirit*, we immediately find that all kinds of Kantian epistemological and Cartesian ontological dualism have been done away with: sensual perception is just a lower level and partial form of conceptual rationality, and as to ontology there are not two or more substances, but just the parts and the wholeness of phenomena, the opposition between which will eventually be overcome by means of the same kind of dialectics that overcomes the opposition between sensuality and rationality.

As we know, any kind of dualism was similarly abhorrent to Dewey, who kept to his principle of continuity throughout his whole life. Thus, even though he was an empiricist this did not mean that he saw empirical material as basically devoid of rationality, or intelligence, as is his preferred term for a more action oriented concept of rationality. Empirical material is shoot through with action, potential or real, and vice versa, no less than it is filled with communality, nor confined within the privacy of the mind of British empiricism.

Then, there is the historicist perspective of Hegel, where his rather scholastic dialectics makes evolutionary history move towards greater wholeness, to reveal this wholeness or *Geist*, step by step through different social institutions, philosophies, or spiritual shapes. Thus in art the *Geist* is made apparent in sensual form. Beauty is a complete sensual glimpse of *Geist*. But ultimately this very same *Geist* will become conceptualized in philosophy of art, or aesthetics, leading to his famous theory of the end of art.①Likewise, *Geist* is also revealed in religion, only to find its ultimate expression in conceptual philosophy, and in a society organized as a just, rational whole, no longer hampered by internal contradictions and governed by freedom through law. Clearly, this must be a good substitution

---

① G.W.F.Hegel.*Lectures on the Philosophy of Art.*Trans.Robert F.Brown.Oxford:Oxford University Press.(1823)2014.

for the old, community based religion of Dewey' childhood and adolescence. At least it so appeared to be to Dewey.

III　Consummatory Experience

In *Art as Experience* Dewey repeats Hegel's feat in his *Aesthetical Lectures* . Just as Hegel there claims that high art, in so far as it is beautiful, makes the *Geist* appear in sensual form, Dewey in *Art as Experience* claims that art works, but also other artifacts and situations and activities, through being experienced, make experience appear in its most complete or consummatory form. If you ask Hegel: What or how is *Geist* ? One of his answers is given by referring to art and beauty. Similarly, if you ask Dewey: What is experience? That is, experience in its fullness, he would answer by advising you to have an aesthetical experience, either by means of an encounter with artworks, or by participating in other activities that also give this kind of experience. Thus, consummatory experience corresponds for Dewey to the wholeness that Hegel denotes as *Geist* .

I shall now give an overview of what I take to be a Deweyan perspective on what experience is, as revealed in its fullest form in consummatory aesthetic experience. Nevertheless I shall present this theory as a set of auxiliary hypotheses, similar to how such hypotheses are used in real science, that is, as presuppositions taken for granted for the construction of the theory under investigation, in this case a philosophy of religion. Obviously, I do not have room for a complete justification of my claims in this paper.①

I shall introduce this auxiliary theory by means of an illustration chart, which I shall explain in some detail. According to Dewey an experience is not a purely theoretical and a-temporal entity outside of an observing subject, like it is for the British empiricists. It is fundamentally an activity wherein a subject is in-

---

① See Arild Pedersen. *The Last Conference. A Pragmatist Saga.* Oslo: Akademika. 2014.

separably present as involved in the goings on, that is, by its projects of conduct.①In an aesthetic experience these projects of conduct are not all–absorbing, so that one may observe them somehow from the outside, while still identifying with them.According to Dewey there are two main kinds of such projects of conduct:

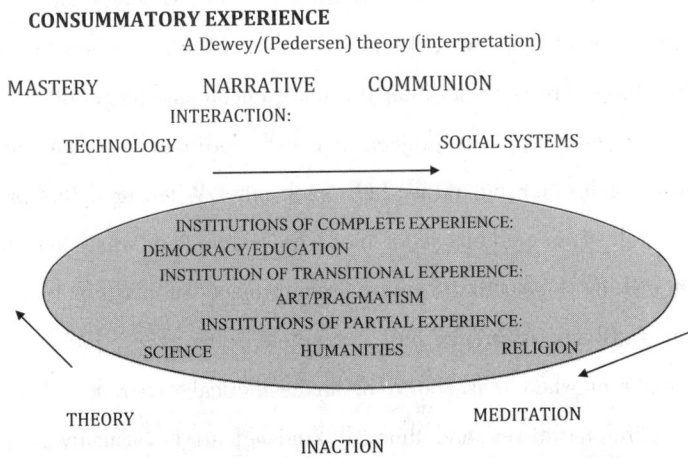

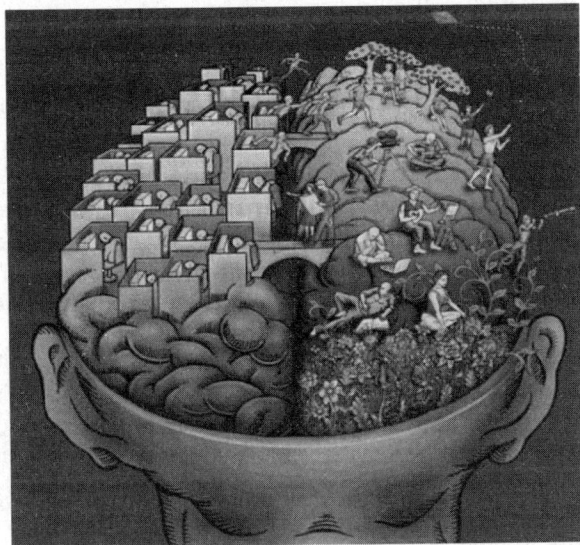

CONSUMMATORY EXPERIENCE
A Dewey/(Pedersen) theory (interpretation)

MASTERY   NARRATIVE   COMMUNION
INTERACTION:
TECHNOLOGY   SOCIAL SYSTEMS

INSTITUTIONS OF COMPLETE EXPERIENCE:
DEMOCRACY/EDUCATION
INSTITUTION OF TRANSITIONAL EXPERIENCE:
ART/PRAGMATISM
INSTITUTIONS OF PARTIAL EXPERIENCE:
SCIENCE   HUMANITIES   RELIGION

THEORY   MEDITATION
INACTION

---

① See John Dewey.*Human Nature and Conduct*.Mineola, New York: Dover Publications, Inc. (1922) 2002.

those that are directed at establishing mastery of ones surrounding, and those that aim at establishing contact and communion with ones fellow beings, either humans, animals, living nature or the universe at large.① These two kinds of projects are common to all living beings, but in humans they are more complex and make use of technological and institutional means. Although each of the projects has problems of their own, like how to build a bridge, or how to establish a love relationship, there is in addition the more encompassing problem of how to make these two, often opposite projects become coordinated so that they do not interfere with each other, but rather help each other. When or if this problem of transition is solved, or perhaps more modestly, elucidated, where one makes or reflects on making a smooth transition from projects of mastery to projects of communion, and back again, one has a complete experience, which becomes reflectively apparent when it is shown in an aesthetical experience. This is done through temporal narratives, and thus all kinds of art is basically narrative, or parts of narratives. While all experiences are narrative or parts of narratives. All complete narratives are about how to resolve the conflicts between mastery and communion. That is the theme of Shakespearean narratives, like *King Lear*, which demonstrates how to fail in such a transition, as well as of more popular Hollywood narratives, as the *Die Hard* movies of Bruce Willis where the hero's fight against evil masters is intertwined with his difficult love relationship with his wife.

However, as can be seen in the nether part of the chart, I have also taken a step further by relating Dewey's consummatory experience with some modern neuroscience. In 2009 Ian McGilchrist published a book, where he argues for a specific relationship between modern neuroscience and philosophy and culture.② I have discussed how this also may be applied to Dewey's consummatory expe-

---

① See Chapter Two of John Dewey.*Art as Experience*.New York:PerigeeBooks.(1934) 1980.
② Ian McGilchrist.*The Master and His Emissary, The Divided Brain and the Making of the Western World*.New Haven,Connecticut:Yale University Press,2009.

rience elsewhere, and will just mention this in passing here.①At the end of this lecture I shall briefly relate this perspective to Dewey's philosophy of religion.

IV The Religious Aspect of Consummatory Experience

In the first chapter of *A Common Faith* Dewey introduces his project by stating: "The heart of my point (...) is that there is a difference between a religion and the religious."②He has some difficulty finding a definition of religion, but settles on the Oxford Dictionary definition: "Recognition on the part of man of some unseen, higher power as having control of his destiny and as being entitled to obedience, reverence and worship."③Naturally, a pragmatist, who from the beginning is a naturalist anti – dualist, and with an anthropological perspective which stresses man as being primarily initiating actions instead of just being a passive, inactive theorist, (the *bios theoreticos* of Aristotle,) will reject religion in this sense. Among Dewey's predecessors Hume, Marx and Nietzsche, did so on a full scale, Marx in particular deeming religion to be a dangerous sedative opiate that should be replaced by science, and Nietzsche seeing it as a means for the slaves to attack their masters, who in their turn rather should adhere to a mythology of a Dionysian Greek and Wagnerian type.

But Dewey is different by finding something valuable hidden in religion, a mistreated baby, which he does not want to throw out with the bathwater. Something positive and progressive within religion has been corrupted by religion being constructed as described in the Oxford definition. Dewey thus proposes "the emancipation of elements and outlooks that may be called religious."④

---

①   Arild Pedersen. *The Last Conference.*

②   John Dewey. *A Common Faith.* Chelsea. Michigan: BookCrafters, Inc. (1934) 1991. p. 3.

③   John Dewey. *A Common Faith.* Chelsea. Michigan: BookCrafters, Inc. (1934) 1991. p. 3.

④   John Dewey. *A Common Faith.* Chelsea, Michigan: BookCrafters, Inc. (1934) 1991. p. 8.

These religious elements and outlooks should not be confused with specific religious experiences, which is a common misunderstanding. One might believe that there are examples of such specific religious experiences, for example, mystical experiences, which are then supposed to be the original source of a religion, but which then become corrupted by being institutionalized, and transformed into an abstract theological system. This is rejected by Dewey: There are no pure religious experiences able to give an objective basis for religion, just as there are no pure sense data, as imagined by the logical positivists, to be able to give objective justification for science. Not that Dewey denies that we may have mystical experiences, but such ones are always interpreted by the religion they are supposed to justify. Instead Dewey claims that " 'religious' as a quality of experience signifies something that may belong to all these experiences"①referring by 'these experiences' to such experiences as aesthetic, scientific, moral, political experiences, or experiences of companionship and friendship.

Thus, if we now make use of the illustration chart of consummatory experience presented above, religion is a partial institution within the wholeness of consummatory experience, but this institution functions more than the others as a kind of narrow bottleneck that tends to arrest the movement through the different narrative stages of a cyclical consummatory experience. The religious aspect of experience, on the other hand, is the very human power, which makes us move through and experience all these stages. Thus the religious is not really coming from or belonging to religion. It is the other way around: It is captured and transformed by religion into a stiff fortress of partiality.

So why call this movement towards consummatory experience 'religious', when it is equally present in or rather active through science, art, politics etc? I am not sure that Dewey answers this question, but, and this is one of my main points: I take it that Dewey believes that religion is particularly able to arrest this

---

① John Dewey. *A Common Faith*. Chelsea, Michigan: BookCrafters, Inc. (1934) 1991. p. 10.

movement, and that by using the vocabulary of 'the religious' he makes us particularly able to focus on this dangerous passage through religion, to accomplish the needed emancipation.

What Dewey wants us to become aware of as the religious, is a capacity to transcend oneself, and to reorient one's life and "bringing about a better, deeper and enduring adjustment in life"①. This is a capacity that religions claim they only have, and that they derails over to the supernatural. Take as an example a drug addict who overcomes his addiction thanks to becoming a member of a specific religion. "It is the claim of religions that they effect this generic and enduring change in attitude. I should like to turn the statement around and say that whenever this change takes place there is a definitely religious attitude."②

The problem with such reorientations when supposed to have their source in a religion, that is, in particular in their theological imagination, is that the imagination that envisions a change of life works from the outside of the personality. Dewey says that such an imagination *supervenes*. However if the reorientation comes from the religious aspect of experience in its emancipated form the envisioning imagination *intervenes*.③It works from within the personality. A supervening imagination has a limited perspective. But the intervening imagination of the religious aspect of experience, on the other hand, as well as "the harmonizing of the self is closer than is usually thought. The idea of the whole, whether of the whole personal being or of the world, is an imaginative, not a literal, idea"④The intervening imagination of the religious imagines ideal ends, and when these are sufficiently imagined, they make us internally motivated to move on within the cycle of consummatory experience.

Thus Dewey emancipates a practical, moral faith from the faith of religions

① John Dewey.*A Common Faith*.Chelsea, Michigan: BookCrafters, Inc. (1934) 1991.p.14.

② John Dewey.*A Common Faith*.Chelsea, Michigan: BookCrafters, Inc. (1934) 1991.p.17.

③ John Dewey.*A Common Faith*.Chelsea, Michigan: BookCrafters, Inc. (1934) 1991.p.18.

④ John Dewey.*A Common Faith*.Chelsea, Michigan: BookCrafters, Inc. (1934) 1991.p.18.

and their theology. The last kind takes for granted the existence of the object that one has faith in. However, the moral faith of the religious aspect of experience imagines ends that are still not existing, seeing them much like the powerful regulative ideas of Kant. What is more: They change as we approach them, no less than the means for attaining them, as Dewey stresses about means and ends rationality in general.①

Nevertheless, "What has been said does not imply that all moral faith in ideal ends is by virtue of that fact religious in quality. The religious is 'morally touched by emotion' only when the ends of moral conviction arouse emotions that are not only intense, but are actuated and supported by ends so inclusive that they unify the self."②That is, in my terminology used her: that they complete or envisage the completion of the circle of consummatory experience.

V   Dewey's Weird Concept of God

So far so good. True, Dewey has twisted our common language in connection with talking about the religious as an active moral faith in the wholeness of the self, while separating this adjective from the substantive it normally accompanies, that is, religion. Still, this is really not so far from ordinary language: We may say of a scientist that he exhibits an enthusiasm and dedication to his work, which is like religious fervor. But in the second chapter of *A Common Faith* Dewey takes a linguistics step from such metaphorical language that definitely moves him over into a new and strange vocabulary.

In that chapter, namely, he tries to change the meaning of the word 'God' from referring to a supernaturally existing particular being, to denoting "the unity

---

① A mainpoint developed in *Human Nature and Conduct*.

② John Dewey. *A Common Faith*. Chelsea, Michigan: BookCrafters, Inc. (1934) 1991. p.22.

of all ideal ends arousing us to desire and actions."①Or in a more specific definition: "...the word 'God' means the ideal ends that at a given time and place one acknowledges as having authority over his volition and emotion, the value to which one is supremely devoted, as far as these ends, through imagination, take on unity."②Thus, we must suppose that not any kind of ideal ends deserves to be denominated God.For example, not the ideals of a narrow specialization, like those of the scientist mentioned above.Aristotle's ideal of the composition of a personality according to the golden mean is lurking in the background, condemning specialization as destroying the balance of a personality.Or even the famous Marxian description of how it will be to live in a perfect communist society, sometimes painting, sometimes fishing, sometimes playing the flute etc, but clearly not in a specialized manner and on a high level, because that would lead to estrangement from the balanced wholeness of the self.

But Dewey is not just hypostatizing an abstract ideal of dynamic wholeness: "It is this *active* relation between ideal and actual to which I would give the name 'God.'③This guarantees that Dewey's God is real and engaged in our world, that is, in a pragmatist sense, and even more so than the supernatural God of traditional theology, which does not seem to answer many or any of our prayers. And as to specialization: Dewey would not be against that in itself, because he sees each individual as a social, collective being, who partakes in the specialization of other individuals.If left alone a specialized individual would certainly be estranged, that is, cut off from the fullness of a consummatory experience, and from its own whole self.But as part of a society constructed so as to further the transition from the different institutions and experiences, the specializations of individuals will only enrich experience for all members of society.I have a scientist

---

① John Dewey.*A Common Faith*.Chelsea, Michigan: BookCrafters, Inc.(1934) 1991.p.42.
② John Dewey.*A Common Faith*.Chelsea, Michigan: BookCrafters, Inc.(1934) 1991.p.42.
③ John Dewey.*A Common Faith*.Chelsea, Michigan: BookCrafters, Inc.(1934) 1991.p.51.

friend who through specialization has invented an apparatus for measuring my blood stream. Good for my health. And in repay I can lecture him on pragmatism. Perhaps good for his religious life.

However, to propose such a new reference for the word 'God' is a rather quixotic project. And Dewey himself was definitely aware of this. As he comments on his own use of the name 'God' : "I would not that the name *must* be given. There are those who hold that the associations of the term with the supernatural are so numerous and close that any use of the word 'God' is sure to give rise to misconceptions and be taken as a concession to traditional ideas."①In this he was definitely more right than he would acknowledge.

However, there are several reasons for Dewey's choice of vocabulary; one of them being his intention to steer between what he considered to be a Scylla and a Charybdis in such matters, where the one extreme is the aforementioned religion posing an existing supernatural God, and the other aggressive atheism of Nietzsche's kind, where all values are dissolved, and everything supposedly is permitted. In between these two Dewey wants to establish a kind of naturalist and active humanism. "Use of the words 'God' or 'divine' to convey the union of actual with ideal may protect man from a sense of isolation and from consequent despair or defiance."②

Looking back at my auxiliary chart it may be used to elucidate further what Dewey may have meant by his concept of 'God'. Thus, there is an active and motivating imagining of an ideal state of experiencing which is in particular shown to us in aesthetical experience, where we get a glimpse of an ideal consummatory experience of cyclical wholeness. We might even claim that what Dewey names God should be identified with such a consummatory experience as an ideal of wholeness, though not as an abstract concept, but as an active motiva-

① John Dewey. *A Common Faith*. Chelsea, Michigan: BookCrafters, Inc. (1934) 1991. p.51.
② John Dewey. *A Common Faith*. Chelsea, Michigan: BookCrafters, Inc. (1934) 1991. p.53.

tor, both in the life of an individual, and in politics at large.

According to Dewey there are lots of benign consequences of this humanistic 'religion': Human beings will take care of themselves, instead of waiting, normally in vain, for help from some supernatural being. No more 'Allah akbar' or "God's willing," and instead "Yes, we can!" Then we will be strongly motivated and act with vigor. But there is a more general pragmatist advantage: Dewey throughout his career opposed any kind of dualism. Traditional religions bolster two kinds of dualism, that between the supernatural and nature. But also from a sociological and political perspective it encourages the dualism between the sacred and the secular. If Dewey's religion should be universally accepted, then there will be no such separation between these two, quite simply because only one of them will prevail. In Dewey's case the ideal is just the ability to make a smooth narrative transition from acts of communion to acts of mastery, and back again.

VI Final Criticism

We may defend Dewey's use of the name God by recalling some of his predecessors. I have already referred to Hegel, who also used a vocabulary about God in a non-dualist manner. But I shall also mention one of the main inspirations of Hegel himself, namely Spinoza. He too, of course, was no dualist, having allegedly proven that there is only one ontological substance, which he denominated alternatively God or Nature. Thus Spinoza too tried to introduce a new vocabulary, which was quite provocative, so much so as to lead to him being the victim of a narrowly escaped murder attempt.

Still, as we know, none of them succeeded in replacing the vocabulary of neither Judaism nor Christianity, and as I have said, neither has that of Dewey. The German sociologist and philosopher, with a general leaning towards pragmatism, Hans Joas, has asked: "Is it really true that organized religion has always inhibited intellectual and moral progress? Can we today, more than six decades later, still share Dewey's optimism that de-institutionalization of religion will release and emancipate authentic religious impulses"①His answer to both questions is "no", expressing particular fear that de-institutionalization will lead to a subjectivization of religion.

My criticism is that a pragmatist should accept what experience teaches about itself: So far it seems like religious impulses belong to religious institutions, and will continue to do so. Also, pragmatists allegedly not being foundationists should not let themselves be trapped by the principle of continuity and non-dualism. A clear distinction between a secular and a religious sphere should not be seen as a threat to pragmatism. And finally: Maybe the force of the religious is just one other form of a more general force of experience itself. We might as well call it the pedagogical impulse, or the political impulse, depending on where in the circle of experience we focus. We might learn from Hegel and call it a spiritual impulse. As I promised we might even see this in a neuro-psychological perspective: As an impulse towards bridging the gap between the two brain hemispheres.

---

① Hans Joas.*The Genesis of Values*.Translated by Gregory Moore.Chicago:Chicago University Press.2000.p.122.

Creative Education—The Task Before Us

Jim Garrison

Virginia Tech

I take my title from John Dewey's essay, "Creative Democracy—The Task Before Us". I want to show that creative education *is* creative democracy. There is little difference between a creative nation and a creative learning community. Dewey's theory of democracy and education arises from his commitment to a pluralistic, open–ended world without an ultimate origin or end, in which human creativity and social connectedness is simply part of the ongoing activity of the universe. It is an understanding of existence, democracy, and education that is perhaps more compatible with Eastern than Western thought.

In the last paragraph of his autobiographical essay, Dewey states:

I think it shows a deplorable deadness of imagination to suppose that philosophy will indefinitely revolve within the scope of the problems and systems that two thousand years of European history have bequeathed to us. Seen in the long perspective of the future, the whole of western European history is a provincial episode.[1]

---

[1] LW 5:159. Citations of the works of Dewey are to the critical edition, The Collected Works of John Dewey, 1882–1953, published by Southern Illinois University Press, Carbondale. Volume and page numbers follow the initials of the series. Abbreviations for the volumes used are: MW The Middle Works (1899–1924); LW The Later Works (1925–1953).

When I look to the East, I believe I see the first rays of a new dawn of Deweyan democracy and education; although, what the light of midday will reveal none may now know for sure.

Dewey thought we live in a world of constantly changing mutually constitutive relations. Hence, human beings are not simply located in space or time; humanity distributes itself wherever it has consequences. We cannot possibility separate the individual from society any more than we can separate an organism from its environment. Always and everywhere, our task, and the best use of knowledge, is to create morally good and aesthetically satisfying relations thereby creating better societies and individual lives.

Much of my paper discusses Dewey's educational psychology. President of the American Psychological Association (1899) before he was president of the American Philosophical Association (1905), Dewey refuted faculty psychology and replaced it with functional psychology. The basic idea is that psychological functions operate to help us coordinate with our environment much like biological functions. That we cannot separate individuals from either social or biological relationship is also the basis of Dewey's critique and reconstruction of the ideals of Western modernity including individuality, rationality, free will, mind, and self. This reconstruction extends to such ideals of classical liberal democracy (now called neo-liberalism) as so-called 'natural' freedom, rights, and equality. None of these exists until they emerge as developing human beings participate in diverse social practices. Democratic individuals are educational creations. I mostly postpone discussion of Dewey's reconstruction of liberal democracy until we finish examining his educational psychology, but because the two intimately interweave, that will sometimes prove impossible.

Dewey (1925,1981) proclaims, "Personality, selfhood…are eventual functions that emerge with complexly organized interactions, organic and social. Selfhood has its basis and conditions in simpler events" (LW 1:162). Good educators attend to their student's physical and biological needs and not just their cognitive requirements.These simpler events are very important for later learning and becoming.

For Dewey, "the life of individual instinctive activity comes first" (MW 14:650).The instincts,or what he usually calls impulses,are species typical responses to stimuli.Because they are unlearned,we sometimes call these impulses "first nature". As organic discharges,they are the basis of all action.Examples include the startle reflex, sucking reflex, and anger as well as such social impulses as emotional contagion.Impulses easily interconnected and readily redirected subfunctions of the biological matrix of learning.

We will say more about impulses shortly.First,though,we must mention that Dewey thought every individual *incommensurable* with every other and born with *qualitatively* unique potential.①Genetically unique,we all also have unique life experiences.Like native impulses,unique potential is important not only pedagogically,but also politically.

We now turn to acquired habits."Habit is second nature," Dewey remarks, "and second nature under ordinary circumstances is as potent and urgent as first nature" (LW 13:108).Habits are neurophysiological electrical and chemical events.Along with impulses and unique potential, they complete the biological matrix of human development.Habits emerge from biological functioning without breach of naturalistic continuity:

Habits may be profitably compared to physiological functions... The latter are,to be sure,involuntary,while habits are acquired.But important as is this difference for many purposes it should not conceal the fact that habits are like functions in many respects, and especially in requiring the cooperation of organism and environment.(LW 14:15)

① Cunningham,C.(1994).Unique Potential:A Metaphor for John Dewey's Later Conception of the Self.Educational Theory,44 (2) ,211-224.

Habits coordinate our transactions with the world. That is why Dewey insists, "We never educate directly, but indirectly by means of the environment" (MW 9:23). Parents, caregivers, and educators should never forget this fact. Habits "are the basis of organic learning" (LW 12:38). For Dewey, "habits are arts" involving skilled "know how." Further, "they constitute the self" and in "any intelligible sense of the word will, they *are* will" (MW 14:21). Educating the will involves modifying the habits that control our conduct. That is why Dewey's naturalism rejects the notion of innate "free will" along with other notions such as innate rationality or innate rights. All these are creative social and political accomplishments not natural endowments.

As dispositions to act, habits constitute the content of our character and form the embodied core of our personal identity. They also explain "the unity of character and conduct" along with "motive and act, will and deed" (MW 14: 33). We are creatures of habit more than of reason or even instinct. All of our genuine beliefs involve biological habits. Of course, we acquire our habits from interacting with our habitat including our social and cultural habitat. Therefore, Dewey also understands "habits as social functions" emerging naturally out of physiological functions (MW 14:15).

We now turn to the social structures of the mind and the self. Socially dependent from birth, humans come to embody cultural meanings as they acquire social habits. Dewey insists the "*meaning* of native activities [i.e., impulses, gestures, etc.] is not native; it is acquired. It depends upon interaction with a matured social medium" (LW 14:65).① Meanings emerge from native impulses and acquired habits. For Dewey, to have a mind is to have meanings and, he affirms, "Meanings do not come into being without language, and language implies two selves involved in a conjoint or shared understanding" (LW 1:226). There are no private languages; hermits take their sociocultural heritage with them.

---

① Nowhere in my paper has emphasis been added to any citation.

"The heart of language," Dewey concludes, "is communication; the establishment of cooperation in an activity in which there are partners, and in which the activity of each is modified and regulated by partnership" (LW 1:141–142). Minds emerge without breach of naturalistic continuity when organisms having the capacity participate in social discourse: "Through speech a person dramatically identifies himself with potential acts and deeds; he plays many roles, not in successive stages of life but in a contemporaneously enacted drama. Thus mind emerges" (LW 1:135). Once we understand how minds appear, there is no need to posit a mind versus body dualism. Since to have a mind is to have meaning and meaning is social, the brain alone is not the mind.

Dewey identifies three elements of selfhood. The first is "a capacity for feeling" (MW 7:339). The second is "the capacity to think of these experiences, to objectify them" (MW 7:339). Finally, there is "the social" (MW 7:340). Without the third, the first two would not cohere into a sense of self. He champions the looking glass self. Dewey also advocates otherness and difference as requisite for self-recognition:

> A contrast is required. When living beings live together under conditions where they have to consult, in directing their experiences and forming their ends, the welfare of others, each is compelled to distinguish others from himself, and, by a correlative process, his own being and aims from those of others. Without the consciousness of *alter*, there can be no consciousness of *ego*; and the more distinct the consciousness of others, the more definite the thought of one's ego. (MW 7:340)

Not only does the self arise through social transactions, it also requires social diversity to fully develop.

Conducting ourselves according to the rules and norms of cultural custom contributes to creating self-identity. Customs persist, according to Dewey, "because individuals form their personal habits under conditions set by prior customs.An individual usually acquires their morality as he inherits the speech of his social group" (LW 1:43).Habits endure across generations when individuals participate in a culture's customary rituals and social practices.Anyone familiar with the Confucian notion of '*li*' knows that whether we translate it ritual,custom,or mores the rules of proper social behavior possess us before we ever posses them.Indeed,if we perform an ancient ritual with reverence and humility, we may feel the impulses our ancestors felt,acquire the habits they used to inhabit the world,value what they valued,and maybe even believe what they believed.However,determining whether past practices are good for future prosperity requires critical-creative reflection on the customs that condition our habits.The habit of reflecting on our habits is a primary educational aim in any democratic society.

Because of the emergent transactional nature of the mind,self,will,and intelligence,Dewey does not think there is some metaphysical fixed and final essence defining human nature.In my dialogue with the Japanese Buddhist leader Daisaku Ikeda and Larry Hickman,director of the Center for Dewey Studies,Ikeda mentions Dewey's essay, "Does Human Nature Change?" Of course,given Dewey's view of human nature,the answer is an emphatic yes! This is of immense importance to educators,but it is equally critical to understanding Dewey's concept of democracy.Again,there is little difference between the two for Dewey. The problem is that most theories of democracy and education assume human nature fixed and final.

While we are not done with Dewey's philosophical psychology,let us pause to sum up several crucial points.For one thing,we should place far greater emphasis on human embodiment;natural impulses and acquired habits are immensely important factors in learning as are good health.We should also remember that we only teach indirectly through the environment. Abstract, symbolic, linguistic learning is essential,but if we cannot embody the meaning in our passions and habits of action, we will not fully comprehend what we learn. This is why so many students that are only average at book learning often excel in actual practice. Further, because we are social beings, we must strive to create good learning communities whether on-line or face-to-face. There is little difference between a good learning community and a good democracy.

We now turn to Dewey's reconstruction of liberal democracy beginning with the ideas of freedom and individuality. At first, it seems the power of cultural customs is so prevalent we might not be able to overcome it:

> Custom is Nomos [law or custom], lord and king of all, of emotions, beliefs, opinions, thoughts as well as deeds...Yet mind in an individualized mode has occasionally some constructive operation. Every invention, every improvement in art...has its genesis in the observation and ingenuity of a particular innovator...Thus, while negatively individuality means something to be subdued, positively it denotes the source of change in institutions and customs (LW 1:164-165).

As powerfully as social customs control the habits constituting the content of our character, free choice and individuality remain possible. "Freedom or individuality, in short," Dewey says, "is not anoriginal possession or gift. It is something to be achieved, to be wrought out" (LW 2:61). Education helps the process while miseducation harms it.

In *Freedom and Culture*, Dewey acknowledges the power of cultural customs to reproduce themselves by inscribing their norms upon individual bodies as habits thereby transforming and standardizing the unique native constitutions of its members. Nonetheless, biological heredity and native individual differences remain important because they continue to "operate within a given social form, they are shaped and take effect *within* that particular form" (LW 13:77). First nature contributes to freedom:

Impulses are the pivots upon which the re‑organization of activities turn, they are agencies of deviation, for giving new directions to old habits and changing their quality. Consequently whenever we are concerned with understanding social transition and flux or with projects for reform, personal and collective, our study must go to analysis of native tendencies.(MW 14: 67)

Impulses are an embodied condition of genuine freedom. Educators cannot constitute new impulses, but they can strive to properly direct them.

Unique potential is another native condition; although, unlike impulses, it is something educators can develop and not just direct. In *Individualism Old and New*, Dewey indicates: "Individuality is at first spontaneous and unshaped; it is a potentiality, a capacity of development. Even so, it is a unique manner of acting in and with a world of objects and persons. It is not something complete in itself" (LW 5:121). Everyone possesses native unique individuality; however, becoming a unique social and moral individual is the work of a lifetime requiring the aid of a great diversity of people, experiences, and explorations.

Traditional notions of potentiality assume some predetermined, fixed, and final developmental goal. Many assume acorns must become oak trees. Actually, acorns become the product of their transactions. To become an oak tree they must transact with sunshine, nutrient soil and water. Most acorns simply decay on the forest floor where they add nutrients to the soil. Many acorns become food for squirrels. According to Dewey in "Time and Individuality":

When the idea that development is due to some indwelling end which tends to control the series of changes passed through is abandoned, potentialities must be thought of in terms of consequences of interactions with other things. Hence potentialities cannot be *known* till *after* the interactions have occurred. There are at a given time unactualized potentialities in an individual because and in as far as there are in existence other things with which it has not as yet interacted. (LW 14:109)

We educate indirectly by arranging individual–environment interactions that help people to appropriately develop unique potential. Dewey's transactional notion of potential depends on otherness and difference in what is, for him, an open, pluralistic, and ever-evolving universe. Dewey believes "the human being is an individual because of and in relation to others. Otherwise, he is an individual only as a stick of wood is, namely, as spatially and numerically separate" (LW 7:227). Since growth is the aim of education for Dewey, diversity, otherness, and difference is as important for his theory of education as it is for his theory of democracy.

Beyond the native endowments of the biological individual including species typical impulses and unique potential, acquired habits are also part of the biological matrix of individuality. Impulses animate the habits that channel them. However, anytime we break a habit or a habit fails us in action, then the "release of some portion of the stock of impulses is an opportunity, not an end. In its origin it is the product of chance; but it affords imagination and invention *their* chance" (MW 14:118). "Breach in the crust of the cake of customs releases impulses" (MW 14:118). When we disrupt cultural customs, impulses are freed; however, Dewey maintains, "it is the work of intelligence to find the ways of using them" (MW 14:118). Such reflection allows us to "use impulse to renew disposition and reorganize habit" (MW 14:117). Dewey lists three things he believes we want in the name of liberty; they are: (i) Efficacy in action and the ability to carry out plans; (ii) the ability to vary plans and change our course of action; (iii) the acknowledgment the power of desire and choice as factors capable of altering the course of events (MW 14:209). He concludes: "Intelligence is the key to freedom in act" (LW 14:210).

Dewey rejects the notion of innate natural rationality, while intelligence is itself an emergent property of individuals that educators can help develop. Here is how he depicts intelligent deliberation:

[D]eliberation is a dramatic rehearsal (in imagination) of various competing possible lines of action. It starts from the blocking of efficient overt [habitual] action, and newly released impulse... Then each habit, each impulse, involved in the temporary suspense of overt action takes its turn in being tried out. Deliberation is an experiment in finding out what the various lines of possible action are really like (MW 14:132).

When imagination releases the possible hidden within the actual, dramatic rehearsal frees us to explore alternative courses of action without explicitly acting. The imaginative aspect of intelligent deliberation provides free choice. Dewey asks,

What is choice? Simply hitting in imagination upon an object which furnishes an adequate stimulus to the recovery of overt action. Choice is made as soon as some habit, or some combination of elements of habits and impulse, finds a way fully open. Then energy is released. The mind is made up. (LW 14:134)

Dewey considers the work of intelligence as creative not just narrowly conceptual.

Dewey explicitly rejects the idea of pure reason. All we have is practical reason impassioned by need and desire. "The intellect is always inspired by some impulse," he finds (MW 14:177). We deliberate for what we desire, although critical intelligence seeks to determine if our desires are truly desirable, if what we value is truly valuable. Dewey rejects the fact versus value dualism. Thus, we should not be surprised when he asserts:

The conclusion is not that the emotional, passionate phase of action can be or should be eliminated in behalf of a bloodless reason. More "passions," not fewer, is the answer...Rationality, once more, is not a force to evoke against impulse and habit. It is the attainment of a working harmony among diverse desires. (MW 14 : 136)

Coordinated habits impelled by impulses drive creative conduct, and thereby transform the world. We cannot become balanced thinkers if we cannot balance our feelings along with our thoughts and actions.

Because we are participants in the affairs of existence and not spectators, our embodied impassioned social selves are involved in every context of inquiry. Dewey insists: "The formation of a self new in some respect or some degree is, then, involved in every genuine act of inquiry" (LW 14 : 70). Indeed, often what most needs transforming in a problematic situation is the self not the world.

Innate impulses, unique potential, and intelligence provide the permanent possibility of freedom. For Dewey, it is the tools, techniques, and attitudes of critical–creative method that liberates individual minds and entire societies. Cultivating intelligent method is a supreme educational ideal in a democratic society. The word "method" comes from the ancient Greek "*meta*", meaning beyond, and "*odos*", meaning way. Most literally, method means "the way" or "a way beyond" and not the fixed expressway to some predestined perfect end. It is Dewey's version of the *Dao*.

There is a hidden irony in the false faculty psychology of classical Western liberal democratic theory. If every autonomous individual is born with the same innate free will and rationality, then everyone should act in the same way in the same situation unless they are morally fallen or in error epistemologically. Ironically, the autonomous individual is not only a fiction, but also a mockery of unique and creative individuality.

In Dewey's reconstruction of the liberal democratic tradition, the social self replaces the autonomous individual without sacrificing individuality. The educational nurturance of unique potential combined with the development of creative intelligence yields a truly irreplaceable individual capable of making their distinctive cultural contribution. Dewey develops an embodied, social, and sustainable ideal of free democratic individuality. Classical liberalism emphasizes individual rights while completely ignoring social obligations. The failure to place social responsibility on the same plateau as political rights has been catastrophic for liberalism.

In *The Declaration of Independence of the Thirteen Colonies* , authored by Thomas Jefferson, we find the famous words: "We hold these truths to be self-evident, that all men are created equal, that they are endowed by their Creator with certain unalienable Rights." Today, many are no longer comfortable with assumptions of self-evidence or even of a creator God. "To put ourselves in touch with Jefferson's position", Dewey realizes, "we have therefore to translate the word 'natural' into *moral* " (LW 11: 174). To comprehend Dewey's reconstruction of classical liberalism's ideal of "Rights" we must translate innate natural rights, freedom, and equality into acquired social patterns of right moral relationship.

In *Confucian Democracy: A Deweyan Reconstruction* , Sor-hoon Tan (2004)[1] makes much of the fact that for Dewey democracy is not just political, but also ethical (see Ch.4). It is ethical because of Dewey's emphasis on the social, relational self that emerges as an individual by participating in human associations and institutions and the social practices they coordinate. Early in his career, Dewey articulated what he called "the ethical postulate":

IN THE REALIZATION OF INDIVIDUALITY THERE IS FOUND

---

[1]　Tan, Sor-hoon (2004). *Confucian Democracy: A Deweyan Reconstruction*. Albany, N. Y. : State University of New York Press.

ALSO THE NEEDED REALIZATION OF SOME COMMUNITY OF PER-
SONS OF WHICH THE INDIVIDUAL IS A MEMBER; AND, CONVERSE-
LY, THE AGENT WHO DULY SATISFIES THE COMMUNITY IN WHICH
HE SHARES, BY THAT SAME CONDUCT SATISFIES HIMSELF. (EW 3:
322)

Recognizing the contingent socially constructed character of human minds
and selves, Dewey remained committed to this postulate through all the many
changes his philosophy underwent over the next sixty years. His thinking about
political freedom, equality, rights, and responsibilities arises out of the social nature of the self and the moral need to create right relationships within the community, thereby creating right relationship within the self.

Dewey replaces "natural" equality, rights, and freedom with "moral"
equality, rights, and freedom. We begin with moral equality:

> The doctrine of equality never meant what some of its critics supposed
> it to mean. It never asserted equality of natural gifts. It was a moral, a
> political and legal principle, not a psychological one. (LW 13:108)

In his essay, "Individuality, Equality and Superiority", Dewey says,

> Moral equality cannot be conceived on the basis of legal, political and
> economic arrangements. For all of these are bound to be classificatory; to be
> concerned with uniformities and statistical averages. Moral equality means in-
> commensurability, the inapplicability of common and quantitative standards. It
> means intrinsic qualities which require unique opportunities and differential
> manifestation. (LW 13:300)

The ideal of moral equality is to educate each unique individual so that they may make their unique contribution to the culture that created them.The ideal is an aristocracy of everyone：

> Democracy in this sense denotes, one may say, aristocracy carried to its limit.It is a claim that every human being as an individual may be the best for some particular purpose and hence be the most fitted to rule, to lead, in that specific respect.The habit of fixed and numerically limited classifications is the enemy alike of true aristocracy and true democracy.(LW 13：297 - 298)

Democratic individuality involves releasing unique human potential to create new values, ideas, things, and institutions.Traditional aristocracies assume a static world with fixed ends, a fixed social hierarchy, and only a few social roles.Democratic moral equality adapts to a constantly changing world where society may not know what it needs or desires until they educate the distinctive individuals able to devise novel ends and innovative means for achieving them, thereby creating a new the social order.

In the following passage, Dewey explicitly connects the false faculty psychology in vogue during the establishment of classical liberalism with its mistaken understanding of natural rights：

> The idea of a natural individual in his isolation possessed of full - fledged wants, of energies to be expended according to his own volition, and of a ready-made faculty of foresight and prudent calculation is as much a fiction in psychology as the doctrine of the individual in possession of antecedent political rights is one in politics.(LW 2：299)

The "faculty of foresight and prudent calculation" assumes innate rationality, which Dewey replaces with the social development of intelligent methods.

Morally, Dewey believes freedom "breaks up in detail into a number of specific, concrete abilities to act in particular ways. These are termed *rights*" (MW 5:394). As opposed to mere capriciousness, moral freedom and rights arise out of the society upon which we depend to develop our humanity. Hence, he continues, "Any right includes within itself in intimate unity the individual and social aspects of activity" (MW 5:394). Thus, "a right, individual in residence, is social in origin and intent" (MW 5:394). Because rights are social and not a native possession, we must recognize something very significant: "A right is never a claim to a wholesale, indefinite activity, but to a *defined* activity; *to one carried on*, that is, *under certain conditions*. This limitation constitutes the *obligatory* phases of every right" (MW 5:394). "Rights and obligations are," Dewey concludes, "strictly correlative" (MW 5:394). Our individual rights should never exceed our social responsibilities.

Freedom is a social function. In the following, Dewey exposes the fallacy of negative freedom:

> The real objection to classic Liberalism does not then hinge upon concepts of "individual" and "society." The real fallacy lies in the notion that individuals have such a native or original endowment of rights, powers and wants that all that is required on the side of institutions and laws is to eliminate the obstructions they offer to the "free" play of the natural equipment of individuals. (LW 3:100)

If we had innate free will and rationality, the lifting of restrictions would be enough. However, as Dewey recognizes,

> The removal of obstructions did have a liberating effect upon such individuals as were antecedently possessed of the means, intellectual and economic, to take advantage of the changed social conditions. But it left all oth-

ers at the mercy of the new social conditions brought about by the freed powers of those advantageously situated. (LW 3:100)

Material conditions matter in the embodied struggle to free our minds for intelligent, deliberative, reflective freedom. For him "the attainment of freedom conceived as power to act in accord with choice depends upon positive and constructive changes in social arrangements" (LW 3:101). Bringing about these changes involves publics identifying shared interests and reconstructing governmental institutions to address them.

Concrete freedom involves social reciprocity and responsibility. Instead of metaphysical free will, Dewey's psychology demands we proceed from human beings in their "concrete make-up of habits, desires and purposes," which is the only reason to hold them personally responsible (LW 3:94). He insists on "the *essential unity of the self and its acts*" (LW 7:288). When we act, we express the present self and form the future self. The primary way that we develop the social, moral, and political self is by looking away from first things such as a putative antecedent free will and toward consequences. This is the quintessence of pragmatism. What it means politically and pedagogically is that by holding people responsible for the *consequences* of their actions it is possible to educate better citizens:

A child as he grows older finds responsibilities thrust upon him. This is surely not because freedom of the will has suddenly been inserted in him, but because his assumption of them is a necessary factor in his *further* growth and movement. (LW 3:94).

Assigning appropriate responsibilities in conjunction with appropriate rights is how we create democratic citizens.

Negative freedom alone makes us slaves to our passions. Responsible citizens who think about the consequences of their actions for others as well as themselves become more, not less, free. Aided by others, they may break bad habits thereby releasing impulses that, in conjunction with intelligent deliberation, enable free choice. In his essay, "Philosophies of Freedom," Dewey affirms: "Freedom is *power to act* in accordance with choice" (LW 3:97). The greater power lies not in mere capacity to act, but to act in accordance with intelligent choice that allows us to imaginatively foresee the consequences of our action and, through passionate commitment, secure socially shared ideal ends–in–view (see LW 11:220).

Thus far, I have ignored Dewey famous *Democracy and Education* having only cited from it once thus far. However, what I have been trying to do is place that book in the context of his larger philosophical and psychological thought. By now, we may readily understand why he declares in *Democracy and Education* :

> A democracy is more than a form of government; it is primarily a mode of associated living, of conjoint communicated experience. The extension in space of the number of individuals who participate in an interest so that each has to refer his own action to that of others, and to consider the action of others to give point and direction to his own, is equivalent to the breaking down of those barriers of class, race, and national territory which kept men from perceiving the full import of their activity. (MW 9:93)

Such living makes, creates, and calls existence beauty, knowledge, and value. It is political *poiesis* .

Recognitive Imbalance and Force On Dewey's Critical Social Ontology of Habit

Italo Testa

University of Parma

Abstract

In this paper I will first reconstruct a Deweyan model of social ontology, based on the process of habituation. *Habit ontology* leads to a social philosophy which is not merely descriptive, since it implies a critical re-description of the social world. I will argue that a habit-modeled social ontology is critical insofar as it includes an account of social transformation and of the inevitability of social conflict. Such an understanding is based on a diagnosis of social pathologies of our life form, and includes an account of the experience of domination, which is described as a matter of an imbalance of recognition which embodies subjugating patterns, and is seen from the critical perspective of freedom understood as emancipation from oppression. This leads to a reconstruction of the genesis of critical attitudes from life's processes of habituation, which leads to an extended naturalist account of social authority.

I Dewey's Habit Ontology

A peculiar socio-ontological approach is to be found in Dewey's writings of

the twenties-mainly in *Human Nature and Conduct* and *The Public and its Problems*-where he raises the question of the status of those kind of entities whose existence depends on human interaction and which are to be distinguished from those facts-such as physical existences – which are not dependent on it.①
According to Dewey, it is proper of social and political facts to be dependent on human activity and still exhibit an "objective reality".Such facts exist out there, have causal consequences, and objectively knowable properties②; they are, to use John Searle's phrase, "epistemologically objective"③.When it comes to understanding how social facts are constituted through interaction, Dewey thinks that we have to take human association as a primitive phenomenon which is proper of our life form and constitutive of social facts. In this sense the question of the socio-ontological constitution of social facts involves an understanding of life's processes, and in particular of the way in which our life form is characterized by "associated life".Association, as such, is not distinctive of human life, since association is, according to Dewey, an ontological law of "everything known to exist" (*The Public and its Problems*).④ If we are to focus on that form of associated life that is ours, we have then to identify its distinctive feature, which according to Dewey consists in the fact that our associated life takes the form of "conjoint", "shared", "common" action.⑤

The first thing to note here is that the notion of "action" is introduced as a manifestation of a life process – as a defining feature of our living nature.⑥Second, action is assumed to be intrinsically social, since its basic form is taken to

---

① Dewey.*The Public and Its Problems* (1927).*LW*2:240;*Experience and Nature* (1925),*LW* 1:153.
② Dewey.*Experience and Nature* (1925).*LW* 1:154.
③ Searle, *The Construction of Social Reality* (1995):8.
④ Dewey.*The Public and Its Problems* (1927).*LW* 2:250.
⑤ Dewey.*The Public and Its Problems* (1927).*LW* 2:257.
⑥ Compare this with the notion of action developed by Michael Thompson in his seminal *Life and Action* (2008).

be "conjoint" action rather than individual action. Third, when it comes to understanding "action", Dewey doesn't take as basic notions neither the concepts of beliefs or desire nor the concept of intention. Habit is rather the fundamental notion that Dewey introduces to understanding associated life as conjoint action, and notions such as 'belief', 'desire' and 'intention' are rather analyzed into patterns of habit①. As Dewey writes "habit is the mainspring of human action, and habits are formed for the most part under the influence of the customs of a group. [...] y" (*The Public and its Problems*). ②

Human action always happens in the context of prior action. It is this structure of action's embedment which Dewey understands as a process of habit formation where actions are cast into patterns, that is, where what is formed are "regulated pattern of behavior derived from prior experience" ③. This means that the dependency of social facts on human interaction involves their dependency on the vital process of habit formation. For this reason habituation is the most basic operator of Dewey's social ontology, since it is habituation which creates human social facts, maintains them in their continued form of existence, and guides their transformation.

Habituation, as fundamental operator of Dewey's social ontology, is articulated into three main levels: habit, custom, and institution. Habit, custom and institutions are here understood as different degrees of systematization of habit formation and establishment of systems of human interaction, which are described respectively at the level of individuals, groups, and social totality. Moreover, in this scheme the notion of custom seems to have some sort of priority over the other notions. As we have seen, the primitive form of human action is conjoint, grouped action − which only makes intelligible what individual action is. The no-

---

① This habit model is what mainly distinguishes Dewey's approach from intentionalist approaches to social ontology such as Jon Searle's, Raimo Toumela's, and Margaret Gilbert's.
② Dewey. *The Public and Its Problems* (1927), *LW* 2:334−335.
③ Dewey. *Lectures in China* (1973):85.

tion of custom as established collective arrangement is then the key to understanding grouped action as constitutive of our life form—which also makes sense of how individual habits are mostly formed "under conditions set by prior customs", and how institutions are established by regulated systematization of custom.①

1.*Does Dewey's social ontology incorporate a critical social philosophy?*

The point I want to stress here is that a social ontology based on the notion of habituation offers us not only a descriptive account of the constitution of social reality, but also a critical approach to it.

To start with, I will argue that habit ontology is a critical one insofar as a) dynamic social transformation, b) plurality, and c) conflict are caught as a structural feature of social reality.

The Dynamic structure of habits

One can infer from Dewey's analysis of habit in *Human Nature and Conduct* many reasons why one should understand habit formation in dynamic terms.

First, habits are acquired. Habits are not given as a property of our first nature but are the result of a process of acquisition. They have to be developed and stabilized into a second nature, and need to be always re-appropriated and thus repeated, transformed or rejected, by those who are brought up with them (from childhood onwards). Hence, habits are only relatively

---

① See Dewey.*Human Nature and Conduct* (1922), *MW* 14:43: "We often fancy that institutions, social custom, collective habit, have been formed by the consolidation of individual habits. In the main this supposition is false to fact. To a considerable extent customs, or widespread uniformities of habit, exist because individuals face the same situation and react in like fashion. But to a larger extent customs persist because individuals form their personal habits under conditions set by prior customs. An individual usually acquires the morality as he inherits the speech of his social group. The activities of the group are already there, and some assimilation of his own acts to their pattern is a prerequisite of a share therein, and hence of having any part in what is going on. Each person is born an infant, and every infant is subject from the first breath he draws and the first cry he utters to the attentions and demands of others".

stable.The transformation of habits is an ambiguous, bivalent process and can take different forms, oscillating between persistency and plasticity, stabilization and readjustment, repetition and creativity.①

2. *The plural and projective structure of habits.*

Habits, due to the dynamic, transformative process of habit formation, have a plural structure. The plurality of habits is connected in a double sense with their embodied character, which is the basis of what Dewey names their "projective structure".

What does it mean for habits to have a projective structure? Habits are embodied in corporeal attitudes, and incorporate objective forces, since they are sensitive to the affordances of the natural environment we inhabit and the social environment we inherit.Such an incorporation of the environment is always projective: it takes places always in a partial, contingent, pluralized way, since "no amount of habits can incorporate the entire environment within itself or themselves" (*Human Nature and Conduct*)②. Moreover, such an incorporation of an environment within habit is not merely an adjustment *to* the environment, but also an adjustment *of* the social environment.Which involves that the environment "is many, not one" as well as habit is plural.This leads us back to the socio-ontological role of habit formation.Habit formation is an ongoing process of pluralized constitution of the objective structure of the social world – adjustment *of* the environment – and of the subjects which inhabit it – adjustment *to* the environment.

---

① On the practical and political side of the creative aspect of habit in Dewey (and Mead) see especially Hartmann, *Die Kreativität der Gewohnheit* (2003) : 181 - 194. On the Peircian roots of the refusal to identify habit with repetition see Hickman, *Pragmatism as Postmodernism* (2007) :274n10.
② Dewey. *Human Nature and Conduct* (1922). *MW* 14:38.

3. *The conflictive patterns of habits.*

Habits, due to their dynamic, plural and projective structure, are conflictive in principle: as Dewey writes, "All action is an invasion of the future, of the unknown. Conflict and uncertainty are ultimate traits" (*Human Nature and Conduct*) ①.

> Customs, as systems of established habits, furnish the horizon of intelligibility of individual action. But due to the intrinsic plurality of habit formation, customs are composed of a plurality of models. This happens not only between different societies, but also within the same society, which is pluralized into different customary groups. Moreover, customs are often hybridized with each other, evolve over time and are relatively unstable. This all means that customs are potentially in conflict with each other. ②

II Patterns of domination and the ontology of groupings

Dewey's habit social ontology can be said to be a critical one also because it can focus on the experience of domination, which is related to the conflictive structure of social practices, and identified as the main cause of the sort of social ills and dissatisfactions which manifest social pathologies of our life form.

When it comes to understanding the intimate dynamics of social conflict, Dewey's social ontological approach again becomes relevant. The idea that the basic form of action is shared, group, conjoint action, understood as a manifestation of customary arrangements of interaction, leads Dewey to criticize the atomist social ontology which conceives society as "made up of collections of individual

---

① Dewey. *Human Nature and Conduct* (1922). *MW* 14:10-11.
② See Dewey. *Human Nature and Conduct* (1922). *MW* 14:38: "Diversity does not of itself imply conflict, but it implies the possibility of conflict, and this possibility is realized in fact".

persons considered as entities"*Lectures in China*)①.Dewey adopts rather an alternative approach according to which we have to understand "society as constituted of people in many sorts of groupings"②.Such an ontology of social groupings is neither an atomist nor a collectivist one, since groups aren't understood monistically as collective entities preexisting social interaction and identical with social totality, but rather conceived of as plural and intersecting social formations. The plural, overlapping and hybridized structure of social groupings, characterized by the phenomenon of multiple and intersecting memberships, is clearly grounded in Dewey's analysis of the dynamic and pluralized structure of habit formation.

This socio-ontological approach leads Dewey to understand social conflict as primarily a matter of "interpenetrating relationship between groups"③.Social conflict is not a matter of conflict between isolated individuals nor a matter of conflict between individuals and their society as a whole, but is rather a matter of conflict among social groups, understood as "collections of people who are united by common interests".

Here we can appreciate why conflict is an inescapable aspect of social reality.As Dewey says in his *Lectures in China*, "society is in a state of imbalance because these many groups do not and cannot develop equally"④.On the one hand, such an imbalance is a structural feature of social groupings.Being constituted of many intersecting groupings, society is in a standing state of potential imbalance. The problem, according to Dewey, arises when such an imbalance turns towards a situation of domination, where "one group oppresses another". Here the social description is coupled with a social diagnosis.Social oppression is understood as subordination of one group to another, which can manifest itself in

---

① Dewey.*Lectures in China* (1973):73.
② Dewey.*Lectures in China* (1973):73.
③ Dewey.*Lectures in China* (1973):65.
④ Dewey.*Lectures in China* (1973):66.

various degrees and forms (tacit acquiescence, latent or more or less organized conflict, explosive open revolt caused by submerged hatred and submerged antipathies).

This causes a diffuse social suffering which affects the well–being of all the groups involved, not only the subordinated, but also the dominating ones, leading to a situation which prevents them from fully developing themselves and which results in an unhealthy situation for the whole of society.

III The imbalance of recognition and social struggles

Conflict between groups is unhealthy when life's structural imbalance develops into domination, leading to social patterns where oppression is exercised by some groups over others. "Subordinated groups", says Dewey in his *Lectures in China*, "are customarily not so recognized" ①. Here social oppression is clearly understood as an embodied habit—a form of customary social arrangement inscribed into the bodily existence of social groups and their individual members – that accords to the dominant ones a "privileged status" over the subordinated. This is where Dewey comes to develop a recognitive analysis of domination and its relation to social conflict. First, domination is connected with the achievement and enjoyment of some sort of privileged social status by some social group. Now let's remind ourselves that habituation is the process by which actions are cast into patterns, which form groups of action. If we follow Dewey's *Lectures on Ethics*, statuses are default positions granted to some actors or objects by an established pattern of habitual interaction, that is, in customs that incorporate an implicit or – depending on their grade of systematization – more or less explicit acceptance/recognition of those statuses②.

---

① Dewey.*Lectures in China* (1973):74.
② Dewey.*Lectures on Political Ethics* (1896):153–162.

Recognition is involved in domination not only for the socio-ontological reason that statuses, even privileged ones, are things which, as contemporary social ontology affirms, exist only insofar as they are to some extent recognized or accepted[1]. When Dewey affirms that subordinate groups are "customarily not so recognized" he adds two further aspects. First, as we have seen, he stresses that the kind of acceptance we need in order to understand how statuses are ontologically constituted, is not just a matter of attribution, but is a matter of customary acceptance, that is, it consists of recognitive habits. Second, Dewey stresses that the recognitive constitution of social statuses is entwined with social power and that this manifests itself in struggles for recognition. Such a recognitive conflict between groups is furthermore understood as an instance of the state of imbalance of society. Domination is thus grasped as a specific form of recognitive imbalance, where some groups obtain a default position of "recognized privilege and power", that is, they obtain a disproportionate amount of "public recognition" for their interests, whereas the "interests being sought by the subordinate group are customarily not so recognized"[2], that is, they do not enjoy such "public" recognition.[3]

Finally, the relation between subordinated and dominant groups is further analyzed by Dewey through the Hegelian paradigm of *Herr und Knecht*, which is thus translated into a customary model of recognitive dependence. The master-slave dialectics is assumed by Dewey to be the general model of social domination. As such it refers not only to subjugating relations between private individuals, but more generally to any system of established relationship of subjugation of some social groups to others, which Dewey exemplifies with children's, women's,

---

[1]　See Searle.*Making the Social World* (2010):8.

[2]　Dewey.*Lectures in China* (1973):74.

[3]　On the different "phases" of the development of "public recognition" in these lectures see Särkelä,"Ein Drama in drei Akten" (2013).

and workers' subordination.①I would like to stress here that the master–slave relationship of subjugation, which is the founding concept of social domination, is explicitly framed by Dewey as a matter of "pattern of dominance – subservience"②. Domination is then again basically understood in terms of embodied habitual patterns of action. These patterns are described as specific forms of recognitive imbalance which affect associated living. These forms of recognitive imbalance are characterized by the fact that they involve some kind of "disparity of status and function" which allows some to enjoy the dominant position of masters, and constricts some others to suffer in the subordinate position of servants. it is important to note that such an understanding of subjugation as a pattern of dominance-subservience leads Dewey to frame domination as a "mode of living".

Domination is understood as a diminished, particular manifestation of our life form, insofar as the relationship between master and servant is qualified as that "mode of living" in which the operation of free and open communication "is at a minimum"③. On the other hand, this means that Dewey understands free and open communication in emancipative terms as liberation from oppression and as enhancement and empowerment of our life form.

"Authoritarian society" is then understood by Dewey as a kind of society where master–slave relationships tend to prevail in social arrangements, leading to a rigid social stratification of habitual settlements of action, and limiting free communication to some restricted and isolated intra–group relationships. Such a society can maintain its existence, remain stable or become integrated, only resorting to "sheer force". And the reason why it also needs sheer force to maintain

---

① See Dewey.*Lectures in China* (1973):92:"The master–slave relationship is not limited to situations in which one person 'owns' another, as was true in parts of America at the time of my birth. It refers to any system of relationship which effectively places one person in subjugation to another – children subject to their parents, wives to their husbands, subjects to their rulers, laborers to their employers".

② Dewey.*Lectures in China* (1973):92.

③ Dewey.*Lectures in China* (1973):92.

and reproduce itself, is that it is affected by massive misrecognition. In an authoritarian society recognitive imbalance embodies patterns of domination−subservience, which engenders a situation where the subordinate members of this society, not being recognized by it, "do not recognize that they have a stake in it"[1]. As a consequence, recognition alone cannot be here the basis of the maintenance and reproduction of social institutions, as on the contrary happens in democratic society, which according to Dewey depends for its stability and development not on sheer force, but mainly on "persuasion" or "consensus" on the part of its members, that is, on their "recognition that they have their stake in it". In this sense an authoritarian society is dysfunctional because higher reflective forms of recognition such as "persuasion" and "consensus" are not here promoted and developed as a dominant force of the social reproduction of our life form.

IV   Recognitive force

It is important to note here that, to my mind, this does not amount to a sheer opposition between "force" and "recognition", nor to a mere identification of "force" with oppression and of recognition with freedom. According to Dewey, in fact, there is "no clear−cut distinction" between physical force, legal force, and mental or psychological or moral force such as reprimand, instruction, and persuasion[2]. There is some continuity between these various manifestations of force, whose difference is a matter of degrees. This is due to the expressivist argument that on the one hand "mental or psychological force can be given expression only through physical force"[3]: expenditure of physical energy is indispensable in every human activity. On the other hand, even the sheer force exercised by the most despotic tyrant does not resort only to physical force, but is entwined with

---

① Dewey. *Lectures in China* (1973) :93.
② Dewey. *Lectures in China* (1973) :127.
③ Dewey. *Lectures in China* (1973) :128.

psychological force as a means to induce obedience. Hence, force, understood as expenditure of physical energy, is a constitutive element of all the manifestations of human life, and habituation is a process through which such a force is deployed and given consistency ①. Such a notion of force is clearly invoked by Dewey's embodied understanding of the habitual human action, since habitual patterns of action need to be bodily inscribed. Properly, there are three levels on which force can be employed according to Dewey: that is "energy", which is "force employed to reach a purpose"; "coercion and resistance", which is "force employed to counter violence"; and violence which is "force expended to accomplish nothing" ②. All these three levels are manifestations of vital force and hence are in some pragmatic continuity with each other. But this does not mean that we cannot introduce levels or degrees in this continuous vital scale in order to critically judge the uses of force and express our evaluation as to which are preferable. In this sense, according to Dewey, our problem is to maximize the employment at the first level, that is, as energy—the conscious use of force to achieve a purpose—and to find ways to avoid the third level—violence—so that we can minimize or even escape the need to resort to the second level—coercion and resistance. Once again, the criterion which supports such a critical judgment of the uses of force, is immanent to life, since it consists in the expansion and enhancement of our life form potential: violence is bad because it wastes human force, coercion and resistance are to be minimized because they negatively constrict life's expansion, whereas energy is good in the degree to which it contributes to the maximum development of our vital capacities, and mainly of knowledge and thought.

Once one understands force as vital expenditure which involves physical expression, then even recognition has to be understood under this model, that is as a manifestation of vital force which may take different forms as for the way in

---

① See Dewey. "The Study of Ethics: A Syllabns" (1984). *EW* 4: 241.

② Dewey. *Lectures in China* (1973): 130.

which it is intertwined with physical force. That's why on the one hand the notion of recognition plays a role in understanding what domination is, and on the other hand, even persuasion, which we have seen is understood by Dewey as a form of reflexive, higher order recognition, is understood as some form of psychological or moral force which may be combined with different degrees of physical force in its manifestation. The state of imbalance of recognitive relations is a direct structural consequence of the fact that recognition is a vital force which manifests itself in different degrees and in plural states. Even imbalanced recognitive relations which are shaped by patterns of domination−subservience are in this sense genuine, even if not full, manifestations of recognition, and not merely apparent one.①For this reason Dewey qualifies the master−slave relationship as a recognitive one: only, the way in which here recognition is intertwined on the one hand with coercion, and on the other hand with forms of misrecognition, makes it something poor, underdeveloped, because it deprives both the mode of living of the subjugated and of the dominant ones.

V   Genealogy of critical attitudes

Habit ontology is a critical ontology because it also reconstructs a genealogy of critical attitudes. The genesis of critical attitudes is tied to conflict, insofar as they arise when a tension between a system of customs emerges, and are a way to cope with such a conflict situation when a customary default disposition does not work anymore. Furthermore, the vital function which critical attitude deploys is that of reorganizing such a conflict, shaping it in a way which promotes the empowerment of the practices of our life form. As such, critical attitudes deploy a function of guidance or direction of life in context where such an orientation cannot be tacitly assumed by existing social patterns.

------

① Ed.By John R.Shook and James A.Good, Fordham University Press, 2010:137.

From this perspective the same notion of reason is reconstructed on the basis of a habit account as a flexible and plastic deliberative adjustment of old habits. That's why even when reflexive and deliberative reason gains a grip on social life as a force of guidance that enhances social progress, this does not mean that we no longer act out of habit, but rather that a new and intelligent purposive manifestation of our vital force has emerged; a reflective disposition that is again involved in a process of habituation, insofar as "every reflective choice tends to relegate some conscious issue into a deed or habit henceforth taken for granted and not thought upon" (*Human Nature and Conduct*) ①.

Critical reason is thus reconstructed as immanent to our social form of life, insofar as it arises from life's exigencies, has to transform it immanently, is to be understood as life's disposition – a manifestation of life's energy, that is, established vital force employed to reach a purpose – and does not respond to life's transcendent normative authorities, but only to 'embodied ideals' that are immanent in the 'authority of life' (*Human Nature and Conduct*). ②

VI   The authority of life

This finally brings us back to the very notion of "authority of life". It is a striking aspect of Dewey's thinking that in some important contexts where he discusses questions of authority, he connects them deeply with the notion of life. First, when Dewey in his *Lectures in China* discusses the notion of "authority", he gives a naturalist account of it based on the notion of pattern habituation: "the pattern of response which enables us to live comfortably in that environment is the authority which controls our behavior". And the absence of some sort of authority in our life is "utterly unthinkable" for the reason that "behavior must be subject

---

①   Dewey. *Human Nature and Conduct* (1922). *MW* 14:193.
②   Dewey. *Human Nature and Conduct* (1922), *MW* 14:58: "The authority is that of life."

to some sort of control"①.In this sense authority is a necessary constituent of life because actions need to be cast into customary patterns which have the economical function to control and make predictable our conduct.The necessity of authority is grounded on the necessity of habit for human action and makes explicit the role of guidance which patterns provide.Authority is thus understood as the guiding force that habit exerts over human conduct. "We cannot dispense with authority"②,says Dewey.For this reason the notion of authority as guidance of action cuts across the distinction between authoritarian and democratic society, since the need for some sort of authority is a functional requirement for every kind of society,including a democratic one.Here Dewey distinguishes between "traditional authority",based on customary patterns dictated by history and tacitly accepted as standards of behavior within unbalanced and often subjugating social relations,and "scientific" or "democratic" authority,which tends to be based on patterns of behavior that have been subjected to reflective scrutiny,and that are consciously accepted as standards of behavior after public examination and deliberation.

"The authority is that of life",as Dewey writes in *Human Nature and Conduct*,because authority is intrinsic to the phenomenon of life.In this sense,life is the first source of authority.And that which originates authority is the very process of habituation through which active life is produced and reproduced,since this involves that some patterns of response have a vital guiding force,that is,exert some sort of authority over our conduct in that they control and direct it.This understanding of life's authority is intimately connected with the notion of "standards", by which he means patterns of behavior that are accepted as authoritative for our conduct.Now,when it comes to the social practices of human life forms,the main sources of standards of behavior are,as we have seen,habit,customs,and institu-

① Dewey.*Lectures in China* (1973):167.
② Dewey.*Lectures in China* (1973):167.

tions, understood as three broad categories of increasingly systematized regulated patterns of human action. Such standards are not abstract ideals or norms, but are rather "embodied"①in action patterns, inscribed in bodily habitual behavior, and are by default tacitly and implicitly accepted in social practices.

The question of what Dewey names "criteria" of action arises when such standards become explicit and are consciously scrutinized, that is, when we critically judge such standards. This does not imply that we cannot assume such standards as criteria of our judgments, that we cannot orient ourselves by willingly following the standards which are already implicitly followed in practice. In this sense habits, customs and institutions are both the sources of standards of action and the "three broad categories of human activity in which we seek criteria for our acts of judging"②.

But according to what Dewey says in his *Lectures in China*, the "chief source" of our criteria for judging, and in respect to which other sources are of "secondary importance", since they are somehow derived from it, is another one. This source of criticism is "associated living", in respect to which we can formulate the "ultimate criterion" by which we are to judge habits, customs, and social institutions, that is, the criterion of "the degree to which the matter being judged could contribute to the development and qualitative enhancement of associated living" (*Lectures in China*)③. In which sense is associated living the ultimate source of the criteria of social criticism, and how are these specified by Dewey? One can see that it is a certain understanding of our natural life form which is relevant here. The ultimate criterion is the qualitative enhancement of associated living, that is, the empowerment of the individual and collective potentials of hu-

---

① Dewey. *Lectures in China* (1973): 86: "Conventions embodied in custom and tradition afford a common power which regulates conduct among individuals and reduces the incidence of conflict which would prevail if each person followed his own whims".

② Dewey. *Lectures in China* (1973): 85.

③ Dewey. *Lectures in China* (1973): 90.

man life.In this sense the other source of critical criteria which Dewey mentions, that is, intelligent thinking and intelligent appraisal, are clearly themselves derived from this "ultimate criterion", since intelligent and reflective habit are both functions and a manifestation of the qualitative enhancement of the force of human life.Intelligent thinking and appraisal are valued precisely because they may free habits from the reified form which blocks their vital force, and therefore emancipate and implement their energy, that is, their living capacity of purposive adjustment to new context.Moreover, the qualitative enhancement of our associated life form is the ultimate criterion by which to judge the standard of social practices, insofar as its sources are not the parochial standards of some specific human practices, but rather human practice as such, that is, the general form of our life form, of our *Gattung*.The qualitative enhancement of associated living is the expansion and empowerment of its main features, that is communication of thought feeling and sympathy, free exchange, mutuality (mutual respect, friendship, and love), and cooperation.Here is the notion of communication which encompasses all the other distinctive features of living association.In this sense communication is not just discourse, but it involves also bodily and emotive interaction.As we have seen, such a notion of expanded communication as an enhancement of associated living is to be understood as a mode of living which emancipates us from domination:that's why Dewey defines the master-slave relation as that mode of living where there is a minimum of communication and which becomes the general social form in authoritarian societies where communication is restricted and atrophied.And such a notion of extended communication has an intrinsic recognitive structure.The master-slave model involves that the "minimum of communication" is understood as a minimum of recognition, that is, as a recognitive relation which is qualitatively poor, whose force is manifested in the form of coercion rather than in the form of affirmative purposive energy.Whereas "full communication", the vital situation where communication is at its maximum, is to be understood as a qualitative enhancement of recognitive force. Hence the social process which leads to the extension of communication is described as a recognitive social struggle, and whose result can be the the establishment of patterns of emancipated recognitive relations as authoritative, as the guiding force of human life.

Extended communication is finally a criterion immanent to life, deeply embodied in its associated form. This takes us back to what Dewey means when in *Human Nature and Conduct* he writes that "the authority is that of life". Even the criterion by which we are to judge the standards which are authoritative in life's social practices, has its source in life itself. Even those who are keen to frame this ultimate criterion as a 'normative' criterion – but, as said, 'criteria' are rather undetermined and orientating, and are more a matter of guidance and direction than of prescription – could here realize that the ultimate source of authoritative standards and norms of social practices is not normative in itself, since associated living may have some immanent standards, and even deploy them in the form of prescriptive norms, but associated living as source of these standards and norms is not itself a norm, but is barely the human life form. In this sense Dewey writes:

> Still the question recurs: What authority have standards and ideas which have originated in this way? What claim have they upon us? In one sense the question is unanswerable. In the same sense, however, the question is unanswerable whatever origin and sanction is ascribed to moral obligations and loyalties. Why attend to metaphysical and transcendental ideal realities even if we concede they are the authors of moral standards? Why do this act if I feel like doing something else? Any moral question may reduce itself to this question if we so choose. But in an empirical sense the answer is simple. The authority is that of life.①

----

① Dewey.*Human Nature and Conduct* (1922), *MW* 14:57.

杜威的"新"逻辑：
一项以定位为目的的探究

孙 宁

复旦大学哲学学院

  杜威哲学的基点是不是他的逻辑，这一问题一直以来都是杜威学者争论的焦点。① 但已经得到公认的一点是：杜威创造了一种新的、独特的逻辑形态，并且，其思想的每一个方面都是与这一逻辑形态息息相关且密不可分的。本文的意图并不是要加入关于杜威哲学之基点的争论当中，也不是要再度阐述杜威逻辑与其哲学的关系，本文的首要旨趣毋宁说是历史性的，即试图在西方思想史当中找到杜威"新"逻辑的位置。这项以定位为目的的探究包含了两个杜威意义上的"可预见的目的"（end-in-view）：首先，让这

---

① 比如，瑟尔（H.S.Thayer）和伯克（Thomas Burke）认为对杜威哲学的正确把握必须从他的逻辑着手。参见 H. S. Thayer, *The Logic of Pragmatism : An Examination of John Dewey's Logic* (New York : The Humanities Press, 1952) ; Thomas Burke, *Dewey's New Logic : A Reply to Russell* (Chicago : University of Chicago Press, 1994)。而另一些学者则对杜威哲学的基点持不同的见解。比如，波艾斯冯特（Raymond D.Boisvert）认为杜威哲学的基石是他的形而上学，希克曼（Larry Hickman）认为理解杜威哲学必须从他的工具主义（instrumentalism）和实验主义（experimentalism）着手，亚历山大（Thomas Alexander）则认为审美经验才是杜威哲学的真正秘密。参见 Raymond D. Boisvert, *Dewey's Metaphysics* (New York : Fordham University Press, 1988) ; Larry Hickman, *Philosophical Tools for Technological Culture : Putting Pragmatism to Work* (Bloomington and Indianapolis : Indiana University Press, 2001) ; Thomas M.Alexander, *John Dewey's Theory of Art, Experience and Nature : The Horizons of Feeling* (Albany : State University of New York Press, 1987)。笔者对杜威哲学之基点问题当然有自己的看法，但是对这一问题的讨论在本文的视域之外，当撰文另述。

一"新"逻辑走出单纯的杜威式语境,或者甚至走出实用主义语境,与西方思想史更为深入地关联起来;其次,在这一定位中,让这一"新"逻辑的后果更为明晰地展现出来,并通过这种展现揭示出杜威对西方思想的推进之处。因此,本文面对的是一个双重性的任务:关联与生发。为了完成这一任务,我将首先对杜威的逻辑进行初步的定位,然后分别从经验性、生成性、想象性、实践性这四个特征着手以期实现对杜威逻辑的具体定位,最后我将给出一个相对简明的结论。

一、对杜威逻辑的初步定位

坚持逻辑形式始终必须和逻辑内容相关联,这是杜威逻辑的"新颖"之处。虽然这一实用主义的逻辑传统可以追溯至皮尔士,即在某种程度上将逻辑扩大为关于科学方法的一般性理论,但是在皮尔士那里,作为科学方法的逻辑本身是固定的(溯因推理),而杜威逻辑的彻底之处在于认为逻辑方法本身也必须是探究的对象,且必须根据探究的目的进行不断调整,也就是说,逻辑方法本身必须是情境化的。这种因为考虑逻辑内容而导致的"非形式性"和变动性使杜威的逻辑基本上游离于弗雷格、哥德尔、塔斯基等人构建起来的现代逻辑语境之外。当然一些历史性的因素也在一定程度上造成了这种游离。我们可以从杜威晚年与亚瑟·本特利(Arthur F.Bentley)的通信中看到,杜威在20世纪40年代才开始接触塔斯基的工作①,而弗雷格的作品则在杜威逝世后的50年代和60年代才开始被逐渐翻译成英文。我们或许可以这样说:与这些现代逻辑范式不同,杜威的逻辑是另一种意义上的"现代"逻辑。

然而,如果我们跳出单纯现代逻辑的语境,将杜威的逻辑放到其同时代的哲学思潮中进行考量,我们会发现前者的游离性依然存在。杜威的逻辑既不同于当时罗素、怀特海、摩尔等人所持的"柏拉图式的"逻辑,即将逻辑

---

① 参见 Sidney Ratner & Jules Altman, (ed.) *John Dewey and Arthur F. Bentley: A Philosophical Correspondence, 1932-1951* (New Brunswick: Rutgers University Press, 1964), pp.251,587-588.

关系的领域同实际存在的领域明确区分开来,又不同于马赫、奥格登(C.K.
Ogden)、里查兹(I.A.Richards)①等人所持的实证主义逻辑,这种逻辑观认
为逻辑法则与自然的实际结构无关,逻辑不过是一种经过语言中介的一般
化的心理学。正如杜威的自然主义在观念论和实在论的论战中所处的尴尬
位置一样,杜威的逻辑也承受着来自两方面的攻击:柏拉图主义者认为将情
境化的内容引入逻辑内部会玷污逻辑的纯洁性,而实证主义者强调的则是
经验对知识总体的验证,而不是作为一般化的心理学描述的逻辑对经验性
研究所起的指导作用。而另一方面,在实用主义内部,杜威还必须抵御詹姆
士的祛逻辑化倾向,这一实用主义内部的倾向可以追溯至詹姆士的精神导
师勒努维耶(Charles Renouvier),并向外延伸至伯格森。在这样的情况下,
我们似乎更容易从这些对立的立场来定位杜威的逻辑,但这样的定位存在
着一个缺陷:杜威逻辑本身的特征并没有得到说明。

　　笼统而言,西方思想史上大概出现了三种基本的逻辑形态。第一种逻
辑形态是形式逻辑。这种逻辑形态以形式化的逻辑范畴作为思维的决定
项,逻辑范畴的运作是抽象的、超越于具体思维内容的。这一形态可以追溯
至亚里士多德,并经过经院哲学的发展一路传承至斯宾诺莎、康德、费希特、
谢林等。第二种逻辑形态是本体论逻辑,其代表是黑格尔。这种逻辑形态
将逻辑范畴视为实在的动态构件,其基本形式不再是三段论,而是一种更为
一般或更为普遍的本体论意义上的辩证统一。否定或否定性不再只是一个
单纯的逻辑范畴,而变成了人类实践的精神工具。作为改变实在的工具,否
定性成为对已有实在的重新评价,并进一步成为发展的契机。虽然这种逻
辑形态超越了形式性与具体性的区分,但它的本体论框架仍然以另一种形
式排斥着"新"内容的进入。也就是说,否定性的展开依然处于本体论的框
架之内,否定性所引入的"异质性"(heterogeneity)在本质上仍然是一种在
"同质性"(homogeneity)内部的运作。第三种逻辑形态便是杜威的探究逻

① 奥格登与里查兹合著的《意义的意义》对艾耶尔于1936年出版的《语言、真理与逻辑》有直接影响。参见 C.K.Ogden & I.A.Richards, *The Meaning of Meaning:A Study of the Influence of Language upon Thought and of the Science of Symbolism* (London:Kegan Paul,1923);A.J.Ayer,*Language,Truth,and Logic* (London:Gollancz,1936).

辑。这种逻辑的基本运作环境不是形式框架,也不是本体论场基,而是情境(situation)。对于前面两种逻辑形态来说,逻辑是一种法则,无论这种法则是基于人类理性的还是内在于绝对精神之中的;而在探究逻辑中,逻辑真正变成了一种方法,并且这种方法随着探究的展开时刻进行着调整和变化。如此一来,逻辑不再是一种自明而确证的东西,逻辑中存在着盲点、误区和暂时的晦暗不明之处。同本体论逻辑一样,探究逻辑认为思维的同质性只有通过异质性才能达到,但与前者不同的是,探究逻辑认为这种异质并不是概念上的,而是具体经验在"质"上的异质。

但是这种分类显然过于简单,并且,这三种逻辑形态之间的关系并没有得到说明。比如一个非常重要的问题是:黑格尔式的逻辑在多大程度上保留在了杜威的逻辑当中?① 然而,无论黑格尔是否在杜威思想中留下了"永久性遗产"(permanent deposit),可以肯定的一点是,在杜威看来,逻辑在精神中本体论式的展开并不是逻辑的真正运作,逻辑的真正运作乃是生成性的,其关涉的对象不是逻辑范畴之间的关系以及由此建构起来的逻辑秩序;相反,逻辑是以存在的类别特征为基础展开的实验性构建。杜威赞同黑格尔将逻辑的展开等同于当下现实,但在杜威这里,这种展开是方法上的,而不是体系上的。因此,这种展开最终依赖的不是绝对精神,而是实验性的想象力。因此,在《经验与自然》(1925)中,杜威这样写道:"在新的机构中的改变客观秩序的想象力绝不仅仅是一种附加的重复。相反,想象力关涉到旧对象的解体和新对象的形成,正是在作为新旧对象之间的媒介的意义上,它可以被认为是主观的。"②显然,这里"主观的"意即"实验的"。

或许还有一个更为简便的方法来表达杜威逻辑的"新颖"之处:杜威的逻辑是达尔文之后的逻辑。换言之,探究逻辑是一种只有在达尔文的演化理论出现之后才有可能出现的逻辑形态。在《达尔文之于哲学的影响》(1909)一文中,杜威提到了达尔文理论在哲学上引发的三个方面的转变。首先,"哲学抛弃了对于绝对始基和绝对终极的探究,而转向为对于产生它

① 参见拙文《从黑格尔式的外衣中解放出来》,《中国社会科学报》2013 年 4 月 15 日第439 期。

② LW 1:171.

们的特殊价值和特殊条件的探究";其次,"古典逻辑认为哲学的必然任务在于证明生命必须因为某些遥远的原因和最终的目标而具有某些性质和价值(无论经验对此如何表述)",但是现在,"为了提高我们的教育、改善我们的举止、增进我们的政治,我们必须诉诸当下的特殊条件";最后,而且是最重要的,"这种新的逻辑将责任引入了理性生活"。① 杜威的工具逻辑(instrumental logic)正是这一达尔文之后的哲学转向的最好表达。逻辑的对象不再是固定的范畴和关系,而变成了特殊的价值和条件;逻辑的任务也不再是单程的推理和演绎,而变成了对于理性生活乃至社会生活的富有责任感的引导。简言之,逻辑由法则变成了工具(instrument)。

在进一步展开之前,让我们先对杜威的探究逻辑稍作剖析。首先让我们来看这一逻辑的部件。在 1916 年对哲学俱乐部所作的一次发言中,杜威批评了罗素的逻辑对象观。在罗素看来,作为逻辑实体的数"既不是物理事物的特征也不只是单纯的主观事物",而是抽象的概念或集合。而在杜威看来,任何逻辑对象都不可能是抽象的观念或形而上学的实体,它们是"我们可以在并且只能在推理中找到的事物(或事物的特征)","它们并不是*通过*推理得到,而是从本身也是经验性事件的推理*中*获得"。并且,数作为集合并不是抽象的,"事物根据推理分成不同的集合"。②

杜威进一步将这种非抽象范畴的逻辑对象称为"存在的类别特征"(generic traits of existence),或者说生成性(genetic)的类别特征(注意,这里 genetic 与 generic 分享着相同的词根)。早在 1915 年,杜威就在一篇题为《形而上学探究的主题》的文章(这篇文章的主要意图是要在自然主义的立场重构形而上学)指出,形而上学应该停止处理那些第一性的或终极的原因,而将"我们在所有科学探究的对象中找到的某些不可化约的特征(irreducible traits)"作为它的主题。③ 比如,多样性(diversity)、互动性(interaction)和变动性(change)便是这样的特征,因为它们存在于任何形式的探究对象中。形而上学应该对这些特征展开经验性的研究,这样,"我们便能够避免

---

① MW 4:10-13.
② LW 10:90-96.斜体为原作者所加。
③ MW 8:4.

以下这些时常出现的做法,即将异质性化约为单质性,将多样性化约为绝对的统一性,将质化约为量,等等"。① 几年之后,这一研究方案在《经验与自然》中得到了进一步展开。杜威希望用"经验性的和指示性的"(empirical and denotative)方法来研究"体现在所有存在类别当中的类别特征"。② 同时他重新界定了"类别特征":"生活和哲学的重要问题在于考量不确定与确定、未完成与完成、重复与变异、安全稳健与危险之间联系的程度和模式。如果我们相信经验到的事物,那么这些特征以及它们之间互动的模式和节拍便是自然存在的基本特征。"③

可以说,在杜威逻辑那里,正是这些类别特征以及它们之间的互动模式构成了作为工具的逻辑。因此,作为工具的逻辑并不是现成在手的,为了获得这种工具,我们必须仔细考察这些类别特征,并将它们当作探究地图上的节点。并且,这些节点同样也是情境化的,而将这些节点作为部件的探究逻辑考虑的永远是这些节点如何能够为我们清晰而有效地标明某条特殊的探究路线。杜威在《经验与自然》中这样写道:"采用经验性的方法并不能保证与每一个特殊的结论相关的所有事物都能够被实际找到,即便找到了,也不能保证它们能够得到正确的展示和交流。但是经验性的方法向我们指明了我们能够在何时、何地、以何种方式达到所描述的事物。这种方法给了我

---

① MW 8:7.

② LW 1:308.

③ LW 1:67.根据笔者的统计,杜威在《经验与自然》中至少举出了四十个"存在的类别特征",它们是:稳定性(stability)、运动性(movement)、安全合理性(safe and sane)、偶然性(contigency)、变异性(variation)、变化性(change)、未决定性(indeterminate-ness)、逻辑性(logicity)、优先性(preference)、价值多元性(pluralism of values)、连续性(continuity)、阻碍性(arrest)、结构性(structure)、不连续性(discontinuity)、危险性(hazard)、模糊性(ambiguity)、开放性(openness)、趋向性(tendency)、方向性(direction)、目的多元性(pluralism of ends)、重复性(repetition)、潜在性(potentiality)、不安全性(precariousness)、未完成性(incompleteness)、不确定性(uncertainty)、不规则性(irregularity)、可能性(possibility)、偏见性(bias)、多样性(diversity)、互动性(inter-action)、统一性(unity)、质性(quality)、完成性(finishedness)、联合性(association)、特殊性(specificity)、时间性(temporality)、确定性(certainty)、持续相关性(constant relations)、量性(qualitative)、个体性(individuality)。我们可以看到,在这些类别特征中,有些是互补的,比如"确定性"与"不确定性"、"未完成性"与"完成性";有些则是独立的,比如"逻辑性"和"时间性"。

们一张地图,上面表示了别人已经走过的道路,如果我们愿意,我们可以重走这些道路,亲自探索沿途的风景。这样,一个人的发现也许能够被其他人的发现订正和拓展……"①

让我们再来看一看探究逻辑得到的结果。探究逻辑的终点并不是某个确定的逻辑结论,而是"有根据的断言"(warranted assertion)。这里引入罗素对杜威探究观的描述,对于我们的理解是有帮助的。罗素曾指出:"在人类可从事的多种行为中,有一种行为叫作'探究',就像许多其他行为,探究的一般目的在于增进人与环境之间的相互适应。探究将'断言'作为它的工具,并且,只要断言能够产生预想的结果,它们便是'有根据的'。但是同其他的实践运作一样,在探究中,更好的工具也许会时不时地被创造出来,而旧的工具则会被抛弃。确实,就像机器能够帮助我们造出更好的机器,探究中的暂时结果也是引向更好结果的手段。在这一过程中并没有最终点,因此并没有一个断言是永远有根据的,有根据的断言只出现在探究的某个阶段。"②简言之,对于杜威来说,有根据的断言不是最终的真理(大写的),而是阶段性的真理(小写的)。但是在《命题、有根据的断言性和真理》(1941)中,杜威对罗素的这一描述进行了补充。在他看来,断言并不是探究的最终结果,也不是工具;并且,断言的根据性并不是因为它们能够产生预想的结果,它们之所以是有根据的,乃是因为作为某一阶段的探究结果,它们是客观有效的。杜威由此区分了在探究之后作出的断言与在探究的过程中被"肯定但没被断言"的命题。在后一种情况中,命题的提出与肯定只是实验性的,用杜威的话来说,它们是"手段和工具,因为它们是运作的媒介,通过它们,有足够理由被接受的*信念*成为探究的*结点*"③。在《逻辑:探究的理论》(1938)中,我们还可以看到这样的表达:"宣告式的命题,无论是关于事实的还是关于概念的(原则和法则),都是能够对控制素材的改造起影响的直接手段或工具(对于事实的是材料性工具,对应概念的则是程序性工具),而对于所有宣告式的肯定或否定来说,素材的改造便是可预见的

---

① LW 1:34.

② Bertrand Russell,*An Inquiry into Meaning and Truth*,(London:Routledge,1995),p.319.

③ LW 14:175.斜体为原作者所加。

目的(或者说最终的目标)。"①

因此,就探究逻辑的结果而言,罗素所描述的"断言"实际上更应该被表达为"命题"。由此我们也可以清楚地看出探究逻辑明显的命题化取向。杜威区分了两种类型的命题:生成性的(generic)和一般性的(universal)。生成性命题在一个未定的情景中找出并规定问题,并为接下来的测试提供证据(知觉材料);一般性命题则表达了那些并不存在的可能性之间的必然联系,这种联系通过"如果……那么"这种形式表达出来。但无论是何种命题,都是获得"有根据的断言"的手段或工具。并且,更为重要的,"有根据的断言"只是探究的阶段性目的,这些断言很有可能在下一步的探究中以命题的形式出现。

因此,有根据的断言并不具有任何处于探究情境之外的"真假值"。杜威写道:"真结论与假结论的区分乃是由运作程序的特性决定的,正是在这些程序中,关于材料和关于推论性元素(意义、观点、假设)的命题得以建立起来。"②也正是在这个意义上,杜威批判了逻辑中的二值原理(principle of bivalence)。在二值原理看来,一个命题要么是真的,要么是假的。不过杜威显然将二值原理同形式逻辑中的排中律(law of excluded middle)混淆了起来。排中律表达是在两个对立的命题中,必有一真,必有一假。但不管怎样,在杜威看来,自然中存在的不确定性、未来的开放性都证明二值原理和排中律是有问题的。在一篇题为《排中律的应用域》(1929)的文章中,杜威写道:"(这一法则)说,门要么是开的,要么是关的,这里的门指示的是一个实际的存在。但这一陈述忽视了两个事实。首先,门也许是正在被打开或关上,也就是说,处于从一个状态到另一个状态的过程中;其次,并没有一扇实际存在的门是百分之一百关上的,也许对于特定的实践目的来说,门关得*已经足够紧*了,但门同时依然是敞开的——裂缝一定会存在。"③在杜威看来,一扇关紧的门便是一个"有根据的断言",但断言并不将门关死,那些依

---

① LW 12:162.

② LW 14:176.

③ LW 5:201.斜体为原作者所加。

然存在的"裂缝"便是探究得以进一步展开的契机。

在对杜威的"新"逻辑展开进一步的定位之前,我们先要对出版于1938年的《逻辑:探究的理论》的语境作简要的考察。这本书是杜威在晚年对于他的探究逻辑的一次总结。此书的一个主要论敌是那些将逻辑与科学方法割裂开来的形式逻辑学家,比如罗素和柯亨(Morris R.Cohen)①。杜威的观点是,逻辑作为关于实际的科学探究的理论不能从探究的语境中抽象出来。然而,在这样的理解下,逻辑不能再是形式化的逻辑,而必须是一种适应于现代需求的新逻辑。杜威将这种现代需求表述为"一种关于探究的统一的理论,通过这一理论,实验性和操作性科学探究的真正形式可以被用来规范常识领域的探究所用到的习惯性的方法;并且,我们可以通过这一理论得出结论,并形成和测试信念"②。在这个意义上,杜威将此书的基本原则归纳为如下两条:首先,"逻辑理论是对可控探究的体系化表达";其次,"在这种控制中,并且由于这种控制,产生了逻辑的形式,并由此产生了作为结论的有根据的断言"。③

因此,作为对探究的探究(inquiry into inquiry),逻辑的有效性并不是先天的,而是建立在"自然事实"之上的。这一立场既有别于经验论的逻辑观(这一观点认为逻辑项只是精神性的实体,或者说其存在只是心理性的),又不同于实在论的逻辑观(这一观点认为逻辑法则表达的是自然中所有可能实体之间不变的关系)。要在这两种立场之外寻找一个变种并不是一件容易的事,如果逻辑形式既不是精神性的,又不是实在的,那么人们就要求杜威说明逻辑形式的性质究竟是什么样的。在杜威看来,逻辑形式是在科学探究的过程中生成的,并且只有在科学探究的过程中才能得到说明。换言之,逻辑不是必然的,而是由探究的过程决定的。这样的逻辑观对于任何寻求确定性的哲学来说都是难以接受的。事实上,如果我们站在传统逻辑观的立场来看,探究逻辑的几个基本特征都具有一定程度的模糊性和不

① 参见柯亨与内格尔(Ernest Nagel)合写的 Morris Raphael Cohen & Ernest Nagel,*An Introduction to Logic and Scientific Method*,San Diego:Harcourt,Brace,1934.
② LW 12:102.
③ LW 12:29.

确定性。首先,逻辑的目标乃是情境化的有根据的断言;其次,命题完全是工具性的;最后,逻辑的对象形成于探究的过程当中,并且是相对的、处于变动之中的。在这种新逻辑中,传统的"主词"和"谓词"完全丧失了原有的意义:主词不再是被指向的(pointed at),而是被指出的(pointed out);谓词则变成了在未来进一步决定主词的手段;系词则代表了这一建构过程的实际运作。为了理解这种新的逻辑形态,整个思维方式的转变是必需的。

在杜威看来,这种工具性的或者说功能性的逻辑正是"哲学的改造"得以实现的关键。在《逻辑:探究的理论》的最后一章"探究的逻辑与关于知识的哲学"中,杜威指出,迄今为止的每一种认识论都是"从可控探究的实际形式中选择性地抽取一些条件和要素"。这些认识论包括感性经验主义,逻辑原子主义,唯物主义,实证主义,直接和批判的实在论,知觉的、理性的和绝对的唯心主义。这些认识论的选择是片面的,因为他们"忽视了,由此实际上是否认了任何其他的条件,正是这些条件赋予那些被选中的要素以思维上的力量,同时又规定了这些要素的应用界限"。[1] 换言之,这些认识论立场的错误在于将材料从语境中抽取出来,并将这些材料"作为结构性的而非功能性的,本体的而非逻辑的"。[2] 如果我们不能意识到探究逻辑的重要性并在认识过程中对此加以运用,那么我们通过哲学思考提炼出来的认识形式对知识的真正更新一定是毫无帮助的。

一些哲学家认同或部分认同了杜威在《逻辑:探究的理论》中所提出的新逻辑,比如胡克(Sidney Hook)、卡夫曼(Felix Kaufman)、刘易斯(C.I.Lewis)、拉特纳(Joseph Ratner)、韦斯(Paul Weiss)、内格尔等人。但对此持反对意见的亦不乏其人。有些评论者则认为杜威的逻辑可以追溯到17世纪的洛克和笛卡尔用探究代替形式逻辑的做法,他们认为杜威的逻辑是这一思潮的高潮;有些则将杜威视作是一个后达尔文时代的密尔,因为他和密尔都认为逻辑是与所有科学都相关的关于"证明的科学"。很大一批形式逻辑学家(其中最为著名的代表是罗素)都批判了杜威的新逻辑,他们认为杜

---

① LW 12:507.

② LW 12:526.

威所谓的"工具逻辑"与黑格尔的逻辑,以及新黑格尔主义的逻辑,比如布拉德利(F.H.Bradley)和包桑葵(Bernard Bosanquet)的逻辑,乃是一脉相承;杜威只不过用体系化的探究代替了固定的实在,但这一逻辑的背后依然是黑格尔式的"精神"和布拉德利式的"绝对"。同时,他们还攻击了杜威试图用方法的有效性来替代逻辑的有效性的做法。另外值得一提的是,还有一部分对探究逻辑的反对乃是基于对科学探究的逻辑本身是否可能的怀疑。对此我们只要引述波普(Karl Popper)与莱欣巴哈(Hans Reichenbach)的话就足够了。波普在《科学发现的逻辑》中写道:"并不存在获得新思想的逻辑方法,也不存在对于这一过程的逻辑重构。"[1]莱欣巴哈的表述则是如下:"我们强调,认识论考虑的并不是发现的语境,而是证明的语境;我们指出,对科学的分析并不指向实际的思维过程,而是指向对于知识的理性重构。"[2]

但毋庸置疑的一点是,杜威的新逻辑将逻辑的绝对性连同任何意义上的终极真理一起都消解掉了。杜威试图阐明,在这种情况下,怀疑主义和相对主义并不是我们唯一的出路。抛弃了绝对的逻辑之后,我们应该走向智性的(intelligent)逻辑。智性逻辑的旨趣不是在于寻找(finding)固定的真理,而是在于通过合理而有效的引导去创造(making)更多、更丰富的意义。在1917年的《哲学复原之需要》中,杜威这样写道:"实用主义的教训在于,不要试图运用思维来达到某些在身体机制或社会存在中已经被给予的目的,而是要运用智性去解放行动和将行动自由化。"[3]正是在这个意义上,我们可以说,杜威新逻辑的最终目标在于用智性的引导去解放人类的行为。

在这一初步的定位之后,接下来我们要从经验性、生成性、想象性和实践性这四个探究逻辑的基本特征着手对杜威的"新"逻辑进行进一步的定位。

---

[1] Karl Popper,*The Logic of Scientific Discovery*,London & New York:Routledge,2002,p.8.

[2] Hans Reichenbach, *Experience and Prediction*: *An Analysis of the Foundations and the Structure of Knowledge*,Chicago:University of Chicago Press,1938,p.381.

[3] MW 10:45.

二、逻辑的经验性与经验性逻辑

我们已经提到,探究逻辑的基本部件是"存在的类别特征",正是这一点从根本上规定了探究逻辑的经验性特征。但需要注意的是,杜威并不是要揭示出逻辑中所包含的经验成分(就像后来的蒯因所做的那样),而是要建立起一种纯粹的经验性逻辑,这一点正是杜威逻辑的彻底之处。杜威坚信的一点是:逻辑的有效性并不是先天的,逻辑的有效性必然且必须基于方法的有效性。因此,经验性逻辑的根本基础在于经验性方法。

在《经验与自然》中,杜威将经验的方法(empirical method)称为"指示性方法"(denotative method),或合称为"经验的指示性方法"。① 杜威指出,非经验的方法的错误并不在于它的理论化上,而是在于没有"将提炼之后的、二级的结果作为一条通路再次回到原初经验"。具体来说,这一方法存在三个失败之处。首先,人们不再作出"测试和检查的努力";其次,经验不再获得"意义的拓展和丰富";最后,基于前两个失败,哲学以及哲学的材料都被抽象化了。② 那么,什么是"经验的指示性方法"呢?"经验的指示性方法",杜威写道,是一种"指向、寻找和展示的方法"。换言之,"指示的到来既处在最先也处在最后,为了解决任何讨论、遏止任何怀疑、回答任何问题,我们必须朝向某个被指向的和被指示的事物,并在那个事物中找到答案"。③ 为了探究的展开,我们必须首先有所指,知道该往何处寻找答案;而在探究告一段落之后,我们又必须知道如何根据已有的探究成果指向另一个新的探究对象。这一定向与再定向的过程实际就是在经验世界中描绘一幅探究地图的过程。

在这一过程中起引导和整理作用的正是"存在的类别特征",但需要注

---

① LW 1:16.可参见 Thomas Alexander,"Dewey's Denotative-Empirical Method:A Thread Through the Labyrinth", *The Journal of Speculative Philosophy*,18:3（2004）,pp. 248-256。

② 参见 LW 1:16-17。

③ LW 1:371-372.

意的是,根据"经验的指示性方法",这些类别特征必须具有两个基本特征。首先,类别特征是一种"交互过程"(transaction)。经验产生于有机体与环境之间的互动,在其晚年与本特利合写的《知与被知》(1949)中,杜威将这种互动称为"交互过程"①。交互过程既不等同于"自我运动"(self-action),也不等同于"互动"(interaction)。因为"自我运动"是承袭自古代和中世纪的哲学观念,比如柏拉图说灵魂的本质是自我运动,而亚里士多德则告诉我们那些自然存在的事物具有一种自我运动的内在动力;而"互动"则是指牛顿式的机械观,在牛顿看来,世界便是固定不变的部件间的、依从机械法则的相互运作。交互过程是对牛顿式互动的改造。在交互过程中,部件本身也在进行着改变,并且它们的改变既影响着交互过程,同时也被交互过程影响。交互过程不是联合式的统一,而是有机的统一。因此,任何一个类别特征都是交互过程中的一个特征,它们并不是固定的。它们或许有一个模糊的内核,但具体的内涵随着过程的展开不断发生变化。杜威不但关心这些特征,更关心"它们之间互动的模式和节奏"。它们不是自我封闭的范畴。它们并不是抽象的,而是"具体的一般化"。

类别特征的第二个基本特征是"质性"。在杜威看来,"质"(quality)并不被直接把握为知识的对象,无论是通过直觉还是通过亲知(acquaintance)。也就是说,"质"是被直接经验到、感觉到,或者说直接拥有的(had)。这一"拥有"(having)和"认识"(knowing)之间的区分是探究逻辑中的关键一步。因为只有如此,对于经验的建构才有可能。这一建构过程可以这样来表述:要建构经验首先必须将经验情境化,情境对经验作出基本区分,并通过这种区分初步定义出所处理的经验的质。在此基础上,有机体与环境的持续互动中不断标示和拓展这些质之间的关系,最后达到一个"质性整体"(qualitative whole)。杜威在《质性思维》(1930)中写道:"艺术创造与审美欣赏的逻辑特别重要,因为它们以精练的形式强调了质的整体是如何掌控,或者说整合,对于细节和关系模式的选择的。"②

---

① LW 16:96ff.
② LW 5:251.

与传统洛克式或休谟式的经验论不同,杜威认为"质"既不存在于对象中,也不存在于主体中,而是存在于具体的情境中,正是因为如此,质一定是具体的。杜威在《经验与自然》中写道:"质从来不在有机体'之内',质永远是有机体与其之外的事物互动时产生的质。"①然而更为重要的一点是,不是说情境中包含了某些质,而是情境作为一个整体其本身便是一种质。杜威在《逻辑:探究的理论》中写道:"……由于其直接而充盈的质,一个情境便是一个整体。当我们从心理学的一面去描述它,我们会说我们感觉到或感受到作为质的整体的情境。但是,这一表达的唯一价值在于从反面告诉我们情境其实并不是这样一种对象。说情境被感觉到完全是误导性的,因为它给人这样一种印象,好像情境是一种感觉、一种情感,或者任何其他精神性的东西。相反,感觉和情感只有被直接放在一种整体的质的情境当中才能得到规定和描述。普遍的质不但将所有的成分都组合成一个整体,同时其自身又是特殊的,它将每一个情境都构建成一个个体性的、不可分割且不可复制的情境。"②

正是基于类别特征的交互过程和质性特征,探究逻辑才能在经验世界中放置和衍生各个相互关联的探究节点,并使这个由指示性节点组成的网络获得具体的语境和内容。

三、逻辑的生存性基础

杜威不像詹姆士那样认为逻辑与人的生存性基础是格格不入的,相反,他将逻辑视作是生命的基本形式。在杜威看来,逻辑是"由生命的活动形式的某些方面发展而来"③,并且,"逻辑中联系性关系的基本重要性乃是植根于生命条件本身之中"④。因此,杜威的问题不在于逻辑是否需要和生命关联起来,而是在于需要何种逻辑来更好地支撑生命。

---

① LW 1:198-199.
② LW 12:73-74.
③ LW 12:39.
④ LW 12:41.

在《逻辑：探究的理论》中，杜威提出了探究的两个生存性"母体"(matrix)：生物性的母体与文化性的母体。① 在杜威看来，逻辑的生长不但是一个自然的生物性过程，而且还浸润在各种社会和文化的因素当中。并且，这两个母体自身又是结合在一起的，它们之间并没有明确的区分。任何脱离这两个生存性"母体"的逻辑都是"死的"、不会生长的逻辑。生存性逻辑的生长一定不是抽象的、形式化的，它必须经历和承受生命所要经历和承受的一切。在1922年的教学大纲《哲学思维的形式》中，杜威写道："经验是一个运动的过程，其中包含着一种做与改变的节奏，或者说，由做带来的内在的扰动。做带来行动，也带来承受，我们要么适应或运用所要承受的，要么就'受苦'(suffering)。为了恢复功能上的统一，我们要坚持、尝试、实验、承受、接收、受苦、'经受'(standing)各种后果。一个经验的特征或质在于在任何情况下都存在的做、承受、继续做之间的那种联系。"②在《经验与自然》中，杜威这样写道："尊重经验不但要尊重它在思维和知识中的可能性，也要强制关注到它的欢乐和悲伤。"③但是人们要问：处在这种生存性视角之下的逻辑保持其应有的严密性和规范性吗？但是这个问题在杜威看来恰恰是毫无意义的。因为如果我们脱离经验的生命史、脱离经验的"欢乐和悲伤"来谈论逻辑，由此得到的逻辑反过来必然对生命的展开毫无建树。第欧根尼·拉尔修(Diogenes Laertius)曾说理性是"冲动的匠人(technites)"④，而杜威正是在这个意义上将逻辑的探究理解为对生命冲动的组织者和改良者，通过前者的运作，后者可以被更好地表达、雕琢并最终实现。

这里，我们不妨针对杜威与皮尔士就各自的逻辑观所作的交流稍作展开，因为这对我们理解探究逻辑的生存论特征是有所帮助的。针对杜威与他在芝加哥大学的学生共同写作的《逻辑理论研究》(1903)，皮尔士曾与杜威进行了一系列的通信。1904年6月9日，皮尔士在写给杜威的一封信中谈到了他将在《国家》(The Nation)杂志9月号发表的评论，这是一封火药

---

① 参见 LW 12:26-28。

② MW 13:379.

③ LW 1:392.

④ Diogenes Laertius, *Lives of Eminent Philosophers*, 7:86.

味很重的信,体现了两位哲学家对于自己所持立场的确定性和严肃性。皮尔士写道:"你提议用一种思维或经验的'自然史'来取代规范科学(Normative Science),而后者在我看来是我们的时代最为需要的。当然这种做法远不会阻碍人类去找到他们正在试图找到的真理了,无论这种真理是什么,但我并不认为自然史可以解决以下问题的,在我看来极为迫切的需求,即人们因为不理解推论的理论而浪费了大量的思考、时间和精力。"①皮尔士认为推理必须是严格的,而"教导人们用思想的自然史来替代规范科学会导致理性上的不严格,事实上在我看来认为您和您的学生正埋头一种堕落而放任的理性思考中。"②而在发表于《国家》的评论中,皮尔士这样写到,思想的自然史可以被称作是逻辑的,那么我们就不再期望逻辑能够"宣称某个思维过程是合理有效的,而另一个则不亦然"③。皮尔士认为逻辑并不是生成性的,而是基于基本范畴的。他在信中继续写道:"我的一些非生成性的研究已经直接获得了数学和其他领域中的一些发现,在这些发现之上建立起来对于实在的实验性研究,这种建构虽称不上坚固,但也不致有问题。简言之,我想知道有哪一个生成的逻辑学家能够接近我在实际科学中所做出的这些成果。"④并且,"我的'连续论'的第一条准则是:我们的结论不能超出前提所明确保证的。你自然有权力说,对于某些哲学问题来说,如果思维及其对象的发展对于这些问题来说是相关的,那么应该把这种发展也纳入考量。但你说的却是:任何与这种发展不相关的探究都是不被允许的"⑤。

从皮尔士的信中,我们可以很清楚地看出杜威与皮尔士在逻辑观上的区别。皮尔士在《小逻辑》(1902)的开篇便写道,逻辑是研究"决定理性思维之安全的条件的理论"⑥。逻辑的目的是"用理性的观点来装备对象",其直接目的只有一个,那便是"认识"。并且,逻辑"最高和最伟大的价值在

---

① CP 8:239.
② CP 8:240.
③ CP 8:190.
④ CP 8:243.
⑤ CP 8:244.
⑥ CP 2:1.

于能够帮助我们理解理性思维的过程"。① 逻辑是"指示性的",或者说"规范性的"科学,这就意味着逻辑在实践中具有比其他学科更广的应用。② 因此,在皮尔士看来,逻辑必须是纯粹的,逻辑不但必须与心理学、历史学、社会学等区分开来,更不能反过来建立在它们之上。而在杜威看来,逻辑研究的是我们的思考行为——我们思考什么,又是如何思考的。逻辑的任务并不是保证理性思维的"安全"或正确性。在《逻辑理论研究》的第一篇文章中,杜威将逻辑理论描述为"对我们的思考行为的生成性考量",或者说,"对反思过程的一般化"③。

　　然而,如果我们更为深入地思考下去,这一区别也许还是不最为根本的。最为根本的一点是:在杜威那里,逻辑的最终目的不是精确性和严格性,而是可能性;并且,这种可能性并不仅仅是理论上的可能性,还是生命实际发展的可能性。在1938年于纽约大学所做的题为《时间与个体性》的讲座中,杜威区分了两种"潜能的范畴":第一种是"目的范畴",这一范畴将个体的发展视为"一种对已经先在或潜在的目的的展开过程";另一种则是"存在范畴",这一范畴认为"除非个体能够拥有在当下并未实现的力量或能力,否则发展就不能实现",并且这些能力"并不从自身内得到展开,而是从与其他事物的互动中获得"④。亚里士多德的潜能显然应该归于杜威所说的第一种范畴,而杜威所提倡的第二种范畴不但剔除了目的论的因素,还将存在过程本身当作实现潜能的唯一基础。

　　在我看来,这两种范畴的区分从本质上来说是基于逻辑观上的差别。杜威在《逻辑中的新要素:回应罗宾逊先生》(1917)中这样写道:"事实上,亚里士多德比我走得更远,因为他将未来的不确定性引入了所有关于未来事件的命题当中,这种引入是至关重要的,因为它影响了任何对于这种不确定之逻辑特征的判断。"⑤但是需要注意的是,这里杜威并不是说亚里士

---

①　CP 2:4.

②　参见 CP 2:7。

③　MW 2:300.

④　LW 14:109.

⑤　MW 10:100-101.斜体为原作者所加。

多德同他一样将"未来的不确定性"真正当作了一个逻辑构件，而是说，亚里士多德虽然意识到了这种不确定性，但他却用目的论的形式将这种不确定性极端化了，于是，"存在范畴"变成了"目的范畴"，潜在性以目的论的形式被固定而僵化了。在杜威看来，只有作为"存在范畴"的潜在性和可能性才具有逻辑上的重要性，任何被目的论预先把握的潜在性和可能性都不能进入真正的逻辑运作，因为逻辑的运作乃是一种探究，任何不变的东西都不是探究的材料。在《时间与个体性》中，杜威又谈道："潜在性必须被把握为与其他事物互动的结果。因此只有在互动出现之后，潜在性才能够被认识。在某个时段，一个个体中具有未实现的潜在性，因为虽然有其他事物的存在，但互动尚未发生。"①从潜能到现实的过程只有在互动中才能实现。在这个意义上，潜在并不是一个有待实现的状态，而是一种功能。由此，潜在丧失了一切形而上学的意味。在写给麦瑟内（Emmanuel G. Mesthene）的一封信中，杜威这样写道："'潜在'这个词是存在性的（时空的），它指的是探究当中一种用处或功能。"②

在《逻辑：探究的理论》中，杜威进一步区分了"潜在性"（potentiality）与"可能性"（possibility）。在杜威看来，潜在性是生存性的，其对应于我们之前提到过的"生成性命题"，而可能性则是非生存性的，对应于"一般性命题"。③但是无论如何，在将未定的情境转化为建构后的、被认识了的情境的过程中，潜在性与可能性都是不可或缺的。逻辑，同生命的进程一样，本质上是由还未实现的可能性组成的。

四、想象性的逻辑艺术

杜威曾在《作为经验的艺术》（1934）中指出，形式逻辑学家所缺少的是

---

① LW 14:109.

② John Dewey. *The Correspondence of John Dewey*, 1871–1952 (*I–IV*), electronic edition (Carbondale: The Center for Dewey Studies). CJW 14685.

③ LW 12:289.

像艺术家那样对生存性材料的关涉。① 在杜威看来,一个好的逻辑学家必须首先是一个艺术家,同艺术一样,逻辑的本质在于改造既有的形式,并赋予经验以新的维度。这种技艺,正如杜威在《经验与自然》中所说的,是一种"为了强化、精练、延长和加深自然事物自发地带给我们的满足而有技巧地和智性地处理它们的艺术"②。而这一切的关键则在于想象力。

在杜威那里,想象或者想象力的作用同他的工具主义立场是一致的。他在《经验与自然》中这样写道:"以改变客观秩序、建立新对象而告终的想象并不只是一个单纯的附加事件。想象的介质包含了旧对象的消解和新对象的形成;并且,这种介质超越了旧对象但又还不是新对象,因此可以被恰当地定义为是主观的。"③想象的作用在这里相当明显:它是旧对象转化成新对象的中介。但是需要注意的是,这里的中介并不是指单纯的中间阶段或过渡阶段,也不是指黑格尔式的辩证片段;在杜威这里,作为介质的想象更应该被理解为是逻辑运作的"实验性场地"。在这一场地中,探究逻辑自由地寻找对象,对此进行定位、探查、修改,从而形成新的对象。只有通过想象的介质,逻辑才有可能真正做到将新的东西(novelty)引入到经验的建构当中来。

在杜威这里,并不存在任何"先验"的想象力,想象力自始至终都是经验的。换言之,想象力不是自发地来自主体,或是先天地内在于主体当中,想象力乃是在实际的探究过程中实际发生的。对实用主义者来说,任何能力都是通过后天教养或教育习得的,探究逻辑的想象力也不例外。然而另一方面,逻辑想象力涉及的又不只是单纯的原始经验。席勒曾经这样表达这种需要经过理性整饬的想象力:"不是这一边旺盛的想象力毁坏了知性辛勤得来的果实,就是那一边抽象精神熄灭了那种温暖过我们心灵并点燃过想象力的火焰。"④然而在杜威那里,想象力必然地同逻辑关联在一起,也就是说,想象力不需要额外的知性或理性对此进行规范或规定,想象力本身

---

① 参见 LW 10:219。

② LW 1:291.

③ LW 1:171.

④ 席勒:《美育书简》,中国文联出版公司 1984 年版,第 50 页。

就具有独特的生长形式,那就是以意义和价值的丰富为目标的探究逻辑。我们不需要像席勒那样用游戏冲动来统一感性冲动与理性冲动①,逻辑想象力是形式与内容、理念与经验的统一。在《作为经验的艺术》中,杜威说想象是"观念在充满情感的感觉中的具体化"②。

逻辑想象力的本质在于它的创造力。这也正是杜威将逻辑想象力同艺术家的工作联系起来的原因。我们之前提到在"艺术创造与审美欣赏"中所达到的"质的整体"。在杜威看来,艺术的创造过程乃是一种经验的整体性展开。但是艺术家并不是在创造这个整体,而是将自己"融入"(absorption)这个整体。③ 这种融入虽然是艺术经验的特征,但它又是"所有经验的一个理想,这一理想也在科学探究者和职业工作者的活动中得到实现,在这种情况下,自我的欲望和迫切需求完全融入了工作的对象当中。"④探究逻辑也是同样,为了更有效地、更深入地进行探究,探究者需要将自己"融入"作为整体的探究情境当中。在杜威看来,只有这种艺术创作式的融入才能保证探究者在探究过程中将情境,而不是将自我以及伴随自我产生的偏见和虚妄之见作为探究展开的前提。然而这种融入又不是"忘我",而是将"自我的欲望和迫切需求完全融入了工作的对象当中",在这样一个过程中,自我与对象的存在都不是独立的,而是同时存在于一个整体的探究情境中。

并且,这种"融入"并不需要任何来自外部的推动力,而是完全出自于一种创作的"自发性"(spontaneity)。杜威说:"艺术的自发性与任何东西都不对立,它完全融入到有序的发展进程当中。"⑤但是需要指出的是,这种自发性并不是产生于艺术家内部的,只有在创作者和创作对象构成的整体情

---

① 在此我们不能忘记席勒的自由游戏说对另一位实用主义哲学家皮尔士的影响。

② LW 10:40.

③ 参见 Ciaran Benson, *The Absorbed Self: Pragmatism, Psychology and Aesthetic Experience* (London: Harvester Wheatsheaf, 1993), chaps.4-6; Ciaran Benson, *The Cultural Psychology of Self: Place, Morality and Art in Human Worlds* (London & New York: Routledge, 2001), chap.11。

④ LW 10:285.

⑤ LW 10:285.

境中,这种自发性才有可能产生,也就是说,艺术的自发性是产生于情境当中的一种功能。杜威写道:"艺术的作品常常展现出一种自发感,一种抒情的性质,就像是鸟儿毫无预备的歌唱。但是人,既可以说幸运又可以说不幸,并不是鸟儿。他最自发的表达性释放并不是内在压力的瞬间溢出。艺术中的自发性完全融入到新鲜的素材之中,这些新鲜的素材能够控制并维持住情感。"①艺术家被情境驱动,也就是说,艺术家时刻留意并反思自己与创作对象的关系,以这种方式,作为质的整体的情境得以"活"起来,正是在这个意义上,我们说好的艺术作品是"活"的,在"活"的艺术作品中,所有的关系都是新鲜的。杜威写道:"这里存在着一种交出(surrender)与反思的节奏。我们打断自己对对象的屈从,询问对象会将我们带向何处,又是如何将我们带向那里的。"②然而另一方面,艺术的自发性并不是说艺术家自身不需要作出努力,为了互动,有机体必须作出自己的努力和贡献,没有互动,情境就不会活动。杜威写道:"诗歌或戏剧必然的自我运动与之前所做的再多的工作都是相容的,如果这些工作的结果能够同新鲜的情感完全地融合在一起的话。济慈诗性地描述了艺术的表达是如何实现的——'在智力与它的成百上千的材料之间发生了无以计数的建构与分解之后,我们才得到那颤栗、精致而微小的美感。'"③以上对于艺术创作自发性的讨论完全适用于想象性逻辑,或者说,想象性逻辑在探究过程中所表现出来的自发性同这种艺术创作的自发性是完全同质的。艺术创作的自发性与想象性逻辑的自发性拥有一个共同的根本目标,那就是通过建构实现经验的协调性与和谐性(在杜威看来,这一目标深植于人性当中);同时,为了实现这一过程,它们采取了相同的步骤:在一个整体化的情境中实现因这一目标而产生的冲动(艺术冲动和探究冲动)。

因此,在杜威看来,逻辑只有成为一门想象性的艺术才能真正指导经验的生长。最高形式的想象力,也就是创造性的想象力,能够让我们通过感觉的形式达到那些隐藏起来的意义,并以一种非机械的(或者说有机的)形式

---

① LW 10:76.

② LW 10:149.

③ LW 10:76.

更新它的对象。创造性的想象力能够敏感地体认到对象的理想形态,并能够将对象从临时的偶然形态中解放出来;较之于把握单纯的存在,它更关注于意义的丰富。而这些特征正是杜威眼中的理想逻辑形态所应该具备的,也正是在这个意义上杜威一定会认同亚里士多德的说法:"诗是一种比历史更富哲学性、更严肃的艺术。"①

并且,我们还需要补充的是,在杜威那里,想象力的创造性一定是与已有经验相关的,想象力不是凭空的创造,而是对情境化经验的创造性把握和重构。为此,杜威区分了"假想"(the imaginary)与"想象"(the imaginative)。他在《民主与教育》中提出:"想象"不应该被等同于"假象",想象是"对于一个情境整体的温暖而亲密的把握"。② 而在《人性与行为》(1922)中,杜威这样写道:"生命的材料在想象的影响下成为一个年轻化的、沉着的、增强的形式",而假想则"以自身为目的。它沉溺于幻想当中,这些幻想从所有的现实中撤退,无法用行动来创造一个世界,又希望能以此带来短暂的刺激"③。想象与假象的最大不同在于它们的产物,想象能带来经验更新,而假象只能是没有根据的虚构。在《作为经验的艺术》中,杜威写道:假想"因为随意而消逝,而想象却持存下来,因为后者虽然初看起来奇怪,但同事物的本质却持久地密切相关"④。只有掌握了想象的艺术,探究的展开才能成为可能。

五、逻辑的实践性基调

我们在第二部分提到的莱欣巴哈的一段表述已经为我们提示出了杜威逻辑的实践维度。在莱欣巴哈看来,关于科学的哲学要考量的是"证明的逻辑",而不是"发现的逻辑"。对于这一观点的彻底拒绝决定了杜威逻辑的实践性基调。在杜威那里,探究逻辑并不是形式化的框架,而是探究的具

---

① 亚里士多德:《诗学》,商务印书馆1996年版,第81页。
② MW 9:244.
③ MW 14:113.
④ LW 10:274.

体运作模式,并且这种运作模式只有在具体的实践过程中才能够成型。

毫无疑问,行动一直以来都是实用主义者的根本旨趣所在。① 实用主义者最为关注的未来维度是由行动引出的:作为工作材料的过去经由以行动为基本形态的当下被改造为新的未来形态。可以这样说,以探究逻辑为指导的行动本身是这一过程当中的唯一形式。更为重要的是,在杜威这里,生长的永久性是由行动本身所决定的,只要行动还在继续,生长就不会停止。

探究逻辑偏爱的不是已被认识或已被把握的(the known world),而是可认识的世界(the knowable world)。在这一前提之下,逻辑之实践性的重要性彰显无疑,因为可认识的世界并不是先天地等候在那里以供我们去发现的;相反,我们需要在已有的世界之上不停地挖掘和改造,并将最新获得的世界作为进一步挖掘和改造的基础。但是需要指出的是,这一过程并不是单纯的行动,而是在探究逻辑引导下的智性逻辑。皮尔士曾经假想的提问者与实用主义者的一问一答很好地回应了这一点。提问者问道:"好吧,如果你选择将做(Doing)作为人类生活的一切与终结(the Be-all and the End-all),那么为什么你不说意义是单纯地由做组成的?"实用主义者答道:"你这个说法是强加给我的! 你的大部分论点都应该被承认。但首先应该被承认的是,如果实用主义真的将做作为人类生活的一切与终结,那么这将会是实用主义自己的死亡。因为如果我们只是为了行动并且作为行动而生活,而不管行动所带来的思想,那就等于是说并不存在理性意义(rational purport)这样的东西。"②不同的是,在皮尔士那里,探究的智性是通过探究者共同体的长期探究实现的,而在杜威这里,探究的智性则是通过对话和建构的逻辑实现的。杜威提示我们以建构性的对话式逻辑取代先在的本体论框架,他在1927年的《公众及其问题》中这样写道:"最完善的逻辑应该回归逻辑这个词的原始意义,即对话。"③而正是这一点让杜威的新逻辑跳脱

---

① 参见 Richard J. Bernstein, *Praxis and Action*, Philadelphia: University of Pennsylvania Press,1971。
② CP 5:429.
③ LW 2:371.

了传统逻辑的狭窄领域，真正进入社会和政治实践的具体应用中。

汉娜·阿伦特（Hannah Arendt）在 20 世纪 50 年代提示我们注意一个由"语言和行动"组成的公共世界的丧失。在阿伦特看来，这一丧失是由资本主义的私有价值体系与日益装置化的政治世界所造成的。① 杜威在《公众及其问题》中同样也意识到了"伟大的社会"（Great Society）在机械时代所遭遇的危险。他指出，在伟大的社会转变成为"伟大的共同体"（Great Community）之前，公众都会处在被遮蔽当中。② 而形成伟大的共同体的唯一途径便在于交流（communication）。在杜威看来，公众最本质的需要在于讨论、辩答、交流的方法与条件的改善，而这一切从根本上来说都处于探究逻辑的实践范围之内。公共世界是由"语言和行动"组成的，但更为根本的，则是由对公共问题和公共现象的探究实践组成的。在这个意义上，教育、培养和发展智性的探究逻辑便成了拯救共同体的关键之所在。

在杜威看来，强调智性逻辑在社会实践中的关键性作用是个体自由的最终保证。如果我们没有把握这一点，也许就会缺失杜威新逻辑背后的助动力。在杜威那里，真正的自由不是静态的系统，而是动态的过程。在《自由的哲学》（1928）中，杜威建议关于自由的争论应该从争论人是具有自由意志的还是被决定的转移到这样一种认识，即"让人认识到自己的责任也许能够在他们*将来的*行为中产生决定性的不同"③。杜威所提示的这种自由指向的是可能性、反思力和责任感，这是一种建构性的自由，而这种自由表达的正是杜威式经验观的根本旨趣。另一方面，杜威认为对于自由的讨论必须从约束性转向创造力，换言之，自由探讨的不是个体与约束条件的关系，而是个体如何自愿而有效地发挥创造力的问题。这种创造力同想象力密切相关，而想象力关涉的则是如何创造性地组织和重构已有的经验，从而在最大程度上获得新的意义和价值。而这一切正是杜威的新逻辑所追求的实践后果。

---

① 参见 Hannah Arendt, *The Human Condition*, 2nd edition. Chicago：The University of Chicago Press, 1998, pp.115-119, 248-257, 301-310。

② 参见 LW 2:324。

③ LW 3:94.斜体为原作者所加。

　　以上我们从经验性、生成性、想象性、实践性这四个特征着手探究了杜威逻辑的"新颖"之处。这一"新"逻辑蕴含着对旧哲学范式的根本性突破：人类认识与实践的出发点不再是主体，也不再是对象，而是以有机体与环境之间的互动为原初规定性的情境。情境是原初的，任何的建构只有在情境的基础上才有可能展开和实现。在杜威看来，情境的原初性(primodiality)和充盈性(pervasiveness)是首要的，主体和对象的规定性则是次要的，或者说衍生的。更为重要地，这一"新"逻辑的洞见还在于：情境本身的规定性也必须在情境展开的具体过程中获得。因此，一切先天的东西(a priori)都必须被抛弃；任何指导经验的东西都必须是方法论式的"地图"，而不是本体论式的"框架"。在杜威那里，哲学的改造必须是彻底的，而正是这种方法论上的彻底性使杜威招来各种批评，而这些批评者要么站在杜威所批判的旧哲学立场上，要么因为残余的旧哲学因素而不能对杜威提出的新方法作彻底的理解和运用。哲学的根本兴趣不在于描述经验而在于改造经验，这是贯彻杜威一生所有哲学思考的主线。对旧哲学范式的改造正是为了让意义的丰富和经验的生长真正成为可能。经验的生长不是抽象的原则，而是具体的操作，也正是在这个意义上，教育成为杜威思想的最终落脚点。

　　杜威用他的哲学思考一再告诉我们，哲学并不一定是对确定性的寻求，但问题是，很少有人能够真正贯彻这一初看起来几乎是常识性的立场。在《逻辑：探究的理论》写作近30年之后，从实用主义者那里汲取养分的普特南(Hilary Putnam)还在试图澄清这一点。普特南在一篇题为《不是必然如此》(1962)的文章中指出："我们不能放弃在与知识主题必然相关的陈述和偶然相关的陈述之间作出的方法论上的区分。但是，传统哲学的那种将必然陈述与偶然陈述永久性地区分开来的做法是行不通的。"①事实证明，一种涉及偶然性与可能性的逻辑并不像听上去那么容易被接受，而这正是杜威的新逻辑所遭遇的困境。事实上，一直到1949年，也就是与本特利合著的《认知与被知》中，杜威还在尝试界定他的新逻辑。大致来看，《所知与被知》希望完成三个任务：批判形式逻辑，从而为杜威的新逻辑辩护；批判逻

―――――――――

　　①　Hilary Putnam,"It Ain't Necessarily So", *The Journal of Philosophy*,59：22（1962）,p.670.

辑实证主义,从而为实用主义辩护;建构一套关于探究行为的新语汇。在杜威看来,完成这三个任务的关键在于改造逻辑。为此,他并没有简单地将逻辑自然主义化,而是试图建构一种终极的自然主义哲学,在这一哲学图景中,逻辑虽然只是有机体和环境进行交互的一个层面,但又是推进这种交互的关键层面。为了证实这一构想,我们不仅需要理论上的论证,更需要来自经验的证据,换言之,我们需要在最广阔的人类活动语境中应用并检验这一构想。正因为如此,这一构想始终是一个开放性的方案。杜威逻辑的根本旨趣在于:逻辑作为探究的方法必须永远向新的探究结果敞开,必须永远从后者那里获得更新的契机和材料。正是因为如此,逻辑必须永远关涉未来的可能性。更为重要地,在杜威看来,只有在具体探究中落实了这一点的逻辑才是真正的"新"逻辑。

[本文是国家社科青年项目"科隆建构主义学派视域中的古典实用主义研究"(14CZX036)的阶段性成果]

个人，行动以及民主的再造

——从杜威民主学说出发的一个考察

孙　斌

复旦大学哲学学院

个人以他的行动来寻求连续的经验，因为生活是连续的。生活的连续不在于旧状态的维持，而在于新状态的再造。这并不是说旧的关于生活的信念就被抛弃了，而是说它们在个人身上获得一种无法替代的特殊性，即与个人独有的感觉和观念联系在一起的特殊性。这就是杜威所说的："人们并不是真的扔掉所有流传的关于现实生存的信念，而是以他们私人的、独有的感觉和观念为基础重新开始。"①在这里，重新开始这个表述是意味深长的，它提醒我们，任何关于生活的信念只要落于个人的行动，它就不是旧的了，而是呈现于再造之中。当然，与这个再造联系在一起的不仅是个人，而且是个人由其融于其中的全部行动所构造出来的生活方式。对于个人来说，他的生活方式的最直接的表现恐怕就是那些每日所发生的事情，如与邻居在街角相遇或者同朋友在家里小聚，等等。这些事情在杜威看来是非同寻常的，因为民主就存在于其中。杜威说："我倾向于相信，民主的核心和最终保证就在于，邻居们自由地聚在街角来回讨论在当天未经审查的新闻

---

① MW 9：304.本文所引杜威著作均出自 John Dewey，*The Collected Works of John Dewey*，1882 - 1953, ed. Jo Ann Boydston（Carbondale：Southern Illinois University Press，1969-1991）.EW 为早期著作，MW 为中期著作，LW 为晚期著作，冒号前为卷数，冒号后为页码。下同。

中所读到的东西,以及朋友们聚在房子和公寓的客厅里彼此自由地交谈。"①不难看出,较之那种将民主理解为一种制度的想法来说,杜威更愿意把民主理解为一种生活方式。正因为民主是一种生活方式,所以它必须随着个人一起得到再造,"每个世代都必须为自身再造民主;民主的本性、本质是某种不能从一个人或一个世代传给另一个人或另一个世代的东西,而是必须根据年深日久我们成为其一部分的社会生活的需要、问题和条件来造出来,这是一种年复一年极其急速变化的社会生活"②。民主的再造也为我们的全部社会生活提供了理解的契机。

一、危险与行动

杜威在《确定性的寻求》中说的第一句话就是:"人生活在充满危险的世界上,便不得不寻求安全。"③这里所说的危险并非是可被指认为某物或某事的敌对的东西,而是一种无法被指认的不确定性,亦即世界本身的不确定与不稳定。这就像杜威所描述的:"世界是一幕险境;它不确定,不稳定,不可思议地不稳定。"④如果是这样的话,那么能被指认出来的敌对的东西,以及能被指认出来借以逃避这种敌对的东西的东西都不是给定的,而只是创造的。在这个创造中,不仅社会的安排、法律以及制度得到建立,而且敌对的东西也得到了规定。而在杜威看来,这个创造从根本上来说乃是指个人得到了创造。他说:"既然确系为真的是,社会的安排、法律、制度为人而设,人不是为它们而设;那么它们就是人的福利和进步的手段和代理。但是,它们不是为个人获取什么东西的手段,甚至不是获取幸福的手段。它们是创造个人的手段。"⑤杜威这里的陈述体现了他对个人的一贯看法,即个人不是某种给定的、既存的东西。事实上,他在这段引文前面就说道:"真

---

① LW 14:227.

② LW 13:299.

③ LW 4:3.

④ LW 1:43.

⑤ MW 12:191.

正的困难在于,个人被当作是给定的东西,已经在那儿的东西。"①毫无疑问,在杜威的考虑中,个人被置于一种前提性的地位并在这个位置上得到追问。在这种追问下,一个在物理学意义上孤立存在的个体并非直接就是个人,一个为福利和进步而勉力奋斗的人也并非当然就是个体,尤其是当这种奋斗是以金钱为尺度和手段②的时候。之所以如此,是因为对于个人这个前提而言,这样的孤立存在和勉力奋斗或者是未及或者是错失。然而,这在某种程度上是不可避免的,因为如果说个人是创造出来的,那么他就总是处在新的状态之中,这就给未及和错失留下了可能。毋宁说,未及和错失是意义重大的,这是因为,它们较之世界本身的那种难以指认的危险来说是公然和坦白的。这种公然和坦白使它们成为对象性的东西,即行动的对象。也就是说,人的行动不是指向这个世界所充满的危险,而是指向他的行动所造成的结果。这既是出于指认和不可指认的缘故,也是出于创造和非创造的缘故。这个时候,危险归根到底仅仅是一种刺激或者说邀请,而它本身是什么我们一无所知,亦即我们对于它无法形成杜威所批评的那种旁观者立场上的知识。与这个刺激和邀请同时发生的是人的行动,"哪里有生命,哪里就有行为、有活动……为了维持生命,就要转变周围环境中的一些要素"③。这样的行动与这样的危险成为一种起始的东西。

唯其如此,我们应当根据行动来考虑环境,而不是根据环境来考虑行动。其原因在于两点:第一,没有什么来自环境的东西是未经行动改造便被交付给我们的,哪怕这个行动只是一种可能性意义上的行动,或者只是将某种设定加诸本身不确定的对象;第二,我们在某物或某事上所意欲取得的实效已经在它们经由行动改造被交付我们时获得标示了,即对象是在行动以及行动所欲求的实效中呈现出来的。这就如同康德在一个例子中所分析的,"医生必须对处在危险中的病人有所作为,但他不了解这种病。他观察现象,判断这可能是肺结核,因为他不知道有更好的判断。他的信念甚至就

---

① MW 12:190.

② 杜威在批评旧个人主义的时候,曾经说道:"旧个人主义的全部意义现在已经缩减为一种金钱的规模和尺度,这么说并不过分。"LW 5:84.

③ MW 12:128.

他自己的判断来看也只是偶然的，另一个人也许可以得出一个更好的判断。我把这种偶然的、但却给现实地运用手段于某些行动上提供根据的信念称为实用的信念"①。在这里，危险（Gefahr）所透露的正是一种不确定和不稳定，它刺激或者说邀请医生采取行动，而医生采取行动的对象不是危险本身，而是他的行动即判断或者说设定加诸其上的东西，也就是这里所说的肺结核。所谓的"实用的（pragmatisch）"由此而得到刻画。而我们知道，从皮尔士开始的实用主义正是在康德哲学中，确切地说，从康德的"实用的"这个概念中获得启发的。事实上，实用主义这个作为皮尔士新理论标题的词就体现了他对康德的"实用的"所做的考虑。他说，在康德的术语里面，"实践的和实用的相距甚远宛如两极……后者表达了与人的某种确定目的的关系。现在新理论最为显著的特征便是它认识到了理性认知和理性目的之间的一种不可分割的联系；恰是这个考虑决定实用主义之名乃是优先之选"②。

我们之所以从"实用的"出发来展开讨论，是想避免一种可能更为人们所熟悉的一般性的考虑，即与作为行动者的人分离的环境对人来说乃是无。这个考虑当然没有错，但是在杜威以及实用主义这里，它有它的特殊的表现。借着"实用的"这个视角，我们再来看杜威所说的寻求安全，就会发现，在这个充满危险的世界上，不管是安全还是不安全其实都是行动的结果，都是由系于人的某种确定目的的行动而获得规定的。换言之，我们的出发点不是环境的顺利或者不顺利，而是行动的妥当与不妥当。由是之故，我们的研究对象就是行动。对于杜威来说，行动既意味着过程，也意味着结果，就像他在工作/作品（work）这个词上所获得的发现："……'work'既指一个过程，也指这个过程所完成的产品，这并不是语言上的偶然事件。倘若没有动词的意义，那么名词的意义就停留在空白之中了。"③也就是说，过程是为着产品的过程，产品是含着过程的产品。就此而言，社会的安排、法律以及制

① 康德：《纯粹理性批判》，邓晓芒译，人民出版社2004年版，第624页。
② Charles Sanders Peirce, *The Collected Papers of Charles Sanders Peirce Vol.5*, ed. Charles Hartshorne and Paul Weiss, Cambridge: Harvard University Press, 1934, p.412.
③ LW 10:58.

度虽然就其本身而言乃是产品或者说名词,但是只有在它们的建立即行动或者说动词中我们才能发现根本的意义。这是杜威在他的研究中所坚持的一个基本思路。不过,在考察杜威的系于行动的民主学说之前,我们还是集中于他在行动这一更为基本的概念上所作的阐述,即经验理论。可以说,经验理论正是对行动的本性与结构的讨论,因而也是对行动妥当与否的讨论。

行动的起始地位使得经验在杜威那里获得了一个完全不同于传统的定义,即一种完全不同于接受性和被动性的定义。他说:"经验变成了一桩首先是做的事情。……活的生灵经历、遭受它自己的行为的结果。做和遭受或者经历之间的密切关系形成了我们称作经验的东西。"①在杜威这个对于经验的经典描述中,做和经历之间的结构性关系得到了揭示。不难看出,在此关系中,做所透露的是作为原因的行动,而经历所透露的是作为结果的行动。在这里,行动的因果性完全是在经验的组织中而言的,但它所起的那种结合和统一的作用与康德所说的范畴相仿佛。不过,这是一条完全不同于先验哲学的进路,即追求实效的进路。实效只有在因果性的行动中才能产生,反过来说,做和经历彼此割裂便无法产生实效。对此,我们可以借助皮尔士给出的一个引起广泛兴趣的例子来加以分析,他说:"……让我们问一下,我们在说一个东西是硬的时意味着什么。显然是意味着,它不会被许多其他的物体所抓破。"②怀特在他的《分析的时代》里,从皮尔士的这个例子中解读出了一种"假如——那么"的形式,即"我们必须把'这是硬的'这个句子,翻译成某种类似于'假使一个人企图用手抓破这个东西的表层,他将不可能获得成功'的句子。总的说来,皮尔士主张,当我们将一个述语应用于一个客体(如'这是硬的'),作一个普通定言单称陈述时,我们就该将它翻译成一个有条件的或假设性的陈述,也就是说,要将它翻译成如同下列形式的一个'假如——那么'的陈述:'假如动作 O 施于其上,那么 E 就将被经验到'"③。

---

① MW 12:129.

② Charles Sanders Peirce, *The Collected Papers of Charles Sanders Peirce Vol.* 5, ed. Charles Hartshorne and Paul Weiss, Cambridge: Harvard University Press, 1934, p.403.

③ M.怀特编著:《分析的时代:二十世纪的哲学家》,杜任之主译,商务印书馆 1985 年版,第 139 页。

在这里，非常明确的是，所经验的东西乃是行动的结果，而所谓的条件和假设所透露的正是作为原因的行动。

杜威在其经验理论中借着做和经历的结构性关系所阐述的行动的因果性，无疑回应了皮尔士所考虑的那种"假如——那么"的形式。当然，这并不是简单地意味着陈述方式的改变，而是意味着行动的因果性以及实效性使得那些不确定、不稳定的东西获得了安排，取得了意义。比如，杜威在谈到美洲的发现时这样说道，美洲的发现不是指一群航行在大海上的欧洲人由于暴风雨而无意中登上了未曾被其他欧洲人抵达过的美洲海岸，因为"美洲的发现包括把这片新接触的陆地插入世界地图之中去。而且，这种插入并非是简单地附加了一点什么，而是改变了原先的世界图像，这涉及它的诸块表面以及这些表面的安排"①。也就是说，就世界图像而言，暴风雨之后登上美洲大陆的欧洲人仍然处在不确定和不稳定之中，他们甚至不知道他们所登上的这块大陆是美洲大陆，或者甚至不知道它是大陆。只有通过"假如——那么"这种探究式的行动——即他们不是停留于暴风雨中，而是通过条件和假设来行动——美洲大陆才可能被插入到世界地图之中，从而获得自身的意义。与此同时，世界图像本身获得了意义上的改变和丰富。事实上，意义由行动而获得也正是实用主义的传统要告诉我们的东西，这就像皮尔士所说的："威廉·詹姆士把实用主义定义为这样一条教义，即，一个概念的全部'意义'或者在被推荐的行为方式中或者在被期待的经验方式中表达自身。在这个定义同我的定义之间，确实似乎没有那种大多在实践中变得短暂易逝的细微理论分歧。"②尽管实用主义在皮尔士、詹姆士以及杜威那里会表现出某些差异，但是，这个传统的核心原则恐怕并没有根本的改变。杜威把在皮尔士那里更多地表现为逻辑上的东西同平常的生活进程联系起来，这是与他对寻求安全的考虑相一致的。

---

① LW 1:125.

② Charles Sanders Peirce, *The Collected Papers of Charles Sanders Peirce Vol.* 5, ed. Charles Hartshorne and Paul Weiss, Cambridge: Harvard University Press, 1934, p.466.

二、自我与实验

对于每个个人来说,最为直接和现实的是,上述的行动构成了他们每天的日常生活。而我们也已经知道,杜威正是从日常生活中自由的邻里讨论或者朋友交谈来考虑民主的。在杜威看来,如果民主同日常生活脱离开来,那么它就会变成一种外在的东西,一种像幻想中的永动机那样永远自行运作的政治机器。也就是说,一旦人们将民主视为一种自行运作的机器,并且将自身以及自身融于其中的行动交付给它,人们就陷入了极大的危机里面。他写道:"当前的深重危机很大程度上归因于一个事实,即,长期以来,我们的行动就好像民主是某样自动使自身永存的东西;好像我们的祖先已经成功地建立起一架克服了政治上永动问题的机器。我们的行动就好像民主是主要发生在华盛顿和奥尔巴尼——或者其他州府——的事情,其动力是男人们和女人们一年左右去一次投票站时所发生的事情⋯⋯"①那么,这个危机的实质是什么呢? 并不仅仅是说人成了外在之物的附属,而且是说人失去了他的生活以及他自身。这是因为,当民主成为机器时,人就失去了作为信念来对其行动做出指导的民主;换言之,他无法通过民主的方式来推进他的生活、拓展他的经验。在民主对经验成长的促进作用上,杜威给出了这样一个判断:"民主是一种信念,即相信人类经验能够产生诸般目的和方法,借着这些目的和方法,进一步的经验将在有序的丰富性中成长起来。"②这个判断是与杜威关于个人并非给定之物的一贯主张相一致的。

我们之所以强调,民主的失去不仅意味着经验的丰富与成长的失去,而且意味着我们自身的失去,还因为在杜威那里,我们自身或者说自我并非是经验的承担或负载,而是被吸收在经验之中的。这就是杜威所说的:"同样失败的是,自我被当作经验的承载者或运送者,而不是一个被吸收到所产生之物中去的因素,就像气产生水的情形那样。"③在这个比喻中,水是所产生

---

① LW 14:225.

② LW 14:229.

③ LW 10:255.

的东西，在它的产生过程中，那个产生它的气并不离开它而独立存在，而是被吸收到它之中了。与之相仿佛，自我也被吸收到经验之中。这样，几乎也可以说，所谓自我就是经验，亦即，不是说首先存在一个作为主体的自我，然后这个自我再去经验，从而形成自我的经验即归属于那个首先存在的自我的经验，而是说，自我首先就以被吸收的方式存在于它所产生的经验之中。对此，杜威的表述是："说'我经验'或'我思考'既不确切也不恰当……经验，即具有它们自身所特有的属性和关系的一系列的事务进程，出现着、发生着并且是其所是。那些被命名为自我的事件就在这些所出现的事务之中和之内，而不是在它们之外或之下。"①在这里，自我并非主体，而是事件。作为事件的自我同作为事物的经验是同一桩事情。

或者，我们也可以将杜威所说的自我与海德格尔的此在作比较。在海德格尔看来，"此在不是一种附加有能够做这事那事的能力的现成事物。此在原是可能之在"②。这个现成事物就是一种承载者或运送者，它负担着行动的能力，但海德格尔并不承认。他所承认的"可能之在"是尚非现实的、尚未完成的，必须在将来呈现出来的，也就是说，它是被吸收进那个在起来的过程的。海德格尔对可能性所做的说明进一步揭示了这一点："可能性作为表示现成状态的情态范畴意味着尚非现实的东西和永不必然的东西。"③如果结合杜威的想法，那么我们可以说，自我也是一个尚非现实的东西，它一方面在经验中不断形成，另一方面又总是没有圆满完成。这就如同杜威所说的："旧的自我被摆脱，新的自我只在形成之中，而它最后所获得的形式将取决于冒险的不可预见的结果。"④之所以冒险的结果是不可预见的，是因为冒险意味着不断摆脱任何特别是来自外部的强制和强加，从而使生活得以推进、经验得以成长。而民主正是使这样一种冒险成为可能的东西，因为民主作为信念："相信每个人都有能力从他人的强制和强加中摆脱

---

① LW 1:179.
② 海德格尔：《存在与时间》，陈嘉映、王庆节译，三联书店1999年版，第167页。
③ 海德格尔：《存在与时间》，陈嘉映、王庆节译，三联书店1999年版，第167页。
④ LW 1:189.

出来过他自己的生活,倘若适当的条件得以提供的话。"①但是,正如冒险一词本身所提示的,事情存在着不确定和不稳定,因此冒险同时还意味着使这种动荡不定发生与有机体的生存状态和要求相适的变化。

这种变化通过实验来达成。事实上,冒险作为一种向着不确定和不稳定而采取的行动就已经是实验了。如果是这样的话,那么将自我吸收于其中的经验就是实验。而我们也正是看到,像"作为实验的经验"②这样非常明确的提法甚至作为标题出现在杜威的著作中。杜威在这个标题下对实验方法作了这样的描述:"但是实验方法的引入恰恰表明,在条件控制下进行的这样一些操作,正是有关自然的富有成效的观念由以获得和检验的途径。"③也就是说,对于自然的了解不在于静观,而在于实验,即在得到控制的条件下对它采取行动、施加改变并观察反应。在杜威看来,实验方法不仅在物理学家和化学家那里得到运用,而且也在看似并不对星辰施加改变的天文学家那里得到运用。他说:"现在,如果一个人,比方说一个物理学家或者化学家,想要知道什么,他绝不会仅仅是冥思苦想。……他着手去做,把一些能量加到那物质上去,看看它如何反应;他把它置于异乎寻常的条件下以便引起某种变化。尽管天文学家不能改变遥远的星体,但他也不再只是凝视。假如他不能改变星体本身,那么他至少可以在它们的光到达地球时用透镜和棱镜来对其加以改变;他会想方设法去发现否则就注意不到的种种变化。他不会对变化采取敌视的态度,也不会因为星体的神性和完美而否定星体的变化,他常常留神于发现他能借以形成关于星体构造和星体系统的推论的某种变化。"④这段描述揭示了实验的实质,即变化。变化既是生命的特征,也是环境的特征。但是,变化在它们那里的地位是不同的:生命是一种能够由于和为着自己的变化而去发现和变化变化的变化,也就是说,一个个变化成为生命的一个个环节。这种变化就生命历程由诸环节构成而言就是实验,就生命历程本身始终是连续不断的而言就是经验。而

① LW 14:227.
② MW 9:280.
③ MW 9:281.
④ MW 12:144-145.

自我无非就是这些变化的总称，民主则是对于这样的变化的信念。

因此，杜威在这里并不是仅仅向我们描述一种在自然科学中得到应用的实验方法，而是在对有机体的生存方式进行哲学思考，亦即借此向我们揭示生命有机体作为能动者与其环境发生关系的基本模式。这种模式被杜威称作实用主义、实验主义和工具主义。而就人的环境总是渗透着人的行动而言，这样的模式同更为广泛的社会事务以及人生事务相关。杜威在他对哲学现状的考虑中道出了这一事实，"哲学现状的另一相位也需要加以注意。……把那定义科学的检验知识的方法从物理学事件和生理学事件延伸到社会事务和明显的人生事务。这种运动就其各个方面而言被称之以实用主义、实验主义、工具主义的名字"①。但是，社会事务和人生事务并不是固定的，正如有机体的生存状态和要求并不是固定的。因此，实验主义之类名字的另外一层重要意义在于：有机体本身就是一场实验。换句话说，当有机体以实验的方式变化对象时，它也正在变化自身并从而使自身处于实验之中。有机体的规定性在这种自我实验中逐步呈现出来。就此而言，人类的历史就是人类实验自身的历史。这个历史尚未结束，意味着人类这种有机体的规定性尚未完全呈现。杜威的哲学考虑让我们明白，社会事务和人生事务在任何时候都不具有神圣的和完美的本性，它们只是实验的展开。实验取得了许多甚至可以被称作是伟大的业绩，但真正伟大的不是这些业绩，而是实验本身；因为那些业绩一旦成为强制和强加，就会变成敌对人的东西，当然是由人自己创造出来的敌对人的东西。在这个意义上，民主也许可以被看作是这些伟大的业绩之一，但是从根本上来说，它应当被看作是实验，或者说，是对实验的信念，对变化和变化变化的信念：这道出了再造民主的实质。而自我就是这样的信念所引领的一系列行动。

三、民主成为一种生活方式

对于实验来说，调整、修正甚至彻底的变革乃是它的本性，它不需要一

---

① LW 15:161.

种外部的尤其是超越的综合、组织和指导。不难发现,这样设想的超越实际上是对行动的超越,并因此而作为知识或者说认识论的东西进入一度被认为是永恒的领域。但是,对于行动的超越恰恰是不可能的,因为行动在生命那里是一切东西的前提与根本。换言之,这样的超越只可能是断裂。这在杜威看来就是,所有的问题都必须在经验之中来加以考虑,他说:"经验在自身之中携带着结合和组织的原理。这些原理并没有因为它们是关乎生命和实践的而不是认识论的就见得差些。……这种生命所固有的组织使得超自然的和超经验的综合成为不必要。它作为经验之中的一种组织因素为理智的积极进化提供了基础和材料。"①杜威在其经验理论中给出的这个基本想法成为理解其民主思想的线索,即民主不需要一种外部的尤其是超越的指导和管理。这就如同前面所分析的,民主不是只在华盛顿和奥尔巴尼,也不是一架政治上的永动机,前者是外在的,后者是超越的。这意味着,民主是生活的固有本性,在日常生活之外没有另外一种可被冠以民主的生活,确切地说,在日常生活之外没有任何一种可冠以其他名目的生活,比如政治形式或者管理政府名目下的生活。

作为结果,一方面,就民主本身之中已经包含了特殊的政治形式和管理政府的方法而言,它是极其宽广的;另一方面,就民主意味着相信人类经验可由修正和变革而获得丰富和成长而言,它又是极其深刻的。正是在这种宽广和深刻的意义上,民主成为一种生活方式,因为在连续的经验中所呈现出来的全部人类生活是最为宽广和深刻的。对此,杜威这样说道:"首先,较之一种特殊的政治形式、一种管理政府的方法、一种依靠全民普选和当选官员来制定法律和从事政府行政的方法来说,民主要宽广得多。它当然是这样。不过,它比这更加宽广和深刻。民主的政治和政府相位是一种手段,目前所能发现的最好手段,该手段要实现的目的在人类关系和人格发展的广泛领域之中。就像我们常说的,它是一种生活方式,社会的和个人的生活方式,尽管我们也许尚未领会这句话中所包含的全部意思。"②在这里,从目

---

① MW 12:132.

② LW 11:217.

的出发的人类关系和人格发展对于成为一种生活方式的民主给出了社会和
个人两个维度的刻画。这个刻画的合法性在于，既然目的既是当下各种倾
向的连续发展又是对作为手段的事情的指导①，那么把目的当作出发点就
是完全正当的，事实上这也正是实用主义方法的题中之义。接下来，我们要
问的是，这两个维度之间的关系是怎样的呢？ 杜威的考虑似乎是从个人入
手的，即每个人都参与到社会生活或者说公共事务之中。

　　之所以这么说，是因为我们看到，杜威紧接着前面那段话写道："在我
看来，作为一种生活方式的民主的主旨可以被表达为，每个成熟的人都有必
要参与到那些调节人们共同生活的价值的形成之中：这从一般社会福利的
立场和个人充分发展的立场来看都是必要的。"②接下来的问题是，如何参
与？ 要回答这个问题，我们首先要明白，在杜威看来，每个人的参与对于民
主而言不是手段而是目的。因此，我们不能简单地把杜威所说的参与等同
于诸如每隔一段时间例行的公民投票之类，从而把民主的参与归结为包括
普选权在内的一系列制度性的东西。在这一点上，杜威明确表示："普选、
再选、执政者对选民的责任以及民主政府的其他因素都是手段，人们发现这
些手段有利于实现作为真正人类生活方式的民主。它们不是最终的目的和
最终的价值。"③如果是这样的话，那么应该怎样理解这种作为民主主旨的
对价值形成的参与？ 回答恐怕是，因为日常生活本身就是那些调节人们共
同生活的价值的形成过程，所以这里的参与是指，每个人都能从他人的强制
和强加中摆脱出来过他自己的生活，这也正是前面在讨论作为信念的民主
时所提及的。事实上，正如我们一再强调的，对于杜威来说，这样的日常生
活中几乎每天发生的诸如邻居和朋友在街角或寓所的自由讨论之类，就是
民主的核心和保证。这使我们得出结论说，我们一再追问的民主参与就是
日常生活中的平等交往或者说交流。

　　杜威说："对于平等的相信是民主信条的一个要素。但是，它不是对自

---

① 杜威的说法是："目的不再是一个处于导致它的条件之外的终结点；它是当下各种倾向
的连续发展着的意义——正是这些被指导的事情我们才称之为'手段'。"LW 1:280.
② LW 11:217-218.
③ LW 11:218.

然禀赋的平等的相信。"①前一句话道出了杜威的基本态度,但是后一句话可能更为重要,因为它表明,这里所说的平等不同于以往有关民主问题的肤浅讨论中一再出现但又充满曲解的平等概念。杜威之所以不把平等归结到自然禀赋,是因为自然禀赋通常被设想为一种给定不变的东西,而给定不变的东西是无所谓平等或者不平等的,即无论将其判断为平等还是不平等都是没有意义的。只有行动以及行动所创造和产生的东西才能被有意义地判断为平等或者不平等。我们可以在杜威对肤浅的评论家们的批评中发现这一点,他说:"早期民主政治自由主义的公式是,人是生而自由和平等的。肤浅的评论家们曾经认为,这个公式可被断然驳倒,因为事实是人类并不在力量、才能以及自然禀赋上生而平等。然而,这个公式从未假定它们是如此。……它是用这种方法说明,政治上的不平等乃是社会制度的产物;一个社会等级、阶级或身份和另一个等级、阶级或身份的人们之间不存在'自然的'内在差别;这样一些差别是法律和社会习俗的产物。"②因此,在杜威对民主问题的思考中,平等意味着,每个人都有平等的机会来发展自身,并摧毁强加在他身上的种种不平等。这些不平等借助制度、法律和习俗的力量披上了永恒不变的外衣,但是世界从来不是固定的序列,亦即杜威所说的:"现在,不管平等的观念对于民主来说意味着什么,我认为它意味着,世界不能被解释为物种、级别或者程度的一种固定序列。"③既然如此,那么平等所刻画的就不是状态,尤其不是给定或固定的状态,恰恰相反,是变化、发展、创造,即行动。换句话说,从天赋才能来说,人与人之间是有差别的,但是每个人从自己的才能出发采取行动的机会是平等的。这个平等的行动机会是极其重要的,因为我们知道,人正是以他的这样的行动来获得他的作为人的生活的。唯其如此,杜威得出结论说:"简而言之,每个人平等地成为一个个人,并且享有平等的机会来发展他自己的才能,不管这些才能的范围是大还是小。"④这个结论恐怕正是点出了平等的要义。

---

① LW 11:219.
② LW 11:369.
③ MW 11:52.
④ LW 11:219-220.

不难发现,这种诉诸行动的平等不可能是一种已然的东西,而只可能是一种尚未的东西。同样,民主所涉及的交流也不是旨在对先行存在的东西进行表达和沟通,而是要促成尚未的东西。杜威说:"政治民主的核心在于,通过讨论和交换意见来裁决社会差异。这种方法粗略地接近于以实验性的探究和检验来引起变化的方法:即科学的方法。"①这种科学的方法也就是前面提到的实验的方法。这意味着,交流对于民主来说是以实验性的方式来进行裁决和引起变化,而裁决和变化所指向的正是尚未的东西。事实上,杜威在另外一处谈及语言和交流的地方,更为明确地指出了交流的这种尚未的特性。他说:"语言的核心并非是对先行的事物的'表达',更不是对先行的思想的表达。它是交流;在一种有诸多伙伴参与的活动中建立起来的合作,在此活动中,每一者的活动都由伙伴关系来加以修正和调节。"②也就是说,对于作为合作的交流来说,行动是它由以发生和由以完成的契机。唯是之故,交流的过程本身就是改变和调整的过程。如果是这样的话,那么当人们在进行民主的交往或者说交流时,他们实际上并不是在表达或者传递既有的东西,而是在再造出一种从未先行存在过的东西,这个东西是他们的全部生活,同时也是作为他们的生活方式的民主。简而言之,通过个人及其行动,民主及其再造深刻而广泛地体现在人们的实验和生活的每一个环节之中。

---

① LW 15:273.

② LW 1:141.

杜威"社会民主"若干问题辨略

董山民

中南大学公共管理学院哲学系

一般而言,人们通常借助新文化运动巨擘之一胡适进入杜威的世界,知悉更多的可能是杜威的"五步法"探究理论。由于蒋梦麟、陶行知等人的介绍,杜威的教育哲学在中国内地也深入了人心。然而,对于杜威的政治哲学,人们往往知之甚少。现代美国保守主义大师列奥·斯特劳斯认为:"杜威堪称美国 20 世纪首要的民主哲学家。在他相当长而又极有影响的一生中,他的主导意向可以这样来概括:试图在生活的各个领域促进民主的实现。因此,他寻求一种无所不包的民主概念,一种对民主的全面的系统阐述,这种阐述不同于以往所有哲学家对民主的理解。"①之所以说,杜威式民主与其他哲学家对民主的理解不同,重要的一点在于,其他哲学家、政治理论家是按照国家政治制度来理解民主的,而杜威式民主却侧重于从共同体生活来理解民主。换言之,杜威理解的民主更具有社会民主的意义。由于社会民主观念本身的复杂性,杜威很难在如下几个方面为自己的民主观进行强有力的辩护:参与主体的资格、民主参与的成本以及民主参与是否有独立的价值、独立的价值有多大。本文将围绕这三个问题进行讨论,以图加深学术界对民主问题的理解。

---

① 列奥·施特劳斯、约瑟夫·克罗波西:《政治哲学史·下》,李天然等译,河北人民出版社 1998 年版,第 979 页。

一、民主参与主体的资格

我们知道,杜威式民主特别强调广泛的参与对于民主践行的意义。杜威说:"选票和多数统治是社会支配的外间和大抵机械的符号与表现。它们是手段,是在某一时期找到的最好办法,但在它们的底下有两个观念:第一,关于自己在社会秩序中的地位,自己福利和那个社会秩序的关系等,个人有权利和义务去形成其信仰,并表达其信仰;第二,在与他人处于平等地位时,每人做一个人计算,最后产生社会意识,作为多数人观念的共同表现。"①杜威在这里把选票和多数统治看作民主运行的外在形式,这与他早年与梅因辩论中表达出来的思想是一致的。当代很多民主理论家也就此大做文章。当我们用数学的方式、以清点人头的形式进行民主实践的时候,我们离民主将会越来越远,离多数的暴政将会越来越近。杜威这句话中另外一个难题是,多数人观念到底如何被共同表现出来?

我们可以把杜威的民主理解为广泛参与的民主,即在公众形成过程中以及在公共体形成后,凡可能受到公共行为影响的人都应该主动参与。杜威的一个基本理由是,只有穿鞋人自己才有资格声言自己穿鞋的感受。但是,这里的问题是,穿鞋人当然有权表达穿鞋的感受,但是对于如何做好鞋子,穿鞋人能够有权威告诉鞋匠如何设计并制作吗? 这就牵涉"主"的内容是什么。纯粹只是声言感受,还是参与决策的全程,甚至控制整个议程,乃至作出最后的决定?

民主实践过程中很明显具有两个层级:其一,"谁"在参与? 其二,如何参与?"谁在参与"和"如何参与"在整个政策形成并被实施的过程中起到什么作用? 如果我们考虑参与活动的质量,我们就还得考虑参与者的能力,就是说,谁能参与。杜威在这些问题上确实缺乏细致的分析。这很好理解,杜威毕竟是一位哲学家,而不是政治科学家,甚至不是政治理论家。但是,杜威谈到的东西确实不能飘在理论的云端,而不落到经验的层面。既要有

---

① 杜威:《人的问题》,傅统先、邱椿译,上海人民出版社 2006 年版,第 27—28 页。

价值的声言,又得顾及实际操作,这也是实验主义哲学基本原则所要求的,因此,深入分析是很有必要的。

　　被称为"当代在民主问题上最为强大的头脑"的意大利裔美籍政治哲学家萨托利曾经分析过"民主"的主体,即谁在统治,demos 到底涵盖哪些人,真正地进入统治权操作的人应该是谁,能够是谁? 这个问题关系到民主的可行性和民主的质量。他列举了有可能填充"民"之内容的 6 种情况:①人民字面上的含义是指每一个人;②人民是指一个不确定的大部分人,一个庞大的许多人;③人民是指较低的阶层;④人民是一个不可分割的整体,一个有机整体;⑤人民是绝对多数原则所指的大多数人;⑥人民是有限多数原则所指的大多数人。在分析中,萨托利很快地否定了第一种情况,因为在实际政治生活中,那些儿童、精神病人、非公民和暂住人口是被排除在外的。萨托利对第二种情况的反驳是,"人民是庞大的许多人"这一论断提出了一个无法满足的程序要求;必须随时确定多少人才构成人民或者足以构成人民。① 因此,第二种情况缺乏程序上的可操作性。至于第三种情况,可能更加适用于亚里士多德对"民"的界定,即那些穷人、暴民,这里并不作此解。问题是,在选择判定"较低的阶层"的标准上存在难度,是经济收入、财产占有方面,还是受教育程度的"较低"? 况且,如果把民主的"民"限于较低阶层的人,那么,处境较好的人被排除在政治参与之外,这种做法显然得不到合法辩护。萨托利认为第四种解释有一个重大缺陷,即它对民主毫无用处,或者说,它无论如何都可以用来为任何政体辩护。萨托利把我们带到了第五种和第六种情况:

　　　　这样我们还剩下以计算原则解释的人民,即所谓(5)绝对多数原则或(6)有限多数原则的人民。这里的绝对多数意味着只有多数才算数:任何既定人群中的多数就代表全体,并有无限权利为全体做出决定。相反,有限多数原则规定,任何多数没有"绝对"(即无限)权力。第一条标准导致的民主,可以定义为单纯多数统治的制度,而第二条标

────────

① 参见萨托利:《民主新论》,冯克利、阎克文译,上海人民出版社 2009 年版,第 35 页。

准导致的民主可以叫做受到少数的权利限制的多数统治的制度。在这两种情况下,我们终于确定了具有操作性或者应用性的标准。①

这个标准是:受到少数的权利限制的多数统治,民主在此标准的规约下就是受到少数权利限制的多数统治的制度。萨托利接下来指出,如果接受单纯多数统治的制度,那就会导致与民主政治相反的结论。因为"假如民主竞争中最初的获胜者要求不受约束的(绝对的)权力,这个最初的获胜者就能够把自己定为永远的获胜者。这样一来,民主便不再有民主的前景了,民主开始之时便是民主寿终正寝之日。按照前面的定义,因为民主前景取决于多数可以变成少数和少数能够变成多数。由此可见,有限多数统治才是民主制度中唯一的民主可行性原则"。②

我们从这段文中可以看出,萨托利的有限多数统治其实设定了一种机制,即多数可能变成少数,少数可能变成多数。只有依靠这种转换机制民主才不至于走向多数的暴政,或者民主的反面,即专权。但是,遗憾的是,萨托利没有具体地阐述多数变成少数、少数变成多数的运行机制。与萨托利不同,根据实用主义准则,杜威并不抽象地分析人民到底指谁,一般都是在具体的"问题情境"中确定"民"的意义及其所指。在他看来,公众是发生在两个人行为产生了超过两个人之外的影响之后方能形成的。只要存在公众,那么,我们就能确定民主的"主体"到底是谁。进入影响范围之内的任何公民都是即将有资格采取参与行动的行为人。萨托利可能会说,婴儿显然也将进入一个国家的医疗保障计划,但是,婴儿能够成为行为主体吗?显然不能。婴儿的利益肯定会受到公共医疗政策的影响,那么,谁来代理他们?一般来说,监护人具有代理资格。但是,监护人对于婴儿的代理资格显然建立在一种假设之上,即道德上和知识上都称职。监护人能预测婴儿未来的各种信息,了解婴儿的利益并愿意为婴儿的利益采取恰当行动。萨托利会进一步追问,还未出生的下一代人将要受到某一地区公共环境保护政策的影

---

① 萨托利:《民主新论》,冯克利、阎克文译,上海人民出版社 2009 年版,第 36 页。

② 乔万尼·萨托利:《民主新论》,冯克利、阎克文译,上海人民出版社 2009 年版,第 37 页。

响,但是在出生并成年之前他们发不出自己的声音,他们是民主行为的主体吗? 按照杜威的标准,"他们"显然不是,得有代理人来作为他们的代表。一样的问题来了,当下这一代的行为人能够有足够的理智资源和道德资源作为下一代人的合法代理人吗? 面对萨托利可能的驳斥,杜威也许可能调整他的策略。他的民主主体是指卷入某一事件的公民。就是说,当某种事件出现时,进入事件影响范围的行为人有资格参与对某种事件引起的公共措施的商议。如果这个观点是得到辩护的,那么,萨托利的原则应该适合它。可是,这里出现了新问题,少数和多数之间是如何转换的? 考虑到这个转换是民主得以可能的关键,因此有必要在此进行进一步的讨论。

　　萨托利并没有对此展开讨论,杜威却有相关的论述。在杜威看来,一般人所理解的人与社会的冲突实质上是群体与群体之间的冲突。其实,群体之间不仅仅存在冲突的可能,也存在合作的可能。因为群体的需要只有在社会整体中才能得到更好的实现,而更好的实现的途径则是,人们都需要理解到他们与他们的冲突方存在联合的利益和联合的可能。社会关系是复杂的,利益转换也经常可能。如果人们能够看到互相交往之后价值共同之所在,他们就会有意地彼此间认识到对方需要的合理性,并因此准备照顾对方利益,承认对方诉求的正当性。杜威特别强调交往活动对于社会公共利益实现的重要价值,正是这种交往使得社区内某一些公民同胞得到另一部分的理解,从而有可能获得对方的帮助。原来属于少数的派别在反复交往,甚至博弈的过程之后变成了多数,而那些先前的多数派则变成了少数。有限多数统治的要义在于,既要保证多数统治,又要保证少数人不被剥夺,其机制是多数人的权力是有限的,他们随时得准备自己这一派变成少数。因此,民主就变成了流动的程序性活动。参与主体的变换让民主得以避免走向绝对多数的暴政。萨托利得出结论:"少数的权利是民主过程本身的必要条件。如果我们信奉民主过程,我们也必须信奉受少数派的权利限制的多数统治。使民主作为一个不断发展的过程存在下去,要求我们保证全体公民(多数加上少数)拥有权利,这是民主的运行方式所必不可少的。"①

---

　　①　乔万尼·萨托利:《民主新论》,冯克利、阎克文译,上海人民出版社 2009 年版,第 45 页。

但是,这里还有一个问题尚未明朗,即有什么样的标准清晰地界定哪些人卷入了某种行为或政策的影响。换句话说,哪些人被合法地排除在外?杜威的"公众"概念看起来是清晰的,其实并不完全明确。部分原因在于,有些影响可能是潜在的、未被当下认识到的,但这些影响很可能是持久的。譬如,我们要在某地建设化工厂,当下的环评报告认为,不会对当地人的身体健康构成影响,但实质上,生产某种产品的原材料和流程可能产生的危险是目前的科技检测能力无法检测到的,它需要一段时间才显示出来。还有一些影响可能是,当下的关联因子并不明显,但是在偶然的情况下,看起来不相关的因素悄然连接了起来。倘若这样追问下去,很多东西就变成了超出经验之外的形而上的恶的怀疑。之所以提出影响的边界如何确定的问题,是希望提醒人们,杜威对"公众"确定的方法并不那么显而易见。如何确定边界,同样需要借助杜威推崇的理智方法和实践判断。

二、民主参与的成本问题

除了民主参与的主体问题之外,另一个令人棘手的问题是如何确定参与的内部成本和外部成本。这个问题处理不好将会出现:(1)决策的成本难以承受;(2)参与价值的流失。接下来我将从达尔的相关论述开始分析与参与相关的一系列问题,譬如参与的机制问题和参与的成本计算及其影响,然后进一步讨论与民主参与相关的一些问题。

达尔曾经提出了理想的民主五要素:投票中的平等、有效的参与、明智的理解、对议程的最终控制以及包容性。[1] 有效的参与到底是什么意思?有效参与确实是政治活动所必需的环节吗?达尔这样予以简单的解释:"在制定集体决策的过程中,包括在把事项列入议程阶段,每个公民都应当

---

[1] 罗伯特·达尔:《多元主义民主的困境》,周军华译,吉林人民出版社 2006 年版,第 6 页。文中的包容性被译者翻译为结论,这是一个错误的翻译。很显然第五点不是对上述四点的结论,而是独立的标准。达尔在他的其他著作中多次提到这五个标准。譬如在《多头政体》中,谭君久把它翻译为包容。还有些译者翻译为包容性。譬如在由林猛译、冯克利校的达尔的另一部著作《论民主》中 inclusive 被译为包容性。我这里采用包容性这一译文。

拥有充足和平等的机会来表达他或者她关于最终结果的偏好。"①这只是理想民主的程序要求。达尔很快发现这种有效参与在操作上的不可行性。在《论民主》中达尔说：

> 做一些简单的算术，我们就能够看到这在时间和数字上必然会造成的后果。我们就从一个小单位开始，假设它是一个委员会，只有十名成员。那么，给每个成员至少十分钟的时间来讨论手边的问题，这应当是符合常理的。这样，会议就需要一小时四十分钟，把这么些时间花在会议上，对委员会的成员来说并不算过分。不过，如果会议议题非常复杂，每个成员需要半个小时的时间，那么会议就得准备开五个小时，或者是开两次会——这点时间还是可以接受的。②

倘若把会议的规模扩大，我们马上会发现会议的拖沓冗长将让参会人员无法忍受，而且人们可能还要冒每天都需要开会的风险。倘若出现了交叉性的身份，需要参加多个议事组织的活动，人们可能每天要开不同的会议，人人都会变成张天翼笔下的"华威先生"。达尔的计算提醒我们，如果按照杜威广泛参与的要求，人们将面对技术上难以解决的难题。当然，现代电子技术和协商民主的发展可以部分缓解这些困难。电子技术在全民公决、总统选举上可以发挥作用，但是，这些技术的应用也受到了很大的限制。在一个公民美德尚未达到高位的国度里，以互联网为代表的现代电子信息技术可能还会遭到滥用，甚至被犯罪性地运用。这就是民主技术活动中参与的成本问题。按照适用范围民主的成本包括内部成本和外部成本。

姑且不管这些难题，人人参与的活动真的有效吗？萨托利指出：参与人越多参与的效能越差。他以嘲讽的口气指出："古希腊民主的弊端：实际上，把人民召集到公民大会，只代表着古希腊政体中壮观的一面，很难说它

---

① 罗伯特·达尔：《多元主义民主的困境》，周军华译，吉林人民出版社 2006 年版，第 6 页。
② 罗伯特·达尔：《论民主》，林猛译，商务印书馆 1999 年版，第 115 页。

有实效的一面。"①设想一下在现代社会中,人们参加听证会,每人限制发言时间不能够超过3分钟。那些严格按照程序发言的人将会发现他的主要观点和理由还没有陈述清楚时,会议组织者就已经试图阻止他继续发言了。至于大规模的政治选举活动,我们看到的一个情况是,很多发达国家出现了投票率急剧下滑的趋势。虽然我们不能说,投票率下滑将会给民主带来致命的威胁,但投票率下滑多少反映了"民主赤字"的严重程度。公民们觉得自己投出的那一票根本无关最后的结局。投票参与很可能变成噱头,不但不能培育公民对国家负责的美德,相反却会诱发公民对参与投票的抵触情绪。考虑到自己的一票可能并不影响大局,根据理性选择的原则,人们为了降低生活中的成本,他们将毫不犹豫地放弃这样的参与机会。那些热心政治活动,对公共事务抱有责任感的人挤出时间去投票站投票,很快就会发现自己只不过是人海中的一朵浪花。此时,他也许会感到自己有点滑稽可笑了。因为相对于花费在辨识候选人政策差异、候选人本身的道德智力水准上的成本,他知道自己的一票甚至连一个汉堡都买不回来。个别公民策略地放弃投票,整个社会甚至形成了大规模的政治冷淡的局面。在现有政治冷淡的氛围下还可能出现投票悖论,即每个人意识到自己的一票并不具有决定政策和候选人最终走向的功能,因此自己放弃投票,而希望他人投票。然而每个人的"他人"无非就是政治圈中的任何人。根据这个行为策略选择,人们很快发现没有人会去投票。民主参与要求人人投票,根据理性预期,最后却出现无人投票的情况,即民主中的投票悖论。当然,事实上,现实政治生活中无人投票的情况并未出现。理性选择学派不会想到很多参与投票的人根本没有按照经济学方法进行成本和产出的无聊计算。这种现象表明,也不能无限夸大政治冷漠,理性选择的逻辑并不完全适用于公民的政治行为。一个基本的结论是,参与的价值不能化约为经济核算。

哪怕参与不足并不是那么严重,但反对民主参与的人可能据此反对"有效的参与"。但是,把"一人一票"当作政治平等形式上之标志的人不会因此放弃这样做。他们提出的理由是,如果没有我这一票,说不定我意向中

---

① 乔万尼·萨托利:《民主新论》,冯克利、阎克文译,上海人民出版社2009年版,第45页。

的候选人就不能当选,或者我支持的政策就不会获得多数票,进而被通过。这就好比谁也不知道水缸里面的水还需要我们千千万万人往其中滴哪怕是一小滴,水缸就满了。这种算术形式上考虑民主的方式虽然机械、笨拙,但还是存在实践上的价值。杜威式民主还有一个理由是,参与本身就是价值,这种价值可以独立于其结果而得到肯定。杜威虽然反对这种外在的机械的民主形式,但是,他还是觉得这是"历史的特殊时期所设计的一些最好的方法"①。

　　萨托利反对参与性民主的另一个理由是,由于大规模的参与活动需要付出巨大的协商成本,参与变得不可取。更多的公民参与进来,固然可以减少把决策结果的负面效果强加给那些没有机会参与决策谈判的人蒙受损失的可能,但是,参与者之间的谈判将会同样地消耗掉极大的社会成本。萨托利说:

　　　　假如每一个参与者都有独立的发言权,则决策者人数同决策成本成正比——它们一起增加。如果是这样的话,无缘无故扩大决策团体(即增加决策成本)便是不合理的。这样一来问题变成了:有什么理由去扩大决策团体? 在许多可能的回答中,我认为最有说服力的回答是:扩大决策团体以便为第三者提供更多的保护,也就是说,以便减少外部风险。如果这样说的是正确的,我们可以进一步确定第二条规则:决策者人数与外部风险成反比——决策团体增加,外部风险减少。②

　　悖论出现了,即扩大参与决策的人数就会加大参与人之间谈判的决策成本,即内部成本;减少参与决策的人数则会增加未参与决策人的外部成本(相对于参与人的成本)。面对互相矛盾却都有道理的境况,我们到底该增加参与的人数,还是该减少参与者? 这个问题不解决显然将会对杜威鼓吹的广泛参与构成威胁。加拿大学者坎宁安更好地表述了这个难题,并认为

---

① 杜威:《人的问题》,傅统先、邱椿译,上海人民出版社2005年版,第45页。
② 乔万尼·萨托利:《民主新论》,冯克利、阎克文译,上海人民出版社2009年版,第244页。

问题可以解决：

  在更大的一些社会里(相对于克鲁索和星期五)，理性个体所赞同的投票规则与需要作决定的人数、外部成本之间将构成一种函数关系。如果某一个人就可以作出具有约束性的决定，那么，其他人预期付出的成本将十分高昂。这些成本(外部成本)是由于他们无力对于结果进行控制而产生的。而如果在做决策时要求全体一致通过，外部成本将降低为零，因为人人都可以否决他不想要的结果。但是，这样一来决策成本——为说服所有人都投票赞同某一决定而投入的时间和其他资源所产生的成本——将十分高昂。在这两个极端之间(我们暂不考虑偏好的强度问题)，两种成本的比例将随着做出决策的人数而变化。理性的人将据此而选择某种规则，使两种成本的总和最小化。①

民主决策活动中可能产生的内部成本和外部成本之间存在冲突。人们有理由同时控制内部成本和外部成本，但是，事实上，在试图减少外部成本时决策成本(内部成本)将会急剧上升，很难控制；同样的道理，在控制决策成本，即最小化决策成本时，外部成本将会急剧上升，也很难控制。要明白的是，上述讨论是用数学和经济学的方法来解决参与难题的理论途径。坎宁安原则上提到了"理性的人将据此而选择某种规则，使两种成本的总和最小化"，但是，他没有找到具体的办法。如何在外部成本既定的情况下减少决策成本？换句话说，如何在确定了参与决策人数的情况下减少商谈时间和交易成本，尽可能经济地达成一致？这个问题的解决恐怕不是数学计量就能解决的。参与决策的人的美德与参与决策的人的专业水平可能更加重要。因为过多地运用专业技能很可能让商谈被锁死在斤斤计较的互不相让上；相反，尊重并容忍他人的观点和利益诉求很可能导致谈判时间减少。这就回到了杜威的观点：共同利益的多少和共享价值的程度决定着民主的

---

① 弗兰克·坎宁安：《民主理论导论》，谈火生等译，吉林出版集团有限责任公司2010年版，第142页。

成败。

　　杜威之所以也不反对外在的机械的看待民主的方式,即以投票、定期选举等方式实现民主,其理由之一是,它可以防止少数专家的专业知识变成妨碍大众利益的私人知识。现在,萨托利提出的挑战是,防止外部风险的可能性总是不可预见的,但是,增加社会决策成本却是实在的。为了阻止决策成本的增加,有两个路径:一是改变决策团体的构成方式;二是简单地减少决策人的数量。如果说,第一种方式是定性上进行控制,那么,第二种方式则是数量上的控制。如果基于原教旨主义的民主理念,民主题中之义即广泛的参与,那么,很显然,数量上控制参与者的方式将得不到民主支持者的支持。那么,如何改变决策团体的形成呢? 萨托利的办法是:

　　　　实际上,形成决策团体的代表制方式允许外部风险曲线迅速下降,而决策规则只会使决策成本有所减少或稳定下来。只要你愿意,会使两个曲线(决策成本曲线和外部风险曲线)显示出非常不同的灵活性。于是代表便成了关键:只有大大削减参与小型代表团体的人所组成的整体,才能大大减少外部(镇压)风险而又不加大决策成本。①

　　根据萨托利的方法,可以说,数量控制是不得已的控制方式。全体一致只有理论上的可能,事实上不可能做到。在控制决策人数的前提下再来考虑决策集团的构成方式,因此,决策人资格核定变成问题的焦点,即代表的构成变成了最关键的环节。谁能够有幸成为被社会挑选出来的代表? 成为代表需要具备什么样的素质? 也许存在两个路径:其一是抽签;其二是程序性的选举。前者听凭运气,它能够保证公正性,但是缺乏道德的、技术的和知识上的支持,考虑到在现代这么复杂多变的社会中,作出任何决策都可能涉及大规模的人的利益受损或者受益,把如此巨大的风险交付运气裁定,没有人会乐于坚持这种方式。另一种方式,即程序性的选举,则自然地回到了

---

　　① 乔万尼·萨托利:《民主新论》,冯克利、阎克文译,上海人民出版社 2009 年版,第 244、249 页。

熊彼特的逻辑,那些政治精英往往能够赢得人们的忠诚。在很多社会主义国家里,代表的构成耐人寻味,某些职业上取得成功、可以作为表率的人往往成为人民代表。萨托利没有言明的是,倘若民主真的要变成可行的,那么,民主不可避免要走向精英式的民主,李普曼的影子又回来了。

三、支持杜威的更多理由

由于杜威是哲学家,而不是实证科学家,他不可能这么细致地思考具体的操作性的问题,对于民主实践中蕴含的精英主义逻辑,他没有萨托利等人认识得那么深入。威斯布鲁克斯注意到了这个问题:"然而尽管在杜威本人的论述中也有暗示,但是,杜威似乎很少考虑过参与式民主的问题和可能性。"[①]不过,杜威仍然可以得到的一个辩护是,他并不反对精英,只是反对精英的产生方式。由此,杜威通向了对资本主义制度本身的批判,而不是对精英主义本身的批判和对参与本身的反思。

也许金蒂斯和鲍尔斯的下述一段话说出了杜威想说的观点:

> 在生产经验构成了重要的学习环境的范围内,资本主义经济的专制特征束缚了自由民主资本主义培育人民普遍地控制个人发展的能力。……经济是一个对其参与者一般来说无责任的公共领域,这些参与者将掌控不了他们自己发展的社会权力,无论他们是作为工人,还是在发展通过工作充塞他们的个性和能力的范围内,作为公民和家庭成员,情况都是一样的。这个问题不仅涉及到作为民主社会的自由资本主义社会的可疑地位,而且涉及到这种社会从长远的观点来看支持和再生产甚至最低限度的自由民主的国家决策体系的能力。[②]

---

① 罗伯特·威斯布鲁克斯:《杜威与美国民主》,王红欣译,北京大学出版社 2010 年版,第 335 页。

② 塞缪尔·鲍尔斯、赫伯特·金蒂斯:《民主与资本主义》,韩水法译,商务印书馆 2003 年版,第 170—171 页。

　　换句话说,资本主义造就了一种反民主的文化,虽然他在形式上保证了民主,但在实质上却抽空了民主的基石。我们知道,杜威对民主的倡导的一个重要维度是道德,然而资本主义的生产方式和意识形态的生产过程却培育了一种不道德的社会基础,从而导致民主伦理遭到破坏。达尔在这个问题上与杜威的立场大致一样。他说:

　　　　由于政治资源的不平等,一些公民比另一些公民对政府的政策、决策和行为有更多的影响。这些侵害权利的行为不可等闲视之! 因而,公民没有获得政治上的平等——远远没有——于是,民主的道德基础,即公民之间的政治平等遭到了严重破坏。①

　　萨托利、达尔等人从技术角度分析了广泛参与的不可欲性,以间接的方式巧妙地论证了精英主义的合理性,从而走向了与熊彼特一样的逻辑。但是,与萨托利等人不同的是,杜威并未过分纠结于技术性的细节,却从这种参与的局限中过渡到对资本主义制度的全面批判。在他看来,正是资本主义资源占有不平等的事实,深刻地改变了社会道德的基础,甚至导致民众中践履民主的能力的匮乏,以及意愿的减退。一旦赚钱能力作为人生价值的测量指标,那么,政治公共空间中民主参与将会萎缩。在能力约束和能量约束下,原先作为连体婴儿的资本主义与民主,现在走向了互相拆台和敌对的状态。

　　单纯从参与的两种成本角度来考虑民主也许存在很大的局限性,我们可以看到司法体系和司法制度的安排也是极度消耗社会资源的,它们会使社会付出巨大的成本,可是,人们一般不会去反对现代司法制度。当然司法制度的被动性可能与民主活动的主动性完全不同,尽管如此,还是不能以成本消耗作为全面否定参与性民主的充分理由。

　　行文至此,只是回到了如何参与和参与的成本问题,与此相关的另一个问题是,如果不考虑参与的后果可接受与否,而来考虑参与活动本身,那么,

————————————

　　① 罗伯特·达尔:《论民主》,林猛译,商务印书馆 1999 年版,第 186 页。

问题就变成参与本身有何价值。在民主漫长的历程中,很多原先被排除在政治参与进程之外的人慢慢地参与进来。譬如说,黑人、印第安人、妇女的选举权和被选举权。政治平等不一定在现阶段实现了,但是,阻止政治平等的力量逐渐遭到失败毕竟是历史中的真实现象。这就说明,除了成本问题不能成为反对民主参与的判决性理由外,参与本身还具有其他重要价值。如果说,从成本角度考虑参与问题更加接近自由主义的思路,那么,从参与本身的价值来考虑参与则更多的与共和主义传统联系在一起。桑德尔点明了这一点:"根据共和主义的政治理念,共享自治包括更多的东西:它意味着与公民伙伴就共同善(the common good)展开协商,并致力于塑造政治共同体的命运。而就共同善展开充分协商,不仅需要选择自己的标准的能力以及对他人做同样事情的权利的尊重,而且还需要关于公共事务的知识、归宿感、对集体的关心和对自己命运休戚与共之共同体的道德联系。因此,分享自治要求公民拥有或者逐步获得某些品质或公民德行。"①参与本身需要美德,参与也可以塑造美德,而民主政治的良性运转需要的条件在托克维尔看来那就是普遍的公民美德。对于参与可以塑造人们的美德,台湾学者姜宜桦作了如下表述:"通过亲自参与公共事务的研拟、讨论、说服或监督其执行人,人们真正与他人共同创造了一个'公共领域',使自己原本局限的观点得以在参与审议的过程中,转化为具有公共性导向的意见。我们在这个过程中,或者可以从别人的意见学习到自己看不到的地方,或者可以说服别人接受自己更具有理性的看法,因此参与兼有教育和转化的作用,可以让一个人领悟到沟通、协调、讲理、容忍等公民德行。而这些德行既是民主政治所需要的文化,也是民主政治所能滋养的文化。"②

人们拒绝民主经常用到的一个论据是,民主是一种无效率的政治形式。资本主义作为一种经济运行的原则和人类文化,其实就是在效率上压倒了其他制度安排及其文化。与资本主义兴起互为伙伴的就是政治上的自由主义,自由主义经常与古典经济学家亚当·斯密的名字联系在一起,这已经变

---

① 迈克尔·桑德尔:《民主的不满——美国在寻找一种公共哲学》,曾纪茂译,江苏人民出版社 2008 年版,第 6 页。

② 姜宜桦:《自由民主的理路》,新星出版社 2006 年版,第 43—44 页。

成了如今人所共知的常识。但是,这种方式与共和主义相对的地方之一是,在谈论政治的时候自由主义经常以经济的方式来思考,试图清除那些不能用数学来处理的东西,譬如道德价值和审美价值。但是,价值中立性何尝不是一种虚构和神话。在很多思想家看来,效率优先原则就是价值中立的具体体现。没有人否认效率的重要性,但是,是不是可以用效率来衡量人类所有的活动?杜威曾经指出,某种观念固定下来成为人们珍视的价值,其实是有条件的,但是人们经常忘记了它们出现的问题情景和依赖的条件。他指出这种思维方式的缘由:"凡是关于它们可以说的话都是关于它们的发生条件和它们所产生的后果的。这种把直接的价值认为是可以思考和可以谈论的概念,乃是由于把因果范畴跟直接性质混淆不清而产生的结果。"①譬如,我们憎恨动荡,喜欢安定,那是因为动荡的东西经常让我们限于困境,我们经常得不到自己需要的东西。但是,我们能不能因此拒绝动荡本身也是有价值的呢?显然不能。同样的道理,政治生活中对活动效率的要求也不能倾覆人们对参与本身的珍视,美德之所以成为美德,是因为它经常以不那么直接的方式维系政治机器的运转。参与可以锻炼人们的参与能力,要学会游泳必须跳入泳池,人们必须在实际性的参与活动中才能学会正当地行使自己的权利。

    杜威式社会民主的概念遭遇了主体资格认定的困难,并在民主参与活动的操作上面临了两种成本互相冲突的困扰。消解这些难题的路径之一是让杜威回到民主伦理学的基本原则,即美德本身就是制度运行的润滑剂。在杜威、达尔等打算为政治活动寻求道德基础的思想家看来,资本主义经济制度及其运行方式才是民主的敌人。因此,重要的是尊重民主参与的独立价值,培养一种民主文化。

---

① 杜威:《经验与自然》,傅统先译,江苏教育出版社 2005 年版,第 251 页。

杜威与中国：百年回溯与展望

徐 陶

中南大学公共管理学院哲学系

杜威在来到中国之前已经是一位享有世界声誉的哲学家和思想家,其整体思想中包含了实验主义、工具主义、进步主义教育哲学、经验自然主义、经验共享式的民主理念、进化发展观等诸多主题,几乎涉及了社会人文的所有思想领域。而 20 世纪初期的中国处于打破传统封建文化与社会制度,谋求进行现代转型的关键时期,爱国志士和思想界的精英们竭力寻求一个拯救中国于危难之中的自救与强国之道。杜威哲学无疑对于变革时代的中国起到了重要的引导作用,杜威思想传入中国将近百年,探讨杜威与中国的交互影响对于研究 20 世纪中国思想史、文化史、教育史、政治史皆具有重要的意义。本文将从以下几个方面来进行论述。①

一、杜威与"五四"时期的社会变革

胡适等人最开始邀请杜威来访中国的目的,是想以他们的老师在世界上的声望来促进他们所倡导的新文化运动。新文化运动旨在解放人们的思想、启迪民智,反对守旧的传统文化。辛亥革命失败以后,受外国势力培养的军阀集团和封建势力相结合,掀起了一股复古尊孔的逆流,这使得新文化

---

① 刘放桐教授曾经以《杜威哲学及其在中国的影响》(《天津社会科学》2010 年第 2 期)为题,撰文阐述了杜威对于中国社会和文化发展的影响,特别是论述了杜威思想与马克思主义的共通之处。本文的写作亦受该文启发,并且试图提供一些新的视角。

运动势在必行。新文化运动的提倡者胡适、陈独秀、李大钊等人深刻地认识到,要想在中国进行具体的社会制度的变革,必先在思想和文化层面进行一次彻底的去旧纳新。杜威的实用主义与新文化运动之精神是契合的,杜威的平民主义教育思想提倡大众均有机会接受教育,并倡导科学的态度和精神,提倡发扬民主理念,以及社会的持续进步,反对教条主义的道德规范。新文化运动两个倾向都可以在杜威思想中找到支持。杜威认为时代是不断更新的,我们必须在具体的环境中构建我们的理论,因此,在世界进入现代化进程的时期,我们有必要采用新的语言(白话文)、采用新的道德观念(反对封建礼教);而且,杜威对于科学方法的推崇和对于民主的关注,这无疑也和陈独秀所倡导的民主和科学两大观念相契合。

　　杜威到上海的第三天,便作了题为"平民主义的教育"的讲演,此后又作了关于社会哲学与政治哲学、伦理学、现代哲学思潮等若干主题的演讲。胡适在其《杜威先生与中国》一文中概括了杜威哲学的方法论,即历史的方法和实验的方法①,而实验的方法又包括:"第一,从具体的事实与境地下手;第二,一切学说理想,一切知识,都只是待证的假设,并非天经地义;第三,一切学说与理想,都须用实行来试验过,实验是真理的唯一试金石。"②杜威在中国各个省市的长时间巡讲,对于新文化运动的深入传播起到了很大的作用。杜威认为当时的中国正处于一种机遇之中,"这就为社会教育作为一种社会进步工具的重要性提供了一个生动的证据"③。

　　杜威来中国不久,中国便爆发了轰轰烈烈的"五四"运动,"五四"运动是一场大规模的反对北洋政府在巴黎和会上与日本签订的不平等合约的群众运动,使得新文化运动从思想启蒙的层面发展到进行现实的社会变革的层面。杜威目睹了当时学生运动的风起云涌和浩大声势,这使得杜威对于

---

① 胡适把杜威哲学称为"实验主义"而非"实用主义",这在一定程度上避免了国人对于"实用主义"一词的误解,因为"实用主义"很容易同"急功近利"、"只求个人的眼前利益、不讲原则"等词语相联系。即使在今天,大多数人仍然是这样来理解"实用主义"一词的。

② 张宝贵:《实用主义之我见——杜威在中国》,江西高校出版社 2009 年版,第 19—20 页。

③ 简·杜威:《杜威传》,单中惠编译,安徽教育出版社 2009 年版,第 42 页。

中国有了全新的认识。当时杜威和其他西方人一样,也认为中国是受传统文化浸染过深而难以自救的民族,但是"五四"运动所表现出来的普遍性的爱国热情使得杜威认为中国能够彻底改变传统的思维方式,进行政治、经济、文化和技术的变革。杜威对"五四"运动高度评价,他写道:"这正是一个学术现象,值得去研究、琢磨、调查和思考。当今世界没有哪个地方发生的事情——包括正沉浸在改造阵痛中的欧洲,能和中国目前的状况相提并论。"①杜威在美国的《新共和》和《亚细亚》杂志上陆续发表文章报告中国"五四"运动的形势。杜威在《中国学生的抗议示威》中描述了学生的行动和政府的反应,认为这显示了独立于政府之外而又能压倒政府的组织团体的威力,而运动中很多年轻人的参与给杜威留下了深刻印象:"很难想象,我们国家 14 岁以上的孩子能够带头发起一场大规模净化并改革国家政治的运动,并能让商人和专业人士感到羞愧而加入到他们的行列中来。这真是一个了不起的国家。"②

杜威对于中国当时的社会处境也有着深刻的思考,他在《中国人的民族情绪》、《中国的政治动乱》、《中国政治的酵母》、《中国是一个民族吗》、《工业的中国》等文章中探索了中国问题,认为中国急需建立稳定的中央政府,统一的货币体系和交通体系,克服地方民族主义。他在《中国的新文化》、《转变中的意识》、《谁阻碍了中国的前进》等文章中强调中国的现代化进程必须根据本国国情来进行,指出:"所需要的是一种新文化,是从西方最为系统全面地思想体系中自由吸取的——但一定要是适合中国国情的、建设欣欣向荣的中国文化所运用的方法和媒介。"③杜威在《远东的僵局》、《在东海的两边》、《从内部看山东》、《中国的噩梦》、《美国在中国的机会》、《在华财团》、《重放山东》等文章中讨论了中国与外国政府的国际交往,谴责了在华外国势力对于中国的侵占。杜威在《中国的新文化》一文中提到,如果军阀的残暴统治长期持续下去,那么必会引起布尔什维克主义者的反抗。

---

① 简·杜威:《杜威传》,单中惠编译,安徽教育出版社 2009 年版,第 360 页。
② 简·杜威:《杜威传》,单中惠编译,安徽教育出版社 2009 年版,第 360 页。
③ 简·杜威:《杜威传》,单中惠编译,安徽教育出版社 2009 年版,第 361 页。

应该说,杜威对于"五四"运动持支持态度,对于当时中国的社会文化的发展和变革是起到积极意义的。但是我们毕竟要看到,杜威思想也只是当时各种思潮中的一员而已,并非唯一的影响。而且很多学者也对杜威思想进行了批评,例如张水淇在《知识果是工具么》一文中提倡为知识而知识,而反对知识的工具主义的观点;朱言均在《驳实验主义》一文中认为知识要分为两类,一类是逻辑和抽象的知识,另一类是经验知识,前者不需要接受实验主义,只有后者才和杜威的实验主义相适应;刘均量在《实验主义者的理想》一文中,痛斥杜威就是一个懦弱的学者,站在旁观者的立场来对中国问题指手画脚。尽管有这些反对的声音,但多数的知识分子还是对于杜威思想持肯定态度,杜威在华的演讲也得到了最为广泛的传播和推广,成为 20 世纪初期中国文化界的一大盛事。

二、杜威眼中的中国文化

杜威在中国待了两年多,不仅进行讲学,还走访各地了解风土人情,他在美国的《亚细亚》和《新共和》杂志上所发表的文章不仅涉及社会与政治,而且还关注中国的文化特质,这为我们反思自身文化提供了一个有价值的外来视角。杜威写道:"这是我学术生涯中最有价值的事情之一。……这是一次绝对超值的体验,与其说学习到了什么新鲜的事物,不如说获得了崭新的看待事物的视角与侧面。西方的任何事物在这里都会变得完全不同,如同年轻人的重生,世界未来的希望指日可待。"①

在当时的国人眼中,杜威在教育方面的成就影响堪与孔子相提并论。②1919 年蔡元培以"孔子与杜威"为题发表演讲,他说:"我觉得孔子的理想与杜威博士的学说,很有相同之点……孔子说学而不思则罔,思而不学则殆,这就是经验与思想并重的意义。他说多闻阙疑,慎言其余,多见阙殆,慎行

---

① 简·杜威:《杜威传》,单中惠编译,安徽教育出版社 2009 年版,第 363 页。
② 关于杜威和孔子的教育哲学的会通之处,笔者亦有专文论述。参见《杜威与孔子的教育哲学:历史视野与当代意义》,《教育科学》2012 年第 4 期。

其余,这就是试验的意义"①,但是很奇怪的事情是,相对于儒家思想,杜威对于中国的道家思想则更为关注。

杜威在《亚细亚》杂志上发表论文《中国人如何思想》,分析了中国传统文化中保守心理习惯的渊源,他认为要归结于道家的无为思想。杜威认为这是一种民族的惰性,而这种文化的来源又是因为中国是个农耕社会,人们对于土地依赖过重。刘伯明在《杜威论中国思想》一文中评述了杜威的这一观点:"在杜威观之,盖源于老子思想之影响。老子最重自然,而视人为受制于天。无为之说,亦即由是而来。凡积极之活动,皆干涉自然之势。此义虽然非中国之所专有,然其影响于此渐染之深,迥非其他民族所及。中国人对于人生之态度,如顺乎自然、安分知足、宽大和平不怨天尤人等,即原于是。其命运之观念,即由是而来。"②杜威在《中国人的生活哲学》一文中阐述了同样的道理,他认为中国文化主要由儒、释、道三家构成。但是和通常的观点不同,杜威认为道家的思想对人们的影响要远甚于其他二者。他认为,自然无为的思想使得人们不思进取和安于现状。其经济和社会根源在于中国是农业社会,几千年的农业社会得以维持,使得这种保守主义变成了一种民族精神。儒家学说虽然倡导建功立业和社会责任,但是它实际上被道家思想同化了,儒家的礼教和制度都因循守旧和极度保守。

杜威提出,东西方文化应该进行互补,他认为精神理想的构造,不仅需要西方的"服务的伦理思想"和对于社会进步的关心,也需要东方的"审美欣赏与冥想"③。杜威在东方文化中发现了一种"对于自然、文学和艺术之美平静而从容的欣赏"和"一种平和的在冥想和沉思之中对于心灵的涵养",而这可以用来纠正西方的行动主义的急躁性。杜威认为他在中国道家思想中发现了一种对于自然的虔敬,道家思想一方面容易导致保守主义和宿命论,从而阻碍社会的发展;另一方面倡导节约自然资源,与自然和谐共存,中国人对于自然的虔敬使得中国人具有"放任自由的、满足、宽容、温

---

① 简・杜威:《杜威传》,单中惠编译,安徽教育出版社 2009 年版,第 396 页。
② 张宝贵:《实用主义之我见——杜威在中国》,江西高校出版社 2009 年版,第 95 页。
③ Dewey, *The Middle Works vol.*13, Carbondale and Edwardsville: Southern Illionis University Press, 1992, pp.265—266.

和、幽默、乐天的生活态度"①。

　　杜威在中国进行了很多的演讲,其宗旨就是告诉中国民众,西方文化的精髓在于其文化,中国必须从改造自己的民族精神开始,来实现本国的复兴。杜威也和新文化运动者胡适、鲁迅一样,指出了中国传统文化中的各种痼疾,例如杜威认为中国人对于国家或者其他人都比较冷漠。他还记载了这样一件事情,他在北京街头看到一个行人被马车撞倒在地,而行人无一上前救助,最后还是一群外国人把伤者送到医院。然而,在一百年后的今天,我们传统文化的这种痼疾仍然存在。

　　杜威在山西发表了"学问的新问题"的演讲,他认为人们要采用进化论的方法来看待社会和时代的变化,用科学探究的方法来分析中国传统文化,中国人必须认清自己的保守主义,但是又不能盲目模仿外国制度,而应该根据本国国情进行创造:"中国这个古国不应纯去模仿,应当自己创造。物质方面,西洋已占先了一百年,中国自然稍稍吃亏。但是社会方面,西洋也还没有用科学的态度去研究,东西两洋,都有新的需要。中国本来很注重社会方面,——像人生问题、伦理问题等——所以希望中国既与西方同处一个新境遇中,应当努力创造,有所贡献于世界文明。"②

三、杜威与中国现代学术的建立

　　新文化运动以前的国学研究泛指以经、史、子、集为基础的中国传统思想,相对于西方现代学术而言,国学有学科分类不够精细、所使用的文言文不易推广和普及、尚古多于批判、论述不够逻辑严密等弊端。并且现代西方学术主要关注的自然科学(进化论、日心说、各种自然科学理论等)和社会科学(自由、民主、平等)的理论是与西方社会的现代转型有内在联系的,而中国仍处于封建社会,国学的研究内容缺乏这些现代理念。因此,在 20 世

---

①　Dewey.*The Middle Works vol.*13,Carbondale and Edwardsville:Southern Illionis University Press,1992,pp.222-227.

②　张宝贵:《实用主义之我见——杜威在中国》,江西高校出版社 2009 年版,第 159 页。

纪初期西方已经普遍实现现代转型的时代背景下，国人认识到有必要对国学进行批判性的反思，而建立现代学术制度，促进思想文化的进步。

杜威实用主义对中国现代学术研究之建立的影响主要体现在哲学、史学、文学、教育学等具体领域。在哲学方面，胡适把杜威的实用主义翻译为实验主义，并且概括为"大胆假设、小心求证"的思维方法，影响颇大。胡适在自己的学术研究中也贯彻这种实证的、疑古的学术方法，1919年胡适出版了《中国哲学史大纲》上卷，这本书具有四个重要特征：第一是把哲学从经学、考据等其他研究中独立出来（明确学科分类）；第二是把传统学术顶礼膜拜而缺乏可靠史料的尧、舜、禹、汤、文、武、周公去掉，直接从老子、孔子开始讲（以哲学史料为基本依据，采用实证性的学术研究方法）；第三是把孔子与其他诸子相提并论，把儒学回归为诸种学说中的一种，打破了经学的学术垄断地位（批判性的学术精神）；第四是采用系统的方法，传统国学都采用平行的记叙，而胡适则阐明了学派之间的内在脉络（内在的学科逻辑）。

而在历史方面则体现为顾颉刚为代表的古史辨派。"五四"运动之后，顾颉刚先生发表了论文《与钱玄同先生论古史书》，提出了新的观念："层累地造成的中国古史"，从而推翻了由"盘古开天"、"三皇五帝"等观念构成的古史理论，力图摆脱传统经学和史学的束缚，重新对古代典籍和古史传说的真伪和时代作全面而深入的考辨。顾颉刚受到了胡适实验主义的影响，他后来曾说："要是不遇见孟真（傅斯年）和胡适之先生，不逢到《新青年》的思想革命的鼓吹……要是适之、玄同两先生不提起我的编集辨伪材料的兴趣，奖励我的大胆假设，我对于研究古史的进行也不会这般的快速。"①尽管古史辨派有其缺陷，但是总体而言，对于历史研究方法仍然有着不可忽视的重要性。

在文学方面则体现为胡适的《红楼梦》研究。胡适把实验验证的研究方法运用到对《红楼梦》的研究上，创立了考证派的红学研究模式，抛弃了索隐推测的传统红学模式，俞平伯深受胡适思想的影响，将这种红学研究模式进一步深化。而在教育方面，杜威对中国的影响最大，杜威的学生陶行知

---

① 顾颉刚：《古史辨》第1册，上海古籍出版社1982年版，第80页。

先生不仅是杜威教育理论的大力传播者,而且是其理论的发展者与实践者。他吸收了杜威的"教育即生活"的理念,结合中国的具体环境,提出了"生活即教育"的学说,并在全国多地成立了杜威式的实验学校。陶行知先生所开创的现代教育体系影响至今。

诚然,杜威在中国的这些弟子以及理论追随者在不同的领域发扬和推广了杜威的实验主义、进步主义教育思想,对于现代中国学术的建立和发展有着重要的推动作用,但是也不可避免地出现了一些偏差,例如古史辨后来演变为"古书辨",胡适的哲学史也被冯友兰的哲学史所超越,俞平伯的红学研究受到批判,等等,不过总体而言,还是功大于过的。

四、杜威与20世纪初期中国发展的两条道路

新文化运动是对于中国传统封建文化和社会习俗的彻底清扫,但是在去旧革新之后,中国道路通向何方,这仍需要国人去探寻。当时的道路主要有两条:一条道路是胡适、孙中山等人所主张的效仿西方的民主制度,另一条道路则是陈独秀、李大钊等人所主张的效仿俄国的社会主义,后一条道路被毛泽东等人改造为根据本国国情来进行无产阶级革命和建立社会主义国家,杜威与这两派皆有交流。

1919年5月,民国前总统孙中山先生拜访了杜威,他希望能够借助于杜威的影响来实现自己的民主事业,同时也和杜威讨论了他"知难行易"的思想,即鼓励人们勇于实践和行动,而非退缩不前。杜威对孙中山的民主思想和哲学思想都颇为赞同,他也认为实践比知识更基本。但是杜威却对于孙中山试图模仿日本快速发展模式的想法并不赞同,因为杜威很反对日本的军国主义传统,甚至还拒绝日本天皇的授勋。

中国共产党的早期领导人陈独秀在接触到杜威思想后,认为实用主义可以和马克思的唯物史观相提并论,并且表示"相信并且尊重杜威的实验哲学"[①]。1921年杜威到广东进行演讲,陈独秀亲自去主持了杜威的演讲

---

① 陈独秀:《本志宣言》,《新青年》第7卷第1号,1919年第12期。

会。毛泽东也曾受到杜威思想的影响,他在《湘江评论》的创刊宣言中写道:"(中国)就成功或者将要成功许多方面的改革。……见于思想方面,为实验主义";1919 年他在长沙发起成立了"问题研究会";1920 年,杜威在上海演讲时,毛泽东是听众之一;而 1920 年杜威来湖南长沙发表演讲时,毛泽东更是亲自担任记录员。另外,周恩来在《天津学生联合会报》创刊号上也称"现在世界的最新思潮是'实验主义'"。①

不管是保守主义者梁启超,还是资产阶级民主改良主义者胡适、资产阶级革命主义者孙中山、马克思主义的早期领导者陈独秀、李大钊,以及青年时期的毛泽东、周恩来,他们都曾对杜威的实验主义有着亲切感。但是随着中国社会和政治形势的继续发展,杜威的实用主义哲学开始在和其他思潮的交锋中,慢慢减弱对于中国社会的影响力,甚至处于被批判的对象。杜威在政治方面的改良主义和反对暴力革命论,背离了后来中国共产党所开展的革命运动,因此逐渐被革命者所遗忘。但是杜威认为不能简单效仿俄国的社会主义革命模式,还是很有启发意义的。

胡适与李大钊著名的"问题与主义之争"是实用主义和马克思主义的差异的端倪初现,胡适认为在当前不要空谈主义,而应该多根据具体情况采取对策,获得社会的进步,这是杜威式的改良主义。而李大钊认为,实际行动很重要,但是主义的号召性和引领性也很重要。客观而言,胡适与李大钊的争论并非是实用主义和马克思主义的公然对立,而实际上还是一种协商和交流的态度。而在 20 世纪 30 年代初,马克思主义者瞿秋白就开始大力批判杜威思想,这标志着实用主义已经和马克思主义处于完全的对立面,瞿秋白认为实用主义是唯心主义的,这和马克思主义的实践第一、物质第一的观点相悖;实用主义是多元论的,这和马克思主义者所主张的马克思主义是唯一的信念相悖;实用主义是改良论的,这和马克思主义所要求的无产阶级革命相悖。最后,瞿秋白得出定论:实用主义绝不是革命的哲学。

胡适所主张的效仿西方的民主制度之具体实现是蒋介石的国民政府,而另一条道路则是毛泽东所领导的无产阶级革命以建立人民民主共和国,

---

① 参见元青:《杜威的中国之行及其影响》,《近代史研究》2001 年第 2 期。

随着时间的推移,这两条道路越发显示了其不可兼容性。胡适担任蒋介石的国民党"国防参议会"参议员,1938 年被任命为中国驻美国大使,已然顺从于前一条道路。而在当时,马克思主义所引领的中国共产党人正在不断发展和壮大。两条路线之间的斗争逐渐尖锐,胡适及其作为思想基础的杜威哲学也被顺其自然地置于马克思主义的对立面。在 20 世纪 30 年代中期,杜威否定了斯大林对于托洛茨基案的审判,杜威从苏联的友人变成了反动人物,其在中国的地位也成为彻底被批判的对象。新中国成立以后,中国在 1955 年左右发起了对于以实用主义为代表的资产阶级思想的批判运动,胡适和杜威被全盘否定,这种情况一直到改革开放以后才被扭转,1980 年以来,我国才开始重新评价杜威及其实用主义。

五、杜威思想与当代中国

那么,探讨杜威思想对于当代中国的发展又有何现实意义呢？杜威的思想重要的是方法,而非理论,他的一系列方法论对于当前我们的社会、政治、文化之发展仍然具有重要的启示作用。

第一,杜威的实验主义与当代中国的社会发展。虽然杜威并不主张在中国复制苏联的社会主义革命路线,也对苏联社会主义模式进行了批判,特别是直接参与了对于斯大林领导的肃反运动的调查与批评。但是,正如刘放桐教授所指出的那样,杜威的实验主义与马克思主义也有相通之处。杜威反对的只是教条主义和机械地照搬他国的经验,他多次强调中国的发展要结合本国的历史和社会条件,实验性地探索发展之路。毛泽东领导的农村包围城市的道路就是在经历了照搬俄国进行城市武装起义而失败的教训后确立的,而邓小平的中国特色社会主义道路的最终确立,可以看作是在坚持四项基本原则的基础上大胆采用实验主义,在具体语境下探索如何逐步发展马克思主义。中国是当代世界唯一的社会主义大国,要想借鉴他国的社会主义发展经验已不可能,只能凭借国人探究性的智慧,采用实验主义的精神,不断开创中国特色的社会主义之路。

第二,杜威与跨文化的交流。从蔡元培把杜威称作"西方的孔子"以来,杜威无疑可以看作是东西方文化沟通的一个最佳桥梁。很多学者都指出,杜威的实验主义、经验自然主义、人本主义都与中国传统哲学关注现实问题、人生问题、伦理问题的学术精神相一致。国外一些学者对于儒家与杜威的社群主义民主思想以及教育哲学等方面进行比较研究。新文化运动涤荡了传统封建文化,但是把优秀的传统文化也一并加以抛弃,而新中国成立后则以极"左"的阶级斗争路线为主。改革开放后各种西方思潮与文化又涌入中国,因此如何在当代以社会主义价值观为主导,融汇优秀的中国传统文化与西方文化,这仍然是一个重要的探索领域。在这方面,杜威与孔子一样,是一个奉行"中道"的哲学家,他哲学中的融通立场值得我们学习。

第三,杜威的全球视野。当代世界是一个全球性的世界,特别是中美两个大国之间的交流日益频繁,正如有的研究者指出,在某种程度上,了解杜威就是了解美国。对于杜威以及美国的研究,可以促进我们更好地进行国际交流与合作。同时,杜威所倡导的民主主义、科学精神、进步主义教育观等思想在西方世界有着广泛的影响,我们可以借此更好地了解世界并走向世界;并且,当代英美分析哲学已经深受实用主义的影响,新实用主义哲学是当代英美哲学的重要流派,了解杜威哲学也可以帮助我们更好地融入世界哲学的前沿研究。同时,杜威思想对于我们不断完善社会主义民主、深化政治体制改革、发展现代公民教育,皆有一定的启示作用。

杜威的工具主义与罗伊斯的绝对主义

杨 兴 凤

广西大学政治学院

杜威是从作为一名绝对唯心主义者开始其哲学生涯的,但其成熟时期的工具主义思想所呈现的却是对任何超自然、超人类的"绝对"的极端拒斥,而关注探索的进程性。他的思想的这两个端点不仅吸引着杜威研究者的注意力,也对研究绝对唯心主义的学者构成兴趣点。不管这两种观点看起来如何的相异,当我们将其放在一起来考察,就会发现他们"对立的思想"的存在并不只产生毁灭性的论战,杜威的工具主义与罗伊斯的绝对主义只是各以不同的思维视角来看待人类的存在,并以不同的方式来处理人与世界打交道的方式,而且从更深的层次来分析,两者是互补的。

一、杜威的工具主义思想的变革作用

（一）工具主义逻辑①对传统认识论中思维与存在二元对立的消除

在《逻辑理论的研究》(1903)中,杜威区分了认识论的逻辑学家和工具主义的逻辑学家。在他看来,认识论的逻辑学家错误地对待反思性思维并

---

① 对杜威在这一系列文章中使用"逻辑"一词,罗素有异议,他指出"他称为'逻辑'的东西在我看来并不属于逻辑……",参见 Bertrand Russell, Professor Dewey's "Essays in Experimental Logic", *The Journal of Philosophy, Psychology and Scientific Methods*, Vol. 16, No.1.(Jan.2,1919) ,pp.5-26,5.

最终得出实在与思维的两个端点,而这两个端点如何联系起来就成为不可解决的问题。杜威认为这是一个不真实的问题,因为根本就不存在这两个端点。相反,工具主义逻辑学家拒绝设定"思维本身",而将反思看作是对"特定刺激的回应"①。杜威当然是赞同后者的。他反对任何神秘的、幽灵般的精神实体,认为反思性思维的价值,只在于其是否回应了唤起它的那个特定刺激。而且,反思性思维也只是通过与现实相关的、公开的、可观察的探索活动而获得其意义,不会有一个空的、普遍形式的"思维本身"的存在。杜威认为,接受这种工具主义的逻辑方案,传统认识论产生的思维与实在二元鸿沟就根本不会出现。因为,思维是对问题的一种适应性回应,它只是人类在生存斗争中使用的工具,评价它的唯一方法是它对于生存是否具有价值。据此,思维的自然史研究就成为一个关键的问题,"进化的方法"就取代"是否符合最终实在"这种真理性与谬误性区分模式的研究。

而且,按照杜威的工具主义方案,认知就与人类适应生存需要的其他功能并置到了一起,而不再像传统哲学那样将其奉为核心。进一步,杜威将认知视为人类的一种生理功能。他认为,认知所得出的结果——思想——只是经验的一个方面,它能使人获得更进一步的丰富经验。而思想只是技艺——technē——中的一个方面,因为技艺是包含着思想、感觉、意志的创造性过程,它是作为无所不包的人类经验而存在的。换言之,对杜威而言,对世界的把握是"多于认知的"。这样,在传统知识论中思维与实在的二元对立中,独占一端的"思维"就被消解掉了;而在经验中显现其特征的自然也绝不仅仅是思想,它是一种比知识的对象更多的东西。

(二)工具主义的知识理论沟通了理性和经验

杜威并不信奉唯心主义者的"理性在经验中无所不在"的主张,而是在某种程度上倒置了这个主张,他相信"在经验之外无理性"。这一倒置使大量的非反思性经验在"经验"所标识的领域中凸显,并打破了理性和反思性思维成为一种本体论范畴的唯心主义传统。但这种打破使杜威必须处理非

---

① John Dewey, *Essays in Experimental Logic*, New York: Dover Publications, Inc., 1953, p.93.

反思性经验与理性的关系,否则,理性和经验的关系就得不到恰当的理解。

杜威的做法是将经验理解为一种生物有机体的功能、一种生物现象,它与有机体周围环境互相依赖,而且它本身就是一组有秩序的材料,具有一定程度的对未来情况的预测与判断,"反思性思维产生于一种已经组织化了的经验并且是在这样一种有机体中运行的"①;当有机体的处境变得有问题时,探索或特定的反思性思维就出现,并就有问题的处境给出一个新的解决方案。据此,探索的作用并不是将经验到的世界转化为理性的内容,而只是对成问题的处境找到一种安全和有效的解决方法。这样,杜威就将很多认识论术语转化为工具性的使用,他的工具主义理论就消解了理性的独立的本体论范畴性质,理性不再是唯心主义者所主张的是一切经验的源泉,理性思维也只是生物有机体的一种功能性运用。

但杜威也认为,理性思维并不仅仅是一种功能性工具,它还参与了"实在"的构造,使最终呈现的"实在"世界是经过理智参与塑形过的经验所呈现的世界。② 杜威由此而主张,并不是理论具有实践内涵,而是理论本就是某种类型的实践,它将有问题的经验材料转化为清晰和连贯的材料,以应对要面临的处境。

(三)工具主义的知识理论在真理问题上的变革

杜威功能化地界定了真理的本质,在他看来,"真理"就是一个观念去做它所要做的事并实现其功能时就"为真"。在他看来,人类的观念和判断是人作为一种生物有机体适应自然世界的努力的一部分,检验观念和判断的方法和标准就是使人有效地保存生命和使生活更加稳定、安全,而那些具有此种价值的判断和观念就是真理。简言之,观念和意见是工具,真的观念就是使人类适应其生存及更稳定地生活。观念并不是要成为与事物本身完全符合的东西,而是使成问题的经验材料成为清晰有条理的工具,并且在这

---

① John Dewey, *Essays in Experimental Logic*, New York: Dover Publications, Inc., 1953, p.129.
② 也就是说,在杜威那里,事物在探索中被改变了,并且探索以这个"被改变了的"事物为起点,因此并不存在某个固定的、不变的自然事物等待着观念与其相符合。

个过程中经验材料因观念的理解而被改变了。据此,就不存在观念与事物符合的问题(这是唯心主义一直存在的问题),最终只有我们根据不断升级的观念系统去经验世界(同时也是转化世界)这个过程。这就是杜威所理解的"思想具有实践的特征",它的激进性在于"并不仅仅是理论具有实践内涵,而是,理论就是变化中的经验材料"①,这样,理论就是某种类型的实践,也是某种经验。既然如此,整个世界就是经验的世界。

杜威对真理问题的工具主义方案就使人们摆脱了传统哲学认知主体如何认识独立其外的客体世界的问题,同时也摆脱了本体界和现象界之间的区分与沟通问题,统一了知与行,即"真"就是"起作用",真观念就是在实践活动中起作用。对杜威来说,知识的目的并不是去符合大写的真理(且也不存在大写的真理),而是去占有和享受经验的价值,把杂乱、不明晰的经验整理成系统明确的有组织经验,以应对有问题的处境。所谓的知识的"真",只是因为它们是被验证的或"可证明的主张"。在杜威看来,所有的观念最终都不是终极真理,它们可能被称为"起作用的概念"更为准确,因为它们起作用,所以称为好的或真的。

基于此,真理在杜威那里是作为一个批判性概念来使用的,在去除它的终极形态和应符合的标准之后,它的存在就完全相对于人类的经验而言。

二、罗伊斯对工具主义的批判及杜威的回应

杜威基于其工具主义立场,对罗伊斯的绝对主义处处挞伐,有时甚至用"不符合于一个同事身份"②的言辞来指责罗伊斯的绝对。对于工具主义的真理观,罗伊斯也表现出直接的反感,并专门在1908年的海德堡国际哲学大会的公开演讲中以此为主题论述了其立场。如果我们呈现他们之间在真

① G.M.Brodsky,"Absolute Idealism and John Dewey's Instrumentalism",*Transactions of the Charles S.Peirce Society*,Winter 1969,Vol.5,Issue 1,pp.44-62,59.
② Frank M.Oppenheim,S.J.,*Reverence for the Relations of Life:Re-imagining Pragmatism via Josiah Royce's Interactions with Peirce,James,and Dewey*,University of Notre Dame Press,2005,p.295.

理问题上的相互批判与回应,则能更深入地理清这两种立场的本质,并看到其联系。

(一)工具主义真理观之私人性、相对性问题的批判与回应

1. 罗伊斯批判:工具主义将真理的价值等同于一种心理价值,而"心理的"只是指向个体的、内在的甚至是转瞬即逝的"意识状态"。

罗伊斯认为工具主义真理观是由当时心理学对于进化过程的兴趣而产生的。这种动机将人类的意见、判断、观念看作是一个活的生物体适应他自身的自然世界的努力的一部分,而真理就是属于这种观念的一种特定价值。但这种价值本身只是一种生物的和心理的价值,它会导致真理随着我们的成长而成长,随着我们的需求而改变,并且依我们的成功来对其进行评价。[1] 据此来论述的真理就是相对的,并易于使人将真理问题等同于个人的权利和自由。而罗伊斯认为,如果工具主义所认为的起作用、成功的观念就是真理,它之为真就不应当只是帮助"这个人"或"那个人"的成功,它之为真就应是基于超越每一个个体人的经验、验证和成功的事实,但事实是没有一个人曾经验到那个事实。因此,罗伊斯认为,工具主义它本身从未有过要构建任何真理理论的动机[2],从而也就从未严肃地对待过真理。

2. 杜威回应:一个活的生物体最基本的特征是它具有一种种族生活的连续性,在客观的人类经验和主观的个体经验之间并不存在鸿沟。[3]

杜威对于罗伊斯指责其将真理价值等同于个体的、私人的心理价值所作的回应首先从反驳罗伊斯所理解的"个体的"、"个人的经验"开始。他认为"个体的"、"个人的经验"等这些观念是历史所产生的错觉概念,是什么东西致使人得到这样一个"个体"的概念,是什么导致将个体等同于私人并将"个体经验"界定为是排他的和隔离的? 杜威认为对这些问题的回答直

---

① 参见 Josiah Royce,"The Problem of Truth in the Light of Recent Discussion",collected in *William James and Other Essays on the Philosophy of Life*, New York:The Macmillan Company,1912,pp.187–254,194。

② 参见 Ibid.,p.222。

③ 参见 John Dewey,"A Reply to Professor Royce's Critique of Instrumentalism",*The Philosophical Review*,Vol.21,No.1(Jan.,1912),pp.69–81,73。

击唯心主义者的要害,正是唯心主义者错误的哲学起点致使其产生了这种遗留问题。而他的工具主义观点拒绝这种"虚无主义的、无政府主义的自我中心的个体概念"①,他所要做的是将所谓的"个体"解释为符合生命功能的活的生物体。而一个活的生物体最基本的特征就在于具有一种种族生活的连续性,在这种连续性当中,"个体人"的生命、经验(包括观念、意见、判断等有机活动)完全是互相渗透的,且具有社会的传统遗产和参照性。另外,教育、语言和其他交流工具会创造"意义的共享体"从一开始就包裹着单个人生命始终。杜威认为,所有这些都使主观的个体经验与客观的人类经验之间根本不存在鸿沟。简言之,生命与经验的连续性和传递性关系保证了对个体来说的成功观念会在社会进程中自然地成为客观的人类经验。② 所以,罗伊斯所指出的这两者之间的鸿沟只是基于罗伊斯假定工具主义者具有这样狭窄、排他的"个体"概念的情况下的工具主义,这只是罗伊斯按他自己的理解所接受的"工具主义"。③

(二)工具主义真理的验证问题的批判与回应

1. 罗伊斯批判:个体经验根本无法验证他接受为真的大量的观念和意见有效性;人类的需求并不止于生命得到保存和安全。

罗伊斯认为,按照工具主义的真理观,观念的价值是使特定的人有效地控制他的既定经验处境而被实际验证,但我们是社会的存在物,并且具有无以数计的和变化的理智上的需求,我们不断地界定和接受大量的观念和意见为有效的,而它们的真理性我们个体根本无法一一去验证,而只是依据其信用价值而接受为真。④ 大量观念的信用价值并不能兑现为我个人的经验

---

① John Dewey, "A Reply to Professor Royce's Critique of Instrumentalism", *The Philosophical Review*, Vol.21, No.1(Jan., 1912), pp.69-81,72.

② 杜威因此而主张一个人会发现自己的经验与别人的经验的界限是无法划定清楚的。

③ John Dewey, "A Reply to Professor Royce's Critique of Instrumentalism", *The Philosophical Review*, Vol.21, No.1(Jan., 1912), pp.69-81,72.

④ 参见 Josiah Royce, "The Problem of Truth in the Light of Recent Discussion", collected in *William James and Other Essays on the Philosophy of Life*, New York: The Macmillan Company, 1912, pp.187-254,224,225。

的"现金",但它们却包含着真的信用价值。

罗伊斯还认为,工具主义依据"作用"和"成功"两个概念界定了真理的本质,但是真理不能仅仅依据我们获得这种控制"作用"的"自己的成功"来界定,每一个人都被限定在他的当前经验中,对"成功"的界定也依不同的经验者而相异。按工具主义者的论述,并不存在一个经验到所有不同个体的成功事实的主体,那么对成功的界定最终就是多元的、冲突的,随情况而定的任意的东西。而且对于人类这种有精神生活的生物体来说,他的要求并不止于生命得到保存和安全这个标准,而这却又是工具主义者常诉诸的标准。基于以上原因,罗伊斯将工具主义定性为一种"个体主义",并断言:"无论是谁,将真理等同于他自己的个体利益而作出任何主张时,这种主张都可能只会因他自己的混乱而一败涂地……这是一种自我决定。"①

2.杜威的回应:工具主义者也接受经社会验证的有效观念为真,但这是假设性的试用,待探索进程来确定其真与否;环境、行动的中介的社会性使一个人的经验结果与他人的经验结果的界限是难以清楚划分开的。

对于罗伊斯指出我们依据观念的信用价值而不仅仅是个体的经验验证而接受为真的观念,杜威首先指出"接受"这个词本身就反驳了罗伊斯对工具主义的指责,因为"接受"这种行为准确说来就是在更直接的个人验证的基础上的承认与接纳,这本身就服从了工具主义者的检验类型。

其次,工具主义者不会任意地接受观念的社会信用,而是在条件允许的范围内假设性地试用,通过作用再次确证时才对接受授予真正的信任。

再次,环境、行动的中介都是社会性的,而且生命的社会载体本身也是连续的,这就使得一个人自己的经验与他人的经验和更多人的经验的界限是无法划清的,某种公共性的标准已经渗透在个人的验证标准中,绝不存在纯粹的私人的经验验证与成功标准。简言之,个人的经验本身在起源、内容

---

① Josiah Royce, "The Problem of Truth in the Light of Recent Discussion", collected in *William James and Other Essays on the Philosophy of Life*, New York: The Macmillan Company, 1912, pp.187-254, 232.

和前景上都是社会的。①

三、杜威的工具主义与罗伊斯的绝对主义之差异与互补

杜威与罗伊斯相互批判与反驳是基于两位哲学家的哲学理念与信仰基础的不同,但在呈现他们的思想差异的同时,会看到两者的相互需要与联系。

(一)两种思想的差异

1.对"绝对"的理解与态度不同。

杜威的整个哲学排斥任何超自然的、超人类的绝对存在,他所关注的是探索的进程性。他认为,心灵在经验和自然的交互作用中起一种持续的作用,任何绝对的设定都是窒息经验与自然互动的进程性的;知识是逐渐形成并且在不断的形成中,而不是一个固有的、现成的、绝对的东西。杜威对超自然的绝对之反对使他确信,我们所理解的自然栖居于经验中,而经验是在自然的界限内——"自然的"对杜威来说就是绝对主义者的"实在的",并不需要一个绝对的他者来作为符合的标准。在杜威看来,超自然、超人类的假设是寻求安全感的绝对教条,他的工具主义是放弃了对终极原理的探求,而只关注于在时间进程内人类有机体的不断探寻。为此他指责罗伊斯的绝对是一个"经过防腐的"东西:"这个固有的或绝对的理想,不仅不可解释,而且是假设的和现成的。"②对杜威来说,罗伊斯的"绝对"这个概念相对于现实的经验丰富性和具体性来说只是"一个苍白的和形式的符号";而且罗伊斯为了能够解释个体的意义和经验又强调每个个体具有独一无二性,这就设定了两个世界——绝对与个体——之间的对立,所以他断定罗伊斯的哲学在进行

---

① 参见 John Dewey,"A Reply to Professor Royce's Critique of Instrumentalism",*The Philosophical Review*,Vol.21,No.1(Jan.,1912),pp.69-81,79。

② John Dewey,"The Study of Ethics:A Syllabus"(1894),EW4:258,*The Early Works of John Dewey*(1882-1898),Vol.4 editor by Jo Ann Boydston,Carbondale:Southern Illinois University Press,c 1991,p.258.

着"一项自我矛盾的任务",其形而上学有着"双重视野的幻象"①。

罗伊斯却始终坚持"绝对"对于人类的存在以及解释是不可少的,并且认为存在着"绝对"。无论(1)从道德生活的严肃性来考量,还是(2)对知识的最终内涵的明确性的说明,以及(3)人类意志的逻辑②的共同性与确定性,最后是(4)纯粹数学科学的存在所证明的绝对真的命题,这些只有在"绝对"存在的前提下才能得到说明。就(1)和(2)两点,罗伊斯曾在1911年的哈里森讲座的系列文章中对"绝对"的双重内涵进行过阐述。他认为,"绝对"的第一层含义是意味着意识到过去的绝对性,即每个行为都不可撤销地开始于不可改变的过去;这种意识表达了人类道德生活的基本严肃性,因为其意味着行动的责任。"绝对"的第二层内涵是一种断言或判断绝对地命中或错失它的意向对象(目标)。也即对罗伊斯来说,是一种知识,虽然杜威式的持续探索是必要的,但如果观念的确切的、固定的(绝对的)内涵没有被揭示出来时,则这种知识就是不充分的。在罗伊斯看来,杜威所主张的探索依赖于时间的进程性具有不充分性和模糊性。对此罗伊斯是继承了皮尔士所强调的真观念之为真必有绝对的逻辑前提的主张。就(3)来说,罗伊斯在《近来对真理问题的讨论》中就明确表述了一种"意志的逻辑"的绝对性。"我主张:所有的逻辑都是意志的逻辑。"③而意志基于其本质是完全的和有意识的自我占有的渴求、对生命完整性的渴求,它界定的真理将会无止境地寻求一个具有彻底性、全体性、自我占有的因此是绝对性的真理。意志的逻辑类似于康德所界定的先验模式的客观必然性,在纯粹数学科学的方法和概念的研究中就可揭示出这种意志逻辑在确定我们行为模式

---

① John Dewey , *The World and the Individual by Josiah Royce* , *The Philosophical Review* , Vol. 11 , No.4(Jul. , 1902) , pp.392–407 , 406 , 404 , 405.

② 罗伊斯认为存在着一种意志的逻辑,与理智的逻辑一样是真的,甚至对罗伊斯来说,所有的逻辑都是意志的逻辑。相关论述参见 Josiah Royce , "The Problem of Truth in the Light of Recent Discussion" , collected in *William James and Other Essays on the Philosophy of Life* , New York:The Macmillan Company , 1912 , pp.187–254 , 234。

③ Josiah Royce , "The Problem of Truth in the Light of Recent Discussion" , collected in *William James and Other Essays on the Philosophy of Life* , New York:The Macmillan Company , 1912 , pp.187–254 , 234.

中的绝对性。罗伊斯最终以数学研究为例说明了绝对的真理是关于创造的意志的本质,也即意志本身的根本和内在的律法是绝对的,我们有限经验范围内的所有相对真理必然要服从那个界定了我们的活动的绝对条件。

基于以上论述,罗伊斯必然要反对杜威的工具主义立场对于"绝对"的消解。虽然这个"绝对"在他思想发展的不同阶段有不同的表述,但寻求统一、寻求某种遏制相对主义的多元性、个体主义之恶的思想初衷一直未改。

2. 两种思想在时间观上的不同。

杜威的工具主义知识观要说明的是,对知识的追求是基于我们对问题所在的世界的负责任态度,知识并不需要诉诸于一种先在的实在,其成果就在于对问题的解决中。因此,杜威的探索就止步于问题所在的世界,相应的探索过程就在于问题所在的世界的时间中。所以探索是在时间界限内的,表现为种族生活的连续性和社会载体运转的连续性。这个过程不会溢出时间性的经验界限之外,因此,他反对超自然的时间概念。詹姆斯的心理学给了他一种对知识的解释方法,它是生理学的、进化概念占主导的,而这使他强调时间的进程性,因此他并不关注自然进程之外的无时间性永恒。

罗伊斯的世界则是由时间性和永恒性两个时间层次构成的。罗伊斯坚持主张,一个真的观念中永恒的和时间性的成分的共同构成,不变的和活动的元素都在其中有其位置。对真观念的永恒的和不变的成分的坚持,是基于罗伊斯大胆捍卫皮尔士的关于观念的概念性内涵所需的逻辑条件是固有的和不变的的主张。关于这一点,罗伊斯认为康德关于先验结构的客观必然性已经做了类似阐述,只是新的逻辑以更清晰、意义更深远的方式确证了康德的分析。在经验领域当中的真观念是相对的,但所有的相对真理都须服从界定了它本身的绝对条件。因此,时间性的领域以我们的有限意识来表现无时间性的绝对。罗伊斯因此而反对杜威和詹姆斯的模糊的、在流变的时间性进程中的"作用"(workings)来作为验证标准。另外,皮尔士在坚持观念内涵的逻辑条件的必要性时,也同时强调人的创造性行动模式、机会和自由游戏的重要性,这两个方面就构成两个时间层次的模式,这对罗伊斯也是直接的启发。而且,在罗伊斯那里,从伦理的角度来看,某种无时间性的"应当被主张的东西"的存在对于时间进程中的人类来说是需要的。就如康德从纯粹理性到实践理性的思想进展就已透露出：实践理性的伦理力量可以破除理论理性上的限制——你无法在人类的认知经验中用知识来证明绝对或上帝，但上帝和绝对却是道德行动的前提，一旦承认存在着道德行动，也就把绝对或上帝作为"存在"来看待。据此分析，罗伊斯的两个时间层次的存在有其合理的论述依据。

3. 两种思想持不同的自然观。

杜威的自然主义只是在有机社会所能产生的理想和现实之间的活动关系。在此基础上，杜威所理解的自然就必然是和经验相关的，他反对按"世界的本来面目"和"向人类显现的面目"区分的这种永恒和流变的二分法，而是在活动和事件中自然向人类显现自身，经验的深度和广度决定了自然的显现程度。总之，自然就是一个现实可能性的、人类有机体所能联系到的条件总体。这样，杜威的自然是一个充满确定性的自然，同时也就是排除了沉思乐趣的、最终无疑惑的自然，它向人的探索敞开。在人的探索中，自然并不神秘。

罗伊斯对自然的理解与杜威不同。罗伊斯所理解的自然除了经验科学所能研究其法则的类型之外，还包括他所说的"超自然"，因此就不仅仅是杜威所说的时间连续性内的自然，它还包括通过无限意识的真正判断所能认知的世界，超自然的世界，它是显示启示和真理的让人敬畏的精神性领域。对罗伊斯来说，超个体或超自然的元素是渗透到人类的所有认知当中的。罗伊斯是一个带有神秘主义色彩的思想家，而杜威在很大程度上是拒绝神秘的。

4. 两种思想的宗教气质不同。

杜威的思想整个地看，较少显露出宗教性。杜威哲学整个关注的是社会公民运用自己的能力在一种民主的共同体中不断开拓可能的经验领域，这并不需要超自然的对象为探索者提供精神的直接支撑。但从他对民主共同体这种理想的组织机构的依赖中，在他的探索者以负责任的求知态度对问题的世界承担起"勇气和主动责任感"中，以及在他论述自然在面对探索的人们所呈现的敞开性时，无一不渗透着和谐的精神。这种和谐精神使杜威信任自然对人的行动的永恒支撑，信任自然会在人的主动探寻中回馈于人、滋养于人,由此可见一种宗教性的情感。但必须要指出的是,他的宗教信仰基础是局限在自然之内的,并不超出自然之外去寻求一个上帝。不过,杜威晚期在《一个共同的信念》中强调的人类联合体却与宗教相联系。他认为"上帝的观念"与自然和环境相关,它有助于推进理想的成长并推进其实现。由此,杜威在理想与现实之间的积极关系的意义上肯定了"上帝的观念"。不过,杜威的宗教性是渗透在所有经验当中的普遍性,而致使神圣与世俗之间的二元论瓦解。他区分了"宗教"与"宗教经验",他的作为一种生活方式的民主共同体虽有一种通向宗教的启示力量在其中,但这仅是对生活方式的民主和经验主义的意义进行深层思考的结果,他的共同体概念并没有跃出世俗与自然。

罗伊斯则是一个宗教气质极浓的哲学家,从他一生的著作的主题就可确证这一点。① 他的"绝对"论证透露其思想的有神论背景,即作为"绝对思想"必然有一位拥有此思想的无所不知者——上帝,这是基于罗伊斯深觉宗教力量对于维系美国的伦理共同体的重要性。而杜威的工具主义思想则不在自然的界限之外寻找精神上的支撑。罗伊斯的思想借重于宗教的力量在于他对于人类存在的看不见的根基的关注,以及从整体上构造有意义的伦理世界的追求。而杜威的工具主义产生背景是基于对世界整体上是不安全的判断,所以他关注的是在世界中生存的人自身应对这种处境所需要的技艺,故而并不需要一位神也并不信赖任何神的允诺。

(二)两种思想的互补性

1.罗伊斯的唯心主义方案与对自然化陷阱的逃离。

杜威的工具主义的理论背景是进化论的盛行。进化论将人的生命仅看作是一个巨大进化过程的偶然,其结果不但是使人从世界当中边缘化,而且使人的内在意义和精神成果技艺化、相对化,最重要的是,它难以彻底地解释观念现象。而罗伊斯的绝对主义并不是要逃离这个世界,而是使人脱离

① 罗伊斯的主要著作如《哲学的宗教方面》、《世界与个体》、《上帝的概念》、《忠之哲学》、《宗教观念的来源》、《善与恶的研究》、《基督教的问题》等,从标题上就可看出他的哲学思想与宗教思想不可分离。

自然化陷阱。基于这种主旨,罗伊斯主张首先从探查观念的核心实质开始。他采纳的是康德在第一批判中的策略,追溯经验知识的根源,认为当这样做时,就会发现"任何一个观念都包含着心灵去形成一个观念的固有的东西"①。观念所负载的先验结构能有力地反击自然主义的经验化进程。而且,罗伊斯指出,在纯粹数学和逻辑中的新发现(例如狄德金关于连续性与无理数的发现等)就是对客观真理的领域的证明,具有绝对性,而不是任由喜好或利益而去创造或抛弃。相反,工具主义真理观上的相对主义是浅薄的,它去除了真理之为真须超越工具主义所强调的真理是作为成功的导引这一点,也忽视了皮尔士所一再强调的观念之真的不变逻辑前提。

按杜威的工具主义思想,经验的自然世界是简洁的,它并不负载形而上学的沉重假设,其亦是有利于指导人对于其处境的控制。但罗伊斯的绝对主义方案使我们在信念和动机上有更清晰和精确的自我意识,这个自我意识使我们只有在找到知识的原则、行动的原则时才满足,且这些原则不是暂时方便的权宜,也不是主观的任性;它要求界定一种更严格的真理概念,揭示思想和行动的必然性形式。据此,绝对主义者相较于工具主义者是过于严苛而无趣味的理智主义者,易被当作抽象理性的同路人,但他们也是有勇气地肩负起"使陨落于地的真理再度升起"使命的理想追求者②,这对于人类精神文化的延续与发展是极其重要的。

2.在个体与共同体关系上的借鉴与趋同。

皮尔士、詹姆斯、杜威和罗伊斯都以不同的方式强调美国人必须负责任地平衡个体主义与促成一种名副其实的共同体的关系。③ 据此,杜威和罗伊斯的思想方法虽殊异但意旨归同。

---

① Josiah Royce, *The World and the Individual*, Vol., I, New York: Macmillan, 1899, pp.121-122.

② 参见 Frank M.Oppenheim, S.J., *Reverence for the Relations of Life: Re-imagining Pragmatism via Josiah Royce's Interactions with Peirce, James, and Dewey*, University of Notre Dame Press, 2005, p.297.

③ 参见 Frank M.Oppenheim, S.J., *Reverence for the Relations of Life: Re-imagining Pragmatism via Josiah Royce's Interactions with Peirce, James, and Dewey*, University of Notre Dame Press, 2005, p.ix。

杜威通过主张"融入化"的个体而反驳了罗伊斯指责工具主义"私人化的"、"隔离的"个体经验与客观的人类经验之间的沟通。这个"融入化"的个体首先具有种族生活的连续性,这就取消了客观人类经验与个体经验的鸿沟;其次,生命和经验的连续性与传递性使文明世界的活动成为一个"传播过程"——即教化,致使"一个人自己的经验与另一个人的经验之间是难以划清界限的"①。杜威通过具有这两个内涵的"融入化"的诸多个体形成了一个人类经验的"意义共享活动"的共同体,这样就会逐渐使诸个体持有共同的价值观,实现对大家所面临的问题的解决。这就是杜威在《公众及问题》以及《一个共同的信念》中的共同体观。

从杜威晚期回到共同体,可以看出黑格尔哲学对统一性的追求一直深沉地潜伏在他的哲学思想当中。这不但使人反对传统的二元论,而且杜威晚期反对原子式的个体主义而建立民主共同体亦反映了黑格尔主义的影响力。杜威具有浓厚社群主义色彩的自由主义使得晚期的他能对个体的生活进行整体的、全方位的关照,他主张的"民主共同体"因而与罗伊斯晚期(1912—1916)的"伟大共同体"合流,他也明确表示应回到罗伊斯的"伟大共同体"。而罗伊斯哲学的最深动机一直都是共同体观,在 1915 年的一次采访中他说道:"我强烈地感觉到我最深的动机和问题是在于共同体的观念,虽然这个观念在我意识中是逐渐清晰的。"②这种动机最集中的表述是他最后的著作《伟大的共同体》。

3. 实存与意义并不存在鸿沟之认识的归同。

按照唯心主义的思路,理性能够构造一个理想的对象,它具有清晰性和经验上的先行性,从而不断引导将经验性材料转化为观念,当我们有限的知识越来越具有全面性时,最初的抽象观念就变得越来越具有确定性、具体性,因此而越来越与自然事物相似。唯心主义者这样的思路中蕴含着他们

---

① 参见 Frank M.Oppenheim,S.J.,*Reverence for the Relations of Life:Re-imagining Pragmatism via Josiah Royce's Interactions with Peirce, James, and Dewey*, University of Notre Dame Press,2005,p.78。

② Edited and Introduced by Randall E.Auxier,*Papers in Honor of Josiah Royce on his Sixtieth Birthday*(1916),Theommes Press,2000,p.282.

意识到,观念应抛弃其抽象特征,因此而能够使经验具有我们直接经验到世界的力量与生动性。尤其是在伦理领域,唯心主义者普遍理性下的道德只会是观念的虚妄,它最终还是须落实到一个活生生的个体的具体的实存方式上。罗伊斯当然也意识到这一点,而且在杜威等人的批判之下,他的哲学思想从强调认知(绝对作为全知者)到强调意志和经验(绝对作为绝对经验),再到最后多元个体在解释的共同体中为所有人而解释所有作为实存个体,这一思想发展轨迹不仅是说明了其从绝对向个体实存的滑动,而且说明了这个"绝对主义者"意识到"实存和意义并不存在鸿沟",而这正是杜威所要强调的。杜威反对唯心主义者将思想与经验分开,他认为,通过"实存和意义并不存在全盘的区分"这样的主张,就不会产生观念与实存之间是否相符的问题,观念只是在功能上不同于其他经验性的材料,这样还保存观念作为观念独有的特征。

罗伊斯比杜威更进一步的地方在于,他主张更高于有限经验的"绝对经验",因为"假设整个经验的世界只是一个碎片式和有限的经验,是一种包含着矛盾的尝试",而只有从一种超越于它的更高观点来看这种碎片性的主张才是可能的。[①] 而且,"我们所尝到的有限性经验之痛苦,就意味着比它们包含更多的东西、意味着超越于它们的东西……"[②]罗伊斯的意图在于指出人类有更深刻地追求——经验世界的统一性,而不只是杜威的探索中经验的多元性、进化性。

据此可以看出这两个思想家理论上的互补性,杜威的工具主义思想在说明人的现存的探索世界的成问题性与解决策略,而罗伊斯的绝对主义则更进一步指出人不止步于现实的探索与可控,还在精神世界中追求更完美的东西,而这种精神追求也构成人的实存的一部分。

---

① 参见 Josiah Royce, Joseph Le Conte, G.H.Howison and Sidney E.Mezes, *The Conception of God*, New York: The Macmillan Company, 1902, p.41。

② Josiah Royce, Joseph Le Conte, G.H.Howison and Sidney E.Mezes, *The Conception of God*, New York: The Macmillan Company, 1902, pp.47-48.

责任编辑:方国根 郭彦辰
版式设计:顾杰珍

图书在版编目(CIP)数据

实用主义研究.第一辑/刘放桐,陈亚军 主编. —北京:人民出版社,2017.9
ISBN 978－7－01－017430－3

Ⅰ.①实⋯ Ⅱ.①刘⋯ ②陈⋯ Ⅲ.①实用主义-研究 Ⅳ.①B087

中国版本图书馆 CIP 数据核字(2017)第 043924 号

实用主义研究

SHIYONGZHUYI YANJIU

（第一辑）

刘放桐 陈亚军 主 编

陈 佳 孙 宁 副主编

人 民 出 版 社 出版发行

（100706 北京市东城区隆福寺街 99 号）

北京市文林印务有限公司印刷 新华书店经销

2017 年 9 月第 1 版 2017 年 9 月北京第 1 次印刷

开本:710 毫米×1000 毫米 1/16 印张:15.75

字数:235 千字

ISBN 978－7－01－017430－3 定价:42.00 元

邮购地址 100706 北京市东城区隆福寺街 99 号

人民东方图书销售中心 电话 (010)65250042 65289539